Break Down & Let It All Out

Printed and bound in the UK by MPG Books, Bodmin

Distributed in the US by Publishers Group West

Published by Sanctuary Publishing Limited, Sanctuary House, 45-53 Sinclair Road, London W14 0NS, United Kingdom

www.sanctuarypublishing.com

ISBN: 1-86074-552-0

Nina Simone

Break Down & Let It All Out

Sylvia Hampton with David Nathan
Foreword by Lisa Simone Kelly

Sanctuary

Contents

Foreword

' "Mommy, I've got your back." The last words I said to my mother, three days before the world turned upside down.

' "My man's gone now…" I hear Mom's voice singing. Wailing…calling… Perfect! I can't believe how much I miss her. Amazing, isn't it? Definitely don't miss the drama! Just that "mother comfort" that remains strong despite dysfunction and abuse: her smell, her touch, her smile (when it was real) and her passion. When she looked at you, you always felt that penetrating gaze weighing and measuring.

'And now, my new life. My destiny became crystal clear the moment I walked through the doorway that her freedom allowed; the only path to superstardom. The price – and there's always one to be paid – is too high; a life-altering price and I will never be the same. I feel as if the Lisa of one year ago was a fantasy. That time seems carefree – which it certainly didn't feel like then. So many traits of Mom I, too, exhibit and am understanding. How do you explain the subtleties of life to the young and ambitious and headstrong? All you can do is watch life work its magic. I fault Mom for not supporting me and using her power to make things easier, or at least attempting to. I fault Mom for not being able to understand that my goal was never to usurp or replace, but to be an extension.

'The next phase: I hear more positive things from others concerning how proud she was of me, yet I rarely received praise from her directly. It's as if she was at war with herself. On the one hand wanting to "be there" and on the other, fabricating some negative reason or situation to have an excuse to persecute me.'

The above is a journal entry I made in November 2003. It was the first time I'd been able to write about Mommy in any capacity. I love her and I miss her terribly. In our last conversation I told her that she had groomed me to be a warrior and that I had her back. I am her daughter and the legacy of Simone continues.

This book really reflects the kind of amazing impact that I'm so proud to say my mother had on people everywhere around the world. As they have lovingly shared, both Sylvia's and David's lives were deeply touched not only by her music, but by the woman I call Mommy. Reading these pages reminds me how just one human being can make such a difference for another, and as I continue my own life journey, that's the commitment I have made through my music and my art.

Lisa Simone Kelly
January 2004

Introduction: 'I Shall Be Released'

I've seen my light come shining, from the west out to the east,
Any day now, any day now, I shall be released.

Deep within, I knew something was wrong. For some unexplained reason my usually cheerful disposition had been overshadowed by a sense of gloom. Speaking to my brother David, I discovered that he too was in a state of melancholy. Was it a full moon? No, what we both sensed was loss, one that would reveal itself within days. On Sunday 20 April 2003, one of the world's greatest performers and most magical beings left us. Dr Nina Simone had passed away. A very small statement for what was, and will always be, a larger-than-life figure.

It took a while to absorb the news. Nina Simone was a woman of great strength and integrity, a friend for almost 40 years and a legend in the world of music. As time put my grief into context I vowed to write this book so the world would know the real Nina. Her life spanned just over 70 years but it was more than just a tale of a musical genius. It was the story of a black woman struggling to fight the oppression of racism, expressing 'radical' views through music and often being ostracised for doing so.

Her life began in America's Deep South and that environment's racist culture was for her a running sore that never healed. As a consequence, she travelled the globe restlessly, never quite knowing where to settle. Sharp dealing in the music business left her feeling exploited and furious.

Yet, more pivotally, she was a woman struggling with the devastating effects of a mental disorder that left her incapable of maintaining the emotional constancy she craved.

State boundaries struggled to contain her. Her spirit broke through every barrier, embellished as it was with a musical gift that inspired and uplifted millions around the world. She crossed the line in so many ways, yet beneath it all she was a woman of integrity, warmth and, above all, human kindness.

As I travelled to France to attend Nina's funeral at Carry-le-Rouet near Marseilles, I wondered how I was going to deal with such a monumental loss.

David had first introduced me to Nina, via her music, when I was just 12 years old. At our very first face-to-face meeting, I was not quite 15. Now I was a grown woman and I could barely recall the time I before I knew her. The impact Nina had on me was profound, as was her music. I had prepared a tribute for her funeral and was trying to figure out just how I was supposed to read it when, each time I looked at the pages my tears obscured the words.

On the morning of the funeral I prayed and asked for God to help me get through the day without falling apart, as I knew Nina would want me to be strong. I was also there to represent David (who was living in Los Angeles and unable to attend). I would try my best to make him proud. As I walked up the hill to the church, carrying a bouquet nearly as large as I was, the tears just refused to stop. Composing myself, I went into the church, which was filled to capacity, and laid down the flowers. As I walked back outside the hearse carrying Nina's body arrived, draped in a large wreath of white roses and a banner that read 'Nina we love you'. I realised I would never again hear the laughter, see that larger-than-life smile, hear the familiar outbursts and be witness to the sheer genius that was Nina Simone.

The service began with a recording of Nina singing 'Ne Me Quitte Pas' and, as I sat next to the casket and listened to those low tones, I knew that on some level Nina would always be with me. Nina's daughter, Lisa, rose and, through her tears, sang a tribute to her mother that touched my very soul.

The service was conducted mainly in French and, even though I was not able to follow it word for word, I knew what was being said. The ceremony started late, so I was unable to read my tribute. I felt relieved, and had a suspicion that Nina was still orchestrating things on my behalf.

Walking from the church I held on to Nina's manager, Clifton Henderson, who had succumbed to his own personal distress, and reminded him that Nina would want him to be strong. I suggested he should picture her admonishing him in those deep, dusky chords that were unique to her. I guess that image worked. He straightened up and walked proudly to the waiting car.

I returned to the hotel with my friend Patsy. We had decided to meet up with a couple of Nina's friends and have dinner later that night. What a night it turned out to be. The four of us sat down at around 8pm, leaving an empty chair at the table in Nina's honour, and began celebrating her life. We talked, laughed, sang, and all the while we remembered the woman we had known and loved. Several others joined the table and, before we knew it, it was 3am. I knew there would be time for tears but right now it was right to celebrate a life that was often lived on the edge, filled with love and laughter and a degree of pain. The day had begun in sombre mood but ended with tears of joy.

The commitment to write this book is based on loyalty to the memory of a remarkable woman and the desire to provide testament to her genius. It is an emotional challenge but one I relish. I can reflect on the many concerts, clubs and, of course, the myriad of music with rapture. Nina was loved and admired by millions, berated by a few and, for those who shared their lives with her, she stood beyond compare. I could not paint her as Snow White because she wasn't, but she was closer to a fairytale figure than scandalised press reports would have people believe.

There's no doubt that being around Nina was like tightrope walking. When she was happy her laughter could fill a stadium. When she was angry…well, let's just say that putting some distance between you and her was the safest course of action.

In fact, her infamous bouts of rage were caused by a chemical imbalance that left her prone to sudden and intense depression, underpinned by bleak, wild fury. Put bluntly, she suffered from a mental illness that often blighted her happiness. Tragically, the illness was a closely guarded secret only a few shared.

I didn't know about it, even though I had been around Nina for years. When I spoke to her daughter, Lisa, following Nina's death she asked, 'How could you not know?' I explained that when I first met her, I was no more than a child. Of course, at that time, questions about her mental health were not uppermost in my mind. I always accepted her for what she was and never sought to explain away her idiosyncrasies.

She was in many ways like a mother to me and, clearly, was not about to confide her problems to someone she instinctively wanted to protect and cherish. But Nina had her own good reasons for keeping her pressing health issues under wraps. She didn't want people to feel sorry for her, she was not one to play the victim. Essentially, she grew up at a time when mental illness wasn't openly debated. When another member of her family showed symptoms of emotional instability he was swiftly installed in an institution.

Thus, Nina had every reason to keep those medical glitches under her hat. Born into a different generation she could have been open and honest about her need for rest and medication. It would have been no big deal. As it was, it became a burden that she had to bear alone. She may well have subscribed to the view that with genius comes madness, that her short spells of insanity were an inevitable consequence of her astonishing musical dexterity.

Would I have treated her differently had I known? I certainly would have been anxious about whether she took her medication and if she washed it down with alcohol. Maybe, though, she didn't want to be treated differently by me and was compelled by pride to stay silent on the issue. She already felt stigmatised as a talented black woman, and would have thought long and hard about stacking up more odds against her. Knowing what I know now, at least I can assimilate all that erratic behaviour.

When it came to her beliefs, Nina never held back. She was an ardent supporter of the civil rights movement, having witnessed at first hand the damage prejudice and bigotry could do. Throughout her life she could never come to terms with the shabby way black people were treated because of their skin colour. In her 1991 autobiography, *I Put A Spell On You*, she wrote, 'The first thing I saw in the morning when I woke up was my black face in the bathroom mirror and that fixed what I felt about myself for the rest of the day – that I was a black-skinned woman in a country where you could be killed because of that one fact.'

Much later, the weight of injustice was revealed when she said she had 'paid a heavy price for fighting the Establishment'.

After her death, jazz concert promoter George Wein explained, 'She was a black woman who never could relate to the position of what it was to be black in America. She couldn't understand it. She was an unhappy person [because of it].'

With considerable perception he continued, 'As an entertainer she had the world in her hands, but she never knew how to grab it.'

Frequently she was frustrated by the ponderous and devious workings of the music industry. She was infuriated by the capacity of record companies to release her material without paying cash rewards and she lumped them together with those who released bootleg LPs that featured her music, but from which she received no royalties. It wasn't until March 1995 that a San Francisco court granted her ownership of 52 original recordings, putting an end to an acutely felt exploitation of artists' rights. In addition, she felt betrayed by a succession of men, including her husband and father.

The press vilified her for 'difficult' behaviour and it was often the more sensational aspects of her life they chose to focus on. It happens to all celebrities. Yet Nina was deeply upset by comments she read about herself in the news. It was at times like these that I saw her more vulnerable side, the one that only a few were privileged to witness. Nina was sensitive, she hated injustice, preached love as mankind's salvation and did not suffer fools gladly.

Her quest for love and her desire for perfection as a performer often turned grown men into shrinking violets. It was her strength as a woman, not just as an artist, that led to periods of loneliness. She literally scared people away, not always intentionally. Deep down, Nina wanted what most of us want: to love and be loved. She married, raised a beautiful and talented daughter, and had devoted friends and family, yet a part of her searched for more. Was she truly fulfilled?

On many levels I believe she was. In these pages she is portrayed as more than a musical genius – she was a woman, mother, activist and philosopher. All of this she achieved with the invisible bonds of mental illness tied, noose-like, around her neck.

Hers wasn't a totally joyous life but it had joyous aspects to it. Despite my own ups and downs with Nina over the years, I would take none of it back, not a single minute. Yes, Nina could charm the socks off you. I witnessed it on many occasions: her voice almost a whisper, she would say to me, 'See, I told you they just needed some sugar, that's all, just a little sugar', and that wicked grin would appear. You couldn't help but laugh to see Nina in action. The periods when the 'backlash' would hit were the only scary times, but then who among us has not let loose from time to time? There are many, like me, whose lives were richer for having Nina in them.

1 'When I Was A Young Girl'

Nina Simone is a name known the world over and it's a name she created for herself. Nina was born Eunice Kathleen Waymon in Tryon, North Carolina, in 1933. Her mother, Mary Kate, was a church minister and her father, John Divine, an entertainer who danced, sang, and played guitar and harmonica. When times got hard he gave up the profession he loved to become a barber. With sisters Lucille, Dorothy and Frances, and brothers Carol, Harold, John and Sam, Eunice would never be a lonely child. Although Tryon was a resort town life was hard, not least because of the economic effects of the Great Depression. If life for black people had long been gritty, at that time it was tougher still. Yet the place had a strong sense of community, one that would be an integral part of Eunice's life.

At the tender age of three – with the aid of several cushions – Eunice sat at the family piano and began to play. Many years later, in an article in a London newspaper, Nina would be quoted as saying, 'Honey, do you believe in miracles? I believe in them. You have to believe in miracles when you can play the piano at the age of three. Just think about that, that's a very strange thing.'

Back in Tryon, her mother declared this musical gift to be God-given and presumed it would be used in worship. Mary Kate had started working for a local white couple, Mr and Mrs Miller, who were equally astonished by Eunice's ability. Mrs Miller offered to pay for a series of piano lessons and consequently, aged six, Eunice began studying with Muriel Massinovitch, known to her as Miss Mazzy. The plan was simple: Eunice would study classical music and become the first black American classical pianist.

Despite the Millers' generosity, Miss Mazzy realised a more permanent funding arrangement had to be found. With the aid of the townsfolk of Tryon, the Eunice Waymon Fund was born. Not only was she being groomed as the first black woman to excel at classical piano, but she was to carry the weight of the town's expectations on her small shoulders. Eunice put away childhood toys to concentrate on music.

Her mother's church upbringing influenced Eunice, and music that was not rooted in religion was referred to as 'real' music. Eunice was discouraged from having anything to do with it. Fortunately, her father had different ideas and, when Mary Kate was out, the pair of them would sit at the piano playing jazz and blues. Hence, Eunice was the apple of her daddy's eye.

Cushioned by the love of her family, and the support of neighbours and friends, Eunice was largely shielded from the horrors of racism.

However, at her first full public recital it would rear its ugly head. In proud expectation, her parents sat in the front row waiting for the concert to begin. However, when a white family arrived, the couple were removed and seated towards the back of the hall. Seething with the injustice of this, Eunice stood up to declare that if her parents did not sit at the front then she would not perform.

The indignant protest was sufficient to bring her parents back to their original seats but the gales of laughter from whites in the audience were echoing in their ears. The incident did much to shape young Eunice's view on the colour bar that existed in her home territory.

Although Eunice's life revolved around her dedication to music, the appearance in town of a young man called Edney Whiteside in her teenage years awoke another side to her nature.

They began dating and for a while life was good. However, Eunice soon had to leave Tryon for Asheville, almost 50 miles away, to attend Allen High School for Girls, where she was given special coaching in music.

For a while the separation didn't seem to matter but, as time went on, the letters and visits from Edney became less frequent. After graduation Eunice had the choice of two scholarships: one to the Juilliard School of Music in New York, the other to the prestigious Curtis Institute of Music in Philadelphia. She decided on a year in New York, where she would be one of the first black women pupils, during which time she could prepare for the entrance examination for Curtis. This immense distance sounded a death knell for their relationship. Edney began dating another woman, Annie Mae, whom he eventually married.

If the broken relationship hurt her, then Eunice had plenty of distractions in New York. Her teacher was Dr Carl Friedburg, a source of inspiration and joy. His musical excellence enabled Eunice to extend herself further than ever before. This, she felt, was what she had been born to do and, invigorated by her own hopes and dreams and those of many others, she prepared for the entrance exam at the Curtis Institute.

However, when the day came her carefully laid plans went badly wrong. Possibly nerves got the better of her and Eunice's playing was under par. Perhaps her colour counted against her. Whatever the reason, her failure to win a place at the Curtis Institute came as a hammer blow to the young hopeful. Hadn't she been told her gift was God-given. Surely, then, God would have wanted her to have the best? She felt strongly that she had the necessary talent and that it was bigotry that had stood in her way. Years later she discovered that another young black woman, concert pianist Marion Anderson, had won admission to the Curtis Institute. That single fact didn't prove the absence of a racist agenda, however.

It was a bitter end to a childhood that had been dominated by a quest for musical excellence. The case for her prowess at the piano was not proven. Eunice had to pick up the pieces and find a new way forward, one of her own making. Proud though she was to be the object of a town's aspirations, she had felt constricted by its ambition for her.

Years later she told the *Evening Standard* newspaper that she had felt frustrated by her lack of options. 'If you are poor and burdened with that amount of talent you don't have much choice in life,' she said.

The day she was turned down at Curtis she died on one level, only to be swiftly reborn in a different guise. The resulting reincarnation was Miss Nina Simone. Maybe it sounded a bit different now, but that unique God-given talent would not be denied.

2 'I Loves You, Porgy'

The rejection by the Curtis Institute left an indelible mark on the young Eunice. Her own hopes and the dreams of all those back home who had invested in her tuition seemed irrevocably dashed. Still trying to come to terms with what had happened, she declared she was through with music but, of course, she had to live. Music had been the focus of her life and she had to survive the only way she knew how. She left Philadelphia for Atlantic City, planning to take a job playing piano in a bar.

Her intention was to send money home to try and repay the family that had invested so greatly in her. She toyed with the prospect of retaking the exam. Then, for the first time, she encountered popular music and the work of singers like Billie Holiday, Sarah Vaughan and Louis Jordan. In addition, there was the sound of the jazz greats including Oscar Peterson and Louis Armstrong. This was the music coming out of bars and clubs all over the States, and Atlantic City was no exception.

Fearful of the damaging effects of modern music, Eunice's mother was outraged, but Eunice felt she had no choice and embraced her new musical existence by adopting a stage name. Nina was the affectionate name a former boyfriend had for her, while Simone was taken from the name of French actress Simone Signoret.

The owner of the bar insisted that she not only played but sang. Following the initial shock, she felt comfortable about this and relished her musical freedom. For years she had loved classical music and the great masters like Beethoven and Mozart. Here was an opportunity to let loose in a totally different way. She discovered, too, that she had some measure of influence over rowdy audiences. If they misbehaved, she simply refused to play. In later years she would be called 'temperamental' for this behaviour, but to Nina it was a matter of respect. When she was shown none she would withdraw to preserve her dignity and self-esteem.

Nina played a circuit of bars and clubs in Philly and Atlantic City, and before long the offers were coming in from New York. She usually played from midnight through until to dawn, with regular breaks. Nobody knew or cared then about the effects of sleep depravation on the brain, least of all the late-flowering Nina. Flexing her new-found freedom she married Don Ross, although the union was doomed to failure, lasting just a year.

Among her best-known numbers was an inimitable version of 'I Loves You, Porgy' from the George Gershwin musical *Porgy And Bess*. One night, without her knowledge or permission, someone recorded her live at a local club and produced an album called *Starring Nina Simone*. Its release by Premier Records resulted in the first of many court battles she had to wage to protect her own music. The seeds of distrust and bitterness towards the music industry were sown.

During her spell in New York she was approached by representatives of Bethlehem Records who asked her to record an album. In 1958 the first legitimate Nina Simone album, *Little Girl Blue*, appeared, featuring 'Plain Gold Ring', 'My Baby Just Cares For Me' and 'I Loves You, Porgy'.

Bethlehem was in fact part of a larger company, King Records, owned by Sid Nathan and based in Cincinnati, Ohio. The label specialised in rhythm & blues recordings and the 'Godfather of Soul', James Brown, began his own career on another of King's imprints, Federal, two years before Nina. Somewhat naively she signed a contract with Bethlehem Records that brought her a cheque for $10,000 in royalties for the sale of the album. With hindsight she came to realise the value of the royalties was many times that figure.

Nina recalled in her autobiography that the first Bethlehem album was recorded in a mammoth 13-hour session. A total of 14 songs were laid down, with Nina accompanied by musicians Jimmy Bond on bass and Albert 'Tootie' Heath on drums.

The album might have sunk without trace if not for the radio disc jockeys who repeatedly played 'I Loves You, Porgy'. It was one in particular – Sid Marx in Philadelphia – who kept playing the song in response to an ever-increasing number of requests. Before they knew it, Nina and Bethlehem had a hit on their hands. When the label released it in the summer of 1959 it became a Top 20 pop and Top 50 R&B smash.

Nina moved to New York shortly after the album was released, taking her husband with her, a man she liked but did not love. She had entered uncharted territory. A hit record, no management and a marriage that lacked real passion. It was a story that would be repeated during her life.

'I Loves You, Porgy' won her fans across the globe – not least my brother and me, listening avidly in our corner of Britain to just one LP, *Nina Simone At Town Hall*, which was wearing thin from constant use.

In 1959 after her first hit with Bethlehem, Nina had been signed by Colpix Records, a division of Columbia Pictures. The label would be her recording home for four years and, in all, she had nine Colpix albums released in the USA – albums that would show her amazing versatility, ranging from Duke Ellington compositions and traditional spirituals to old English odes and African chants. Unfortunately, little of Nina's music had been released in Britain. Pye had issued *Nina Simone At Town Hall* and *Folksy Nina*, and that was about it.

Brought to Colpix by A&R man Paul Wexler, Nina would become one of the label's most prolific artists. Her first album there, *The Amazing Nina Simone*, featured a diversity of music from the old spiritual 'Children Go Where I Send You' to the haunting theme from *Middle Of The Night*, encompassing Rodgers and Hammerstein's 'It Might As Well Be Spring' and Benny Goodman's 'Stompin' At The Savoy' along the way.

Nina's versatility was even more prominent on her live albums, and Colpix released a total of five live albums during her stay with the company. The taping of *Nina Simone At Town Hall* showcased her artistry on a number of standards, including songs like 'Fine And Mellow' and 'Exactly Like You', two tunes associated with Billie Holiday, whom she acknowledged as one of her early influences.

She recalled in her autobiography: 'The day of the show I dressed in a long white gown draped over one shoulder and white satin shoes... I stood in the wings and looked out at the audience, sitting in neat rows with no drinks in their hands, no cigarette girls walking up and down to distract them and no out-of-tune piano to ruin my performance. The MC called my name and I walked on like an Egyptian queen – slow, calm and serious. The reviews were the best I had ever had. I was a sensation. An overnight success, just like in the movies.'

It was this kind of audience reaction that led Colpix to record her at the famous Newport Jazz Festival in June 1960, performing a mix of tunes that included an African chant, 'Flo Me La', Cole Porter's 'You'd Be So Nice To Come Home To' and the traditional folk song 'Little Liza Jane'. Her second studio album for Colpix was the brilliant *Forbidden Fruit*, including songs like Oscar Brown Jr's memorable 'Rags And Old Iron', 'Work Song' and Peggy Lee's 'Where Can I Go Without You'.

While Colpix knew that Nina was an album artist, executives would occasionally have her do recording sessions specifically aimed at producing hot singles. In 1960 she had a Top 30 R&B hit with a revival of the old Bessie Smith blues tune 'Nobody Knows You When You're Down And Out' and then, less than six months later, a revival of another blues classic, 'Trouble In Mind', saw her return to the Top 20 R&B charts once more. One less successful example was an 'answer' song to Ray Charles' classic 'Hit The Road Jack' entitled 'Come On Back Jack', which didn't make the US charts.

It was her albums, though, that defined her increasing importance. Following *Forbidden Fruit* came *Nina Simone At The Village Gate*, recorded in April 1961 at the famous New York Club with then-unknown comedian Richard Pryor as her opening act.

Later the same year Nina married Andy Stroud and he became her manager. She cut a tribute album to Duke Ellington, *Nina Simone Sings Ellington*, including such songs as 'Do Nothin' Till You Hear From Me', 'The Gal From Joe's' and 'Solitude'. She took a mini-break for the birth of her daughter, Lisa Celeste, who was born on 12 September 1962.

It was Nina's electrifying live performances at Carnegie Hall that completed her tenure at Colpix. From her show on 12 May 1963 Colpix producers were able to create two albums – *Nina Simone At Carnegie Hall* and *Folksy Nina*. A couple of years after her departure from Colpix, executives issued an album called *Nina Simone With Strings*, a mixture of new and previously recorded material with strings added. By the time this album came out Nina had moved on to bigger and better things, and had a new international contract with Philips Records.

Nina would change record label several times throughout her life and it was not unusual to find her old label issuing an album to coincide with the release of a new album. This overlap allowed a deluge of bootleg albums to be released, masquerading as bona fide recordings. Not only would the public be unaware of the albums' origins, but often Nina herself had no idea the material was being released. It was a subject that would rear its head several times over the years and justified her conviction that she was being ripped off.

3 'I Put A Spell On You'

It was the early 1960s when I first heard Nina's voice. As mentioned in the Introduction to this book, I was just 12 years old. My brother David's appreciation of her overwhelming talent influenced me greatly.

The swinging '60s had just begun but while our friends were into Manfred Mann and The Kinks, we were spellbound by artists like Dionne Warwick, Aretha Franklin and, of course, Nina Simone. It was not long before Nina became our outright favourite, and even our traditional, Jewish parents were enjoying her sounds.

David recalls buying his first Nina album: 'I was working in a record store in Marble Arch, London, at the time and I'd read an article by one of my all-time favourite artists, Dionne Warwick. In it she mentioned this incredible singer, "Nina Simone". Well, being the curious type I asked the manager of the store if we had any Nina Simone albums. I actually thought she was some French chanteuse and so when he said in a rather dismissive tone, "Yes I think there's one in the negro jazz section" I almost fell over! There it was: *Nina Simone At Town Hall*. I went into the listening booth and as I began to listen to "Black Is The Color Of My True Love's Hair" tears welled up in my eyes. Who was this woman who could go from soprano tenderness to dark velvet in a millisecond? The photograph on the cover gave little clue and there was virtually no information on the back cover of the album to tell me who I was listening to.'

With the release of 'Don't Let Me Be Misunderstood' the spell Nina had put on David and I was complete. I remember listening to her sing, and even at such a young age it filled me with such strong emotions, there were times I was sure she was singing about me. David had always had a love affair with what was then termed 'black' music. Once he heard Nina, he thought there was no other music worth bothering with and I shared his views. Back then I had no idea that one day I would meet Nina, let alone have a friendship that would endure for almost 40 years. I am eternally grateful to David for having such incredibly good taste in music. Without his influence, who knows how different my life would have been.

David would go on to become one of the greatest authorities on 'black' music around and has primarily been a music journalist for over 40 years, as well as a talented blues singer–songwriter himself. His book *The Soulful Divas* recalls how the idea of Nina's fan club came into being: 'The buzz about this mysterious Nina Simone gave me the chance to become part of the "in" crowd: everyone who was anyone in R&B circles had "adopted" a US artist and formed a fan club for the individual or group. Ben E King, Barbara Lynn, Doris Troy, Martha And The Vandellas, Inez and Charlie Foxx, The Shirelles and Dionne Warwick all had fan clubs. To get permission, I promptly tracked down her US manager, one Andrew Stroud, who unbeknown to me, was also her husband. Weeks later, I received my confirmation letter allowing me to set up a fan club for Nina in the UK.'

We had no idea that David's plan to start a fan club would blossom into a worldwide appreciation society, and that those very humble beginnings would eventually see us swamped by sack loads of fan mail from every corner of the planet.

Finally, the long awaited moment had arrived: Nina was coming to England and we would be able to meet her in person! My parents felt I was too young to go to the airport to meet Nina, so I had to make do with David's account of all that transpired on that special day.

'To say I was nervous is without doubt the greatest understatement. I was literally shaking. Here, striding towards me was the object of my adoration – Miss Nina Simone, accompanied by her husband Andy Stroud, daughter Lisa Celeste and a nanny. The closer they got the more I shook. Suddenly the figure was standing right in front of me. I proffered a rather large bouquet of flowers and meekly held out my hand: "Hi, I'm David Nathan." Nina looked at me and grinned: "Oh, so you're my fan club president, it's good to meet you." There, I had done it, I'd managed to speak – what a relief. Andy said to follow them as the record company had arranged for a limo to pick them up and I'd be more than welcome to join them. This was fast becoming too much for me to believe. I'd imagined I'd merely say hello and go home, and here I was being invited to ride along with Nina and company.

'As we drove along my nerves finally began to disappear, partly due to the fact that Nina was chatting to me as if we already knew one another. I remember her asking what other artists I was "into", and I told her how Dionne Warwick was another favourite of mine. With that she turned to Andy, "Have you ever heard of her?" Andy said yes, and she told him when she went home she wanted to listen to her. I went on to explain that it was in fact due to Dionne that I had first heard of Nina. I'd read an interview by her in which she had mentioned Nina, and being the curious type I went in search of her music. Thank you Dionne!

'Nina was interested in another singer, namely Dusty Springfield, and she asked me if I'd heard of her. I told her yes – in fact, she was one of the few "white" artists I listened to. "You know she sounds a lot like one of our singers, Aretha Franklin." I agreed and we continued our journey talking about what I was up to, how was I doing in school, and so on. As we began driving on the overpass, Nina suddenly looked out and with a rather excited voice, prodded Andy: "Oh, look they've all got chimneys. David, do all the houses here have chimneys?" I explained that due to the fact it was cold here…most houses had chimneys to keep warm. "Huh, that's neat, real neat." We finally reached her hotel, The Cumberland in London's West End, and she and Andy bade me a fond farewell and told me to call them later. Wow! As I travelled home on the bus I could not believe it, minutes ago I had been sitting in my very first ever limo, with my idol Nina Simone, chatting as if we'd known each other for ever.

'Upon my return, Sylvia was literally waiting at the door, anxious for me to relay every detail of this first meeting. I did feel slightly guilty that she'd had to stay home, but she was only 13 years old and our mother was trying her best to keep her away from "show business". Fortunately for Sylvia, our mother failed miserably and, eventually, was happy to sit and hear some of the stories we relayed about our adventures. Our father had a more relaxed attitude. Just as Nina had been fortunate to have a father who, over her mother's strong objections, supported his daughter's foray into the world of "real" music, we too were lucky.

Back then we lived in a flat above a restaurant and space was limited. As such, the only hi-fi system was located in our parents' bedroom. One Sunday morning David snuck in and put on the *Forbidden Fruit* album. Our father, the man we termed a gentle giant, awoke to the strains of 'Rags And Old Iron'. Fearing a scolding, David went to turn off the record and was surprised when our father simply sat up and said, 'Leave that alone. I'm listening to that!' It would take the song 'Erets Zavat Chalav' to totally convert our mother – once I had informed her that it was a Jewish folk song, Nina became a real family favourite. This was something that proved vital when David wanted to see Nina live. As he was not yet 18 David was unable to go to a nightclub unescorted, so it was a relief when our father agreed to accompany him to Annie's Room, along with our uncle. David recalls the story of his first encounter with a 'live' performance by Nina.

'Fortunately we'd arrived at Annie's Room early, as on our arrival we had a problem with the guy at the door, who insisted our names were "not on the guest list". I asked my father to find Nina's husband Andy and a few minutes later we were ushered to our front-row seats! The crowd was made up of a rather elite group of "jazz" followers and celebrities. Annie's Room was a club owned by jazz singer Annie Ross, of the famous trio Lambert, Hendrix and Ross, so it was considered the "in" place of the time. It was also a rare treat for my father and uncle, as neither had been to such an upmarket club before, and they were overwhelmed by the whole experience.

'Suddenly the curtains ruffled and there in front of us was Nina, resplendent in a blue silk gown. She made her way to the piano to tumultuous applause. Performing solo, she sang a number of songs from her Colpix albums, but none of her more political protest songs. One of the songs I clearly remember is "Zungo" from her *At The Village Gate* album. The audience seemed completely transfixed – it was as if the spirit was moving everyone as they swayed to the African rhythms, myself included. Following a series of rapturous encores, Nina left the stage and I recall looking at my dad and uncle, both of whom were standing cheering! A few minutes later Andy appeared and escorted us backstage. Nina rose and greeted my dad and uncle, both of whom had obviously had an attack of nerves. It was amusing to watch my dad, a rather large man, seemingly speechless in Nina's presence. I guess not only teenagers get dumbstruck. Finally we left and I listened to my dad raving about Nina all the way home. I had to laugh, as anyone would think he'd discovered her himself!'

As this was Nina's first official visit to Britain, several concerts had been scheduled, along with a live taping of TV show *Ready, Steady, Go*. David was by now part of the Nina Simone entourage.

Several years previously he had become friends with a woman called Vicki Wickham. She was the producer of *Ready, Steady, Go* and their friendship was to prove a blessing: 'I arrived at the studio and, with Vicki, went backstage to see Nina. She was relaxing waiting to go on and, in the background, music was being played over the loudspeakers. The strains of "God Bless The Child" began playing. Nina turned to me seeming rather upset: "Who's that on that tape singing Billie's song? Who's singing Billie's song?" She was obviously angry and with some trepidation I replied, "I think it's a band called Blood, Sweat

And Tears." With that she began shouting "Why are they singing her song, that's her song, man!" So, this was the "other side" of Nina.

'She seemed to calm down a bit and then without warning shouted at me, "DO YOU BELIEVE IN GOD?" I was beginning to get a little scared and said "Yes." With that, she began running round the room screaming, "YOU MUST BELIEVE IN GOD, you MUST believe in GOD!" So here I was thinking, "Okay I'm not quite sure how to handle this," when fortunately Andy walked in and took us outside. What a relief! Had I known this was just part of Nina being Nina, it may not have fazed me quite so much, but back then I'd never been around any performers and it was a shock – one I'd have to get over very quickly if I were to have any kind of relationship with her.

'We went out to the studio and on stage was Doris "Just One Look" Troy (who was to become a lifelong friend). She was just finishing up with her song "Heartaches" and as she came over Nina greeted her cordially enough, although she had no idea who Doris was. As the set wasn't yet ready we stood cooling our heels while waiting. The latest dance music was blasting out of the loudspeakers, and everyone was doing their thing on the dance floor. Nina turned to me, "David do you dance?" I rather sheepishly said "No." So, then she turns to me quite casually and says, "Well if you don't dance, you must have sex." I turned scarlet and half-whispered, "Well I haven't done either." Suddenly she just burst out laughing, "Ha!" I didn't know where to put myself I was so totally embarrassed.

'Just then, Vicki walked over looking rather serious. She informed Andy that due to time constraints, Nina could now only do one song instead of the previously agreed two. He was not at all amused, both by the fact that she could only do one song and also that he had to tell her! She was not at all happy, but to her credit she sat at the piano and gave an amazing rendition of "Children Go Where I Send You". At one point I could see her smiling over at me, and as she did she changed the tempo – it became somewhat sensual to say the least. Was she trying to tell me something? As usual, she had the whole place jumping. Regardless of her anger she was a professional when it came to her music, and very rarely allowed her personal feelings to get in the way of her performance. I did say rarely, as over time she would in fact let her feelings get the better of her on more than one occasion, which resulted in the term "temperamental" being used to describe these outbursts.

'I'd witnessed a temper tantrum, been grilled about my sex life – and this was only our third meeting. I dreaded to think what lay ahead. However, my respect for her as an artist, coupled with my youth, forgave any unseemly behaviour. Afterwards I just thanked her and beat a very hasty retreat, lest I got involved in any more in-depth probing. I saw her again very briefly and then like a genie she was gone. She said she'd had a great time in England, and was looking forward to returning real soon. I determined to become much more worldly before that day came.'

Musically, 1965 was a prolific year for Nina. Philips realised that she was rapidly becoming an international favourite, thanks to the trips she had made to Europe, and wasted no time in having Nina in the studio on a regular basis. In all, she recorded 35 songs during sessions in January, May and September that year, and the diverse material she cut went into four LPs that were released between June 1965 and September 1966. In the summer of 1965 came the classic *I Put A Spell On You*, which contained a number of songs that would remain a staple of her repertoire for many years to come, including 'Ne Me Quitte Pas' and 'Feeling Good' (used in several European television commercials almost 40 years after it was recorded). The title track, Nina's show-stopping version of the song originally made famous by Screamin' Jay Hawkins, inched its way into the British pop charts.

By the end of the year, Philips had issued the *Pastel Blues* album, best known for Nina's spine-chilling reading of the Billie Holiday standard 'Strange Fruit', a song that captured the evil of racism so starkly, along with a tour de force performance of the traditional 'Sinnerman', in which Nina truly let rip. The following year began with *Let It All Out*, a collection based on a number of different sessions and, once again, it contained everything from R&B songwriter Van McCoy's 'For Myself' to the nasty 'Chauffeur', another song (much like 'Gimme Some' on the *I Put A Spell On You* album) that left little to the imagination. While love songs were an essential part of the Simone repertoire, she also made sure she included songs that definitely addressed other areas of romance and relationships, and sex – in all its glory. This was indeed the main and indisputable theme on all these recordings.

The *Pastel Blues* album played a very important role in David's appreciation for what Nina stood for as a civil rights activist. He remembers taking the LP to school as part of a classroom project. 'All my classmates at Kilburn Grammar School were assembled in the library and the teacher had arranged for us to have a record player since he knew I wanted to play Nina's music. I explained to the class who she was and put on "Strange Fruit" for this crowd of pimply, very white teenagers. I told them what the song was about and, after Nina's amazing performance, you could hear a pin drop. I can still see everyone's faces as they sat mesmerised by the raw emotion in Nina's voice. At the end everyone broke into applause. I felt so good that I had presented Nina's music and given the class an insight into what was going on thousands of miles away in the struggle for justice and freedom.'

So David was not content simply to bring Nina into our household, but acted as a miniature 'ambassador' in his quest to have her recognised as a true genius. Her last album for 1966 was *Wild Is The Wind*. The inclusion of a song she wrote called 'Four Women' made the LP a must for fans everywhere and would stand the test of time. Indeed, the last few concerts she did before she died included this classic. The writer Joel Siegel described 'Four Women' as 'brief, incisive portraits reflecting the experiences and generational perspectives of a variegated quartet of black women' and certainly Nina's simple yet stark vignettes left no one in any doubt that she had encountered each type of woman during her life.

In contrast, there were some songs on *Wild Is The Wind* that were obviously aimed at getting mainstream airplay for Nina. Van McCoy's fiery 'Break Down And Let It All Out' gave Nina a chance for fulsome self-expression, while the song 'I Love Your Loving Ways' (written by Bennie Benjamin and Sol Marcus, two of the co-writers of 'Don't Let Me Be Misunderstood') was another up-tempo ditty that framed Nina as a potential R&B hitmaker. Her treatment of McCoy's 'Either Way I Lose' (previously recorded by Gladys Knight And The Pips) was yet another highlight of *Wild Is The Wind*, which was one of her best-selling albums for Philips.

Nina's music was like her life: diverse and inspired. No two albums were ever alike and, over the years, attempts to pigeonhole her failed miserably. She could not be defined as either a jazz or blues singer – her repertoire encompassed every form of music and genre. Although we had yet to hear many of these albums, the small taste of her musical abilities we had sampled had whetted our appetites. David and I would eventually own every 'legitimate' album she ever made and we are grateful to the forward-thinking industry for reissuing these masterpieces on CD. Had it not done so, our original copies would never have survived the countless years of wear and tear they received in our hands.

4 'Take Care Of Business'

Fortunately my being introduced to Nina at such a young age had an added bonus. I began a scrapbook and, to even David's amazement, it is the only tangible thing that has survived my entire life. Thanks to this I am able to reprint extracts from one of the very first newsletters, which is alas undated. However, having researched the material, it seems likely it covers the years 1966–67.

> The Nina Simone Fan Club,
> 21 Deptford High Street,
> LONDON,
> SE8

Dear Members,

The fact is that I have been engaged on the launching of Britain's first 100% rhythm and blues record store, Soul City, and as you can imagine this has taken some considerable effort and time. I now have plenty of important news to report to you regarding Nina's forthcoming trip to this country.

Nina will be arriving in this country for a two-week tour on April 9th. She will be accompanied by her trio and is scheduled to arrive at either 10:40am or 11:00am on Sunday 9 April. I know this is a little early in the morning – but I do hope that as many of you as possible will be able to make it to London Airport to meet Miss Simone.

The balance of the newsletter discusses Nina's tour schedule and the upcoming release of her first album for RCA, *Day And Night*. No sooner had she signed with RCA, Philips decided to release one last album, *The High Priestess Of Soul*. The LP contained gems like 'I'm Gonna Leave You' (written by guitarist Rudy Stevenson), a cover of Chuck Berry's 'Brown-Eyed Handsome Man' and 'I Hold No Grudge', a tune that revisited the ongoing struggle for racial equality.

Nina's personal view on the issue was evident in her choice of songs for her important RCA debut LP. Released in July 1967, just two months after the *High Priestess* album, *Nina Simone Sings The Blues* was a remarkable piece of work containing 'Backlash Blues' from the pen of the famous author Langston Hughes and 'Blues For Mama' written by Nina with fellow singer and performer Abbey Lincoln. Once again, music from *Porgy And Bess* received the Simone treatment. Producer Danny Davis wrote in the sleeve notes for the LP, 'Miss Simone was physically and emotionally exhausted from previous recording, but she sat down at the piano and began to play and sing this moving *Porgy And Bess* tune. The bass picked it up. From somewhere she summoned up the stamina to deliver with even more intensity and spirit a rare, perfect performance that could not be improved.'

Other outstanding songs on that first RCA LP include a great revival of the standard 'Since I Fell For You' and the overtly sexual 'I Want A Little Sugar In My Bowl'.

Well, my time had finally come. Having heard the tales relayed by David about the highs and lows of Nina's personality, I was on my way to Heathrow Airport with him for my first encounter, a bundle of nerves. Here I was, not yet 15 years old, and about to meet my idol. I had a strange feeling that something was wrong with my legs, as they seemed unwilling to move. David finally just grabbed me, my arms straining with the weight of the huge bouquet I was carrying, and half dragged me towards the fur-clad figure walking towards me. I have to be totally honest: I have absolutely no idea what came out of my mouth. I do recall a slender hand reaching out to me, and thinking she seemed a lot smaller in person than I had imagined. Obviously, we exchanged some brief words and then she was gone. As she now had a larger entourage, including her own musicians, things were a little frantic as everyone headed to their hotel and, rather than get caught up in it, we decided to leave. David arranged to call her later. According to David, I drove him completely mad on the journey home, repeating over and over, 'Wow, I finally met her. I can't believe it.' Eventually David pretended he wasn't with me on the bus, so I shut up!

I knew I was going to meet her again shortly, as arrangements had been made for us both to attend her concert at the Royal Festival Hall in London. Prior to this, she was touring England for several concerts, one of which was to be at the Colston Hall, in Bristol. The set included entertainer Dick Gregory as the opening act and they had hired a bus to take them to the venue.

David had been invited to go although, once more, my age barred me from this event. He relayed the ensuing drama, as follows.

'By some sort of miracle I was able to get to the hotel just in time. It was only 6:30am but a long day's travelling was ahead and an early start was imperative. Everyone was milling around – the musicians, Dick Gregory and Andy – but, as yet, no Nina. She finally made her entrance and we boarded the bus. During the ride she chatted to Dick Gregory and I had a chance to talk to some of the musicians, mainly about where they were from, and so on. Finally we arrived in Bristol and headed to the venue. Upon arrival, the promoter had informed Andy that for some unknown reason they had only sold 30 tickets! Andy was understandably furious and it was he who had to tell Nina what had happened. She literally went berserk and the screams could be heard far away. Following this tirade, Andy walked out and asked if I wanted to go for a walk with him. As I hadn't really had a chance to spend any time with him, I agreed.

'As we walked along the seafront, he relayed to me how sometimes she was really difficult to deal with and that being married to her as well as managing her career was hard. "Sometimes, David, I just don't know what to do with her." Being a teenager I really had no answer for him. I'd never had to deal with such a perplexing situation. I felt slightly uncomfortable as I had a strong sense of loyalty to Nina, and any remarks could be seen as a betrayal. He was furious that he had driven half the day, only to discover that sales had been so poor. Had he known prior to departure, no doubt we would have skipped the trip.

'We returned to the concert hall and you can just imagine the scene. Dick Gregory opened to an audience of 30 British people, unable to create an atmosphere. But Nina surprised us all. She came out and immediately told everyone to move to the front. Even though there were only 30 people in the audience, they loved it. She enthralled them with "I Put A Spell On You", "Take Care Of Business" and "Ne Me Quitte Pas". She ended by singing "Day And Night" and "Do I Move You", both from her latest album at RCA, and certainly a reflection of what she'd done to her audience. She did much more than simply move them. Considering the lack of physical bodies, the sound made by this elite group was tremendous. Again she had shown that no matter the circumstances, her audiences wouldn't suffer.'

It was not the only venue in Britain that she failed to fill. In 1967 about 100 people turned up to a concert in Portsmouth and once again she delivered a devastating performance.

One critic called her a wily sorceress and wrote, '[There was] brooding yet smouldering magnetism in everything she did and many of her songs had the sharp tang of bitter poetry.'

If David was concerned about how the ill-fated night in Bristol would end he was in for a surprise.

'Afterwards we all piled back on the bus for the long journey home. We arrived back in London, gone midnight, and Nina turned to me and asked me if I wanted to stay with them, as they had an extra sofa I could sleep on. No guesses for my reply! She came in and made sure I was comfortable and then retired for the night. The following morning she invited me for breakfast, and we talked a bit about how hard it was travelling, performing and trying to be a mother. "It's like a juggling act at times, but it's the road I've chosen. Sometimes I think it's too hard trying to do it all, but then I remember all the hard work I've done, and I look at Lisa and I thank God!" I bade her farewell and thanked her for her hospitality and the great show I'd witnessed. As I went down in the elevator I kept thinking, "Somebody please pinch me." Did I really just spend the night in the same room as Nina Simone? She had been so considerate, and spending this time with her would always be a treasured memory.'

David has many more great memories, but some stand out more than others. The following experience turned out to be much more intense than any that had preceded it.

'During the ride to Bristol Nina had asked me about another venue she was booked to play, the Ram Jam Club, in Brixton, south London. I had told her it was an area mainly populated by West Indians and she seemed genuinely happy, saying, "Great I'm going to be with my people." I never really took much notice of the reference to people of colour at the time. The concert was booked for Sunday 23 April, and I remember it was bitterly cold. Inside it wasn't much warmer, and Nina was reluctant to relinquish the fur coat she was wearing. The audience was predominantly black, and apart from one other guy I was the only white face in the place. The promoter came out to a packed room and announced, "Here from America, is the one and only Miss Nina Simone." She came out smiling, headed to the piano, and began playing "I Put A Spell On You". She seemed to be enjoying herself, when all of a sudden the audience began shouting "My Baby Just Cares". She had no clue what they were shouting about and carried on playing. The shouts started to get louder, and she stood up, stared into the crowd and said "Please be quiet, I'm performing." For a performer like Nina, whose silences were as potent as her piano playing, an attentive crowd was a must. But when she sat back down the audience just kept yelling, "My Baby Just Cares", getting louder with each passing minute. What she didn't realise was the reason they were yelling was because the song "My Baby Just Cares For Me", which was on her first album, had become a West Indian anthem. It had a mix of both ska and blue beat (ska being the forerunner of reggae) and was very popular among most black Britons. It was also hard to find as a single. All of this was unknown to Nina, who had recorded the song way back in 1959 and then forgotten about it. By now the audience was getting really upset. They weren't interested in "Feeling Good" or anything else, they had only come for this one song… Well, she finally lost her temper, got up in true Nina style, slammed the piano lid down, and shouted: "Shut up. If you don't shut up, I'm not performing any more." The audience began yelling and screaming even louder, so she stormed off. I remember thinking I didn't feel too safe as the crowd was getting more and more vocal.

'Sensing a near-riot and to try to calm things down, the promoter came back out and announced, "Miss Simone will be right back." I went backstage to find Nina yelling at Andy, "Why are they yelling at me? What do they want, what the fuck do they want?" Bravely, I turned to her and said, "They want you to sing 'My Baby Just Cares For Me'. Well with that she screamed at me full force, "I'm not singing that piece of shit. I don't even remember the words." So, I was thinking, okay, here we go again. Suddenly she mellowed just a fraction. "David, why do they want me to sing that?" "Well you know Jamaican audiences really like that song." Andy then piped up, "Look Nina, you'll have to sing it." To which all she replied was, "Ha!" I think out of sheer desperation, Andy then grabbed a bottle of gin, handed it to Nina, and said, "Here, honey." Not bothering with a glass, she started swigging out of the bottle. I just stared at her, speechless. All of this was happening while the promoter was frantically trying to calm things down. "Look, Mr Stroud, you've got to get her back on stage, there's a near riot going on out there. If she doesn't go back on stage they're going to tear the place apart."

'Meanwhile, out front the audience was going wild, screaming, "My Baby Just Cares". Finally, a few swigs later, she stormed back on stage opened the piano, and without a word began playing "My Baby Just Cares". Well, the audience went completely crazy shouting, "Sing it, yeah, sing it girl." Nina just glared at the crowd and yelled back, "That's what you wanted!" Minutes later she turned to me and asked, "David, what do you want to hear? My fan club president's here, you know." As calmly as I was able, I replied, "Could you sing 'Since I Fell For You'?" With that, she proceeded to play and gave me one of her by now famous grins, and acted as if the near-riot of the past few moments had never happened. This was just one of those occasions that remain unforgettable.'

When David first recounted the above events, I could hardly move for laughing. Despite the fact that some of it had obviously been difficult, the images of Nina cussing and screaming had me in hysterics. Little did I know that I would later witness many such scenes, that would either have me trying to suppress a giggle or trying to find a place to hide. Now that the arrangements had been made for us to go to the Royal Albert Hall, I looked forward to, at last, seeing Nina perform.

The long-awaited night had arrived and after changing several times I was ready to go. We arrived at the Albert Hall and as we approached the dressing room door, I began to have second thoughts. 'I don't think I'll come in. I'll just go to my seat and watch the show.' David's reply was quite adamant 'I don't think so. You can't just go now. You're coming in and that's that!' With that, he literally pushed me through the door. There in front of me was the regal figure of Nina. Although we had met briefly at the airport, I was sure she had forgotten as she proceeded to look at me as if I was a complete stranger. I was right. My somewhat meek performance at the airport obviously hadn't registered.

Nina greeted David and then she turned her gaze towards me. I was trying so hard to hide in the corner, but she had me in her sights. Nina smiled at David and said, 'So David, this is your "little" sister. Is she a fan too?' David explained how he had been playing the *Town Hall* album when a small face had appeared round the door and that, yes, his little sister was now also hooked. Well, that was my very first experience of her throaty laugh. Two firsts – the smile and the laugh – Nina was on good form that day, thank goodness. It would be a while before I witnessed the other side of her, and scary is not an adequate adjective to describe it. The memory of that first meeting will stay with me for ever.

I finally managed to overcome my fear and told Nina how much I loved her music. 'Thank you, sugar, that's so sweet of you. So how old are you?' 'Oh, well I'm very nearly 15.' I figured that sounded more grown up and I didn't want her to think I was just a child. 'So you're still young and innocent, but you know you have an old soul. I'm an old soul, nearly 2,000 years old you know.' I wasn't quite sure what to say, so I simply smiled and said how great that was. David was by now trying to suppress a huge grin. He had already experienced Nina's penchant for supernature, and was no longer fazed by her comments. Oh well, who was I to argue? If Nina said I had an old soul, then I guess I did.

Having now met Nina, I was even more eager to watch her perform for the first time – and what a performance! Listening to her album was truly amazing, but to see her perform transformed your very being. I sat enthralled as the strains of 'Four Women', 'Plain Gold Ring' and many others enveloped me. I was mesmerised.

Following the performance we went backstage, and I was able to let Nina know just how moved I'd been by her. I guess, looking back, the word 'gushing' would be an apt description, but I was just so overwhelmed. Nina was sitting with a towel draped over her shoulders and sweat was dripping down her brow. It was obvious that performing required a great deal of physical stamina, as well as talent.

Despite my nervousness I just had to say something. 'Nina you were just so amazing. I can't believe how brilliant you are. Thank you so much for the show. I've never seen anything like it.' A huge smile appeared. 'So, you really dug it, did you? Good that's really good, you keep digging me you hear.' Yes I had heard, not that she needed to tell me, I was completely and utterly besotted by her and there was no going back. She then told David to take care of me. I thanked her and told her David always looked out for me and that I couldn't wait to see her again. 'Yes, you come and see me again. Don't let David hide you away okay?'

Nina's husband, Andy, was hovering, and told her she had a number of celebrities and press people waiting outside, and she had to get some rest. With that, we left. Outside I could not get over the events of the night and I drove David absolutely crazy. Over and over I recalled everything she had said, how much I loved the show and how happy I was to have finally met her.

Nina's musical odyssey was in full swing and her concerts included a mixture of old standards and the new more radical material she would include throughout her life. Seeing her live would always highlight her unique ability to translate any song to fit her mood. No matter what tracks she laid down in the studio, seeing her perform had the added bonus of always hearing a new interpretation of her music. In late 1967 RCA released the album *Silk & Soul*, which had its own share of highlights, such as 'Go To Hell' (a strident warning to folks who just didn't want to do right), 'It Be's That Way Sometime', written by Nina's brother Sam Waymon, and 'I Wish I Knew How It Would Feel To Be Free', a wonderful anthem from the pen of jazz musician Billy Taylor. Cover versions of the Bacharach–David classic 'The Look Of Love', The Association's 'Cherish' and John D Loudermilk's saucy 'Turn Me On' were 'Simone-ised', while one of the LP's standout tracks was the magnificent 'Consummation', surely one of her best compositions.

Musically, there was no one to rival Nina. Personally, she was a somewhat complex woman. Her beginnings in America's Deep South had shaped her life, and the path she chose would encompass her varied experiences along the way. It was 1967 and the record-buying public in Europe was discovering just what a versatile performer she was. This was the first of many tours of Europe, and were it not for all those newsletters and the infamous scrapbook, they may not have been so well documented.

In captivating Europe, Nina had altered the lives of two people in particular: my own and my brother's. Yes, we had entered a whole new realm and it would mark our lives for ever.

5 'Mississippi Goddam'

It would be impossible to review Nina's life without discussing her commitment to the civil rights movement, and the impact it had on her and her music. From childhood Nina witnessed racism. She quickly understood that the colour of her skin made a difference, that she was in an underclass as far as the majority of whites were concerned. As a result she became devoted to a quest for equality, and she refused to be inhibited in expressing her beliefs on the subject.

When Nina was growing up in America's Deep South, lynchings were still relatively commonplace. This meant that black people were hung without trial by a white mob as retribution for crimes real or imagined. For example, in 1928, just five years before Nina was born, there were nine lynchings in the American South. This was cause for comment as the number had never been so low. It was also the year that 'Ol' Man River' was a worldwide hit, a thoroughly black song. Lynchings were community occasions, attracting (white) women and children, and picture postcards were sometimes issued to mark these repugnant occasions.

It wasn't until Nina was 21 that segregation in schools was outlawed. She was 22 before a one-woman protest challenged the long-standing custom of segregation on public transport. In 1955, Rosa Lee Parks was arrested after she refused to give up her seat at the front of a bus in Montgomery, Alabama, to a white passenger. A bus boycott lasting more than a year began until the custom was publicly scrapped.

At this point Nina was observing events rather than contributing to them. In 1963, however, the abuse of blacks in the USA reached new heights. In June of that year, Medgar Evers, a civil rights worker in Jackson, Mississippi, was shot in the back near his home. The ex-serviceman was buried with full military honours at Arlington National Cemetery just as assassinated president John F Kennedy would be that same year. Byron de la Beckwith, leader of the local white supremacy group, was twice acquitted of the killing even when his fingerprints were found on the murder weapon. In her autobiography, *I Put A*

Spell On You, Nina recalls her feelings of disbelief and disgust as the state governor walked into the courthouse during one of the trials to shake hands with the man in the dock. (De la Beckwith was ultimately found guilty of the crime in 1994.)

Worse was to follow. On 15 September dynamite was tossed into the 16th Street Baptist Church in Birmingham, Alabama, killing four young black girls who were attending a Bible study class. In the disturbances that followed, two more black people were killed. The rush of fury that enveloped her swept Nina to the heart of the civil rights struggle.

Immediately afterwards she penned 'Mississippi Goddam', the first of many controversial songs she wrote and performed. The words, she said, 'erupted' from her. One emotive verse runs:

'Picket lines,
School boycotts,
They try to say it's a communist plot,
All I want is equality
For my sister, my brother, my people and me.'

In an interview in *Melody Maker* in December 1968 Nina spoke about the writing of 'Mississippi Goddam': 'I was more than angry when I wrote 'Goddam'...I was violent. But I'm not violent all the time. Most of the time I'm the same as everyone. But I know my people need me and I won't let them down.'

The millions who shared her beliefs were inspired and declared her to be their champion. The establishment, however, saw her in a different light. What gave this black woman the right to stand up and highlight the suffering of an entire section of the population?

In a vain attempt to stem the tide of bitterness and anger evoked by artists like Nina, the record was banned, ostensibly for the mention of the word 'Goddam'. This was music to the ears of radio station chiefs throughout the American South, who had no intention of broadcasting 'subversive' lyrics. One dealer in South Carolina sent a crate of copies back to the record distributors with each disc snapped in half.

Nina's friendship with playwright Lorraine Hansberry was significant, too. Hansberry was the first black woman to have a play, *A Raisin In The Sun*, produced on Broadway. She and Nina both shared a passionate belief in equal rights, and saw commitment to civil rights as a matter of duty and honour.

Neither woman, however, permitted those issues to dominate their work to the exclusion of everything else.

When Nina was interviewed on another occasion she tried once more to explain the power of her performances and a connection with activists everywhere: 'I just haven't got the words to describe what I do. It is like love. How do you talk about love? Soul is hard to define, words don't begin to describe the feelings the majority of people have about some things…

'I feel I am upholding the prestige of my people and most of my songs are about their problems. But I never forget that my first purpose is to bring art to the people. Any social feeling I have must not overwhelm the music or be taken to extremes.'

It was Hansberry above all others who impressed upon Nina the fact that she was involved in black rights issues simply by virtue of being black. In 1965 Nina was devastated when her intellectual mentor died from cancer at the age of 35. She took the title of the play Hansberry was working on at the time of her death, *Young, Gifted And Black*, and turned it into a black anthem. It is also the title of the collected works of Lorraine Hansberry, compiled in 1969 by her former husband Robert Nemiroff.

After leaving her place on the sidelines, Nina was drawn to black militancy. She cherished a friendship with Miriam Makeba, a South African singer exiled in 1963 after she gave evidence to the United Nations on the evils of apartheid.

Makeba was married to Stokeley Carmichael who, frustrated by the lack of pace in the civil rights movement, introduced a more proactive agenda under the twin banners of 'Black Pride' and 'Black is Beautiful'. Nina was a loyal supporter. Decades later, at Nina's funeral, Makeba paid tribute to the singer's contribution to the movement when she said, 'She was not only an artist, but also a freedom fighter.'

Nina's involvement in the civil rights movement was such that she became convinced she was at risk of assassination by white supremacists or even the FBI. With considerable courage, she continued to take the stage at concerts, even when she was a sitting target.

Being a rather naive teenager in England, I began to realise that the world was not quite as I had imagined. Ignorance may be bliss in certain situations, but in this instance it was merely ignorance. Fortunately, I had several opportunities to talk to Nina about her views. One occasion in particular springs to mind. She had just come off stage following an explosive concert at the Royal Festival Hall in London, and was sitting in her dressing room preparing to meet several of her closest friends and celebrities. I had watched from the wings as she had delivered one of her most powerful sets. Included in it were the songs 'Mississippi Goddam', and my own personal favourite, 'Pirate Jenny'. Sadly, I would only ever hear her perform that song once more, nearly 35 years later, and she admitted that the song was very 'draining' for her emotionally.

The audience was, as usual, fairly mixed, but Nina had emphasised that these songs in particular 'were for all you black folks out there'. This was something she would repeat over the many years of performing. Being a young white girl I was confused. Had I offended her in some way? I had to find out. 'Nina,' I asked rather meekly, 'Why are you so angry with white people?' Nina turned and with a very serious look on her face replied, 'Sylvia, you know these white folk don't want to hear the truth! You must know the struggles we go through. I'm gonna keep on telling them. They can't hide from *me*!'

Wow! What on earth could I say? After all, wasn't I one of the 'white' folks? I was just about to respond when Nina shot me one of her devilish smiles. Immediately the door was flung open and a whole slew of people descended upon her. I wondered if Nina realised I was white, and figured my huge 'afro' hairstyle must have confused her.

I just couldn't let it drop and I was able to again bring up the subject of her anger, this time with no interruptions. While David and Andy were busy discussing her itinerary, I once again posed the question. This time Nina went into a much longer and more detailed explanation. 'Honey, you're too young to understand. Do you know when I was just a child, I knew that the colour of my skin was different and that because of it, people hated me. Do you know what that *feels* like? You can't know, but it's not your fault; it's part of the system's way of hiding the truth. But the truth is *my* people have suffered for thousands of years, yes thousands! Yes, honey, we've suffered. To be told you're only a second-class human being, and that no matter what you do you will never be equal, hey that's *big*, man.'

I sat very quietly trying to absorb Nina's words fully as she continued, 'Sylvia, I know not *all* white people hate us, just as not all blacks hate white folk, but they are so damn few! The government wants to shut us up. People like Martin [Luther King], Malcolm [X], Lorraine [Hansberry], yes, and all my brothers and sisters. They want us all to just die. Yes, it's true. I don't know if it's the same here, but in America they want to keep us down, shut us up and a whole other bunch just want to bury us!'

Whew! This was far more than I had bargained for, but I really wanted to know. After all, Nina's songs had awakened a lot in me, and left a lot of questions unanswered. An opportunity arose to ask the one person who knew the answers and it was far too important to squander.

A few times Andy had interrupted, asking if Nina was okay and if she wanted anything, but I guess he sensed we were having a heavy conversation, and left us alone. As I sat and listened to Nina my heart felt heavy. I had lived without being aware of the realities of life. I believed we were all just people, that skin colour wasn't important. I had assumed most people felt as I did and was shocked to discover this was not the case. I told Nina that I must have been born 'colour blind', for I had never realised how much hatred there was in the world. I was not stupid. As a girl of Jewish descent I was aware that bigotry and prejudice existed, but to what extent I had never truly understood.

Andy informed Nina that time was getting tight. He wanted her to get some rest, as they had to go for dinner with some friends later. He asked David if we both wanted to come along, but I didn't feel like eating at that moment. I never shared too much of that conversation with David as I felt it was a private moment, and I still had so many more questions I hoped she'd answer. I vividly remember going home and playing 'Pirate Jenny' full blast. As I played it, the anger began to swell up in me and I cried. The song expresses the true extent of Nina's anguish and the passion of her anger as she describes the reality of slavery.

The subject would be one we engaged in many times over the years, and at Nina's suggestion I read books by James Baldwin, Lorraine Hansberry, Dr Martin Luther King, Malcolm X and a whole host of other prominent authors. I must admit to having been envious of Nina. While I could read the books by these inspired writers and humanitarians, she actually knew them. Lorraine had introduced Nina to Dr King and others. South African singer Miriam Makeba had introduced her to Stokeley Carmichael. Nina introduced them, via their writing, to me.

I am eternally grateful that I had such a brilliant teacher, one who knew what it was to do battle on a daily basis just to be respected. Indeed, my original envy at her close association with many of the authors disappeared when I saw how much they had all given for the cause, and I became a lot more militant in my own views.

There was one such occasion during which Nina had explained the whole 'Jim Crow' system to me. These were the long-standing laws that enforced segregation of black and white in the American Deep South on public transport, in education, in theatres and restaurants, even in cemeteries. The term Jim Crow came from a minstrel routine first performed in 1828 and was a derogatory one. It wasn't until 1954 that the first attempts to dismantle the Jim Crow laws were made.

'You've got to understand, Sylvia, down there they don't need a reason to kill a nigger. They just do it. It doesn't matter if you're minding your own business. If the white man wants to have him some fun, hanging's a sport for him. I know Martin [Luther King] says we need to be non-violent, but there's times I just want to get a gun and shoot somebody, just to get it out of me, you know.'

Well, actually I didn't know, but this phrase about not being non-violent became well worn over the years and began to alienate sections of the black community. Do I believe she would have killed someone? Truthfully, I like to believe that her belief in God would have stopped her, but I just don't know. The anger she felt towards a system that saw oppression as acceptable was without doubt justified. Seeing those who had inspired her murdered for their views, was enough to push even the most timid person to violence, and Nina was never 'timid'.

I'm sure there were times when white audience members felt uncomfortable with some of her outbursts. I know I had, but I was determined to find out what was behind them, and of course was fortunate enough to be able to do just that. I once told Nina that as I had been moved to look for answers as a result of her anguish, I was positive others were too. Her response was immediate, 'Yes, yes, that's right. They have to know the truth, and I have to tell them and you have to tell them. They can't hide from me. You see, I've lived there, I know about these rich white folk who don't want to let me in. Oh yes, they want me to play for them, but don't ever think for a moment they respect me – no way, man, it's a lie! But, you know, it's okay, I really don't want to sit about smiling with them acting like it's all right. I'd much rather be with my people, although some of them haven't quite got it yet, but they will.'

These were genuine sentiments, not just the ravings of an angry woman. Would you want to sit down with people that you knew, deep down, disrespected you, or would you prefer to be around people who shared and admired your views? I know which road I'd choose.

Simply being an artist was never what life was all about for Nina – there were many facets to her character. She was an artist, an outspoken civil rights champion, a wife and, of course, a mother. All of these identities had to merge into one person, so it was not surprising that at times the kettle boiled over.

Her dedication to the rights of others was finally recognised, when she was awarded an honorary doctorate in humanities. She would also receive an honorary doctorate in music – both titles richly deserved. Her music spoke to millions and its message was never trite.

Nina was now entering a period that would see her career spiral outwards, and afford her a much more respected place within the industry. Stardom and fame had never been her motivating force. She often said that her talents were a gift from God and that she was merely the instrument he used.

Although Nina would always be aware of just how much influence her music wielded, she never abandoned her full-on style in order to sell more records.

Even when the civil rights movement appeared to have splintered and separated, she continued to enlighten millions through her music and remind them that the struggles were not yet over. Nina was a crusader with a cause, although it would have made her life so much easier had she been willing to forget her ideals and simply sing whatever was popular. Her beliefs had been ingrained at an early age. Regardless of whether or not she travelled first-class and stayed in five-star hotels, the underlying cause of hatred and oppression did not simply vanish with wealth or celebrity. Nina had been born in an age where mankind's inability to accept 'all men as equal' pushed her down a pathway from which she would never wander.

6 'Why?'

Nina had returned briefly to the States but her popularity was such that she soon began touring extensively around Europe. It was early 1968 and she was travelling in considerably more style now. I had taken over as secretary of the now renamed Nina Simone Appreciation Society and I devoted a great deal of time to spreading the gospel according to Nina. I was determined that her fan base would become a force to be reckoned with, and that she would be recognised by the world at large as a true genius.

The second newsletter, which I co-wrote with David, recalls the televised London Weekend Special *The Sound Of Soul*, during which her music was transmitted to households across the nation. This one-hour show highlighted the diversity of Nina's music, and her appearance in African garb only added to the mystique.

Nina felt a powerful connection with her forebears from Africa that sometimes revealed itself to her audience. I remember the very first time I had seen 'the spirit' hit Nina on stage, and she had gone into what I can only describe as a trance-like state. Whether it was the souls of African spirits that possessed her, or just a throwback to her African roots, I have no idea, but when she danced it blew me away. I tried to perfect that dance for years, with some minor success. In fact, Nina once caught me, shoulders shaking up and down, and burst out laughing. 'David, come quick, the spirit's got your sister and she's going back to Africa!' Totally embarrassed, I stopped rather abruptly. I turned round to find Nina, Andy and David trying hard not to fall over with laughter. 'See, honey, I knew you were an African soul.'

Being around Nina could be a sheer delight; it could also at times be scary. More than once I would see her flip out when things were not just so. She was a perfectionist. Those long hard years as a child prodigy had taught her to be the best, and she expected excellence in others, especially where her music was involved. 'Goddam it, can't they just do what I want? Are they dumb? Why do I have to do *all* the work round here? I'm tired. Just once, can't someone else get it right without me.' At these times I learnt that the best remedy was to give her a wide berth and wait for the storm to subside. She would either stomp about for a few minutes or, if it were a major incident, the fireworks could be heard miles away and sometimes lasted for hours.

I understood why she got so angry. She gave everything when she went on stage and she expected everyone else to do the same. Obviously humans tend to make mistakes but, in Nina's world, that wasn't an excuse. Following one of her famous tirades, I suggested that she calmed down as it wasn't good for her to get so upset, and that her band were, after all, only human. Big mistake! The wrath of Nina turned on me full force. 'What do *you* know? You don't have to do shit. You just use me like all the rest. You don't care about *me*, nobody does. If I dropped down dead now no one would give a damn. Don't tell me to calm down – they should know what the fuck to do by now. I ain't no teacher. Everyone just wants a piece of me – sing this, do that, smile Nina – it's all bullshit, you know.' Okay, I thought, don't get upset and don't let her see you cry. After all, I had never asked anything of her, I'd shown her respect at all times and I really didn't deserve this. Whether it was shock or just my stubborn streak that prevented my feet from moving, I don't know. I just knew this wasn't right, and I'd be damned if I'd walk away!

Thank God David was there and saw how upset I was. He turned to me and said, 'Look child [his term of affection for me], she doesn't mean it and you know what she's like. She's tired and, okay, a little bit angry, but you know she cares about you. She's always asking if you're okay and how you are doing, so don't let it get to you. Look, any minute now she's going to stop and forget all about this, so just let it go.'

These were words of wisdom and, of course, he was right. Several minutes passed and Nina went real quiet, then she turned to me and said, 'You know I don't mean to get angry with you. I know it's not you. I'm just so tired of giving, sometimes I feel like no one understands, you know?' Yes, I knew, and even though I was still recovering from the backlash, I smiled and said, 'It's okay. I know it's hard, and I just want you to know I do care. After all, I love you so it's all right.' At that Nina gave me one of the biggest smiles I'd ever seen. 'You love me? Well that's good. You know I love you too, honey.' All was right with the world.

However, I began to realise that this had been a particularly difficult time for Nina. Prior to her departure for Europe, Dr Martin Luther King Jr had been assassinated. I know that a small part of her died with him. Everything

44

she had taught me, all the struggles, the trials and tribulations, were deeply ingrained in me. While preparing for her show at the Westbury Music Fair, the news that Dr King had been shot reached her. I cannot even begin to understand or know the pain and heartache she must have felt. I only know that her willingness to share that part of her life with me gave me an insight that many were not fortunate enough to have. As a result of this tragic event, Nina recorded the song 'Why? (The King Of Love Is Dead)', and to this day, I am unable to listen to it without tears filling my eyes. How she could sit on stage and perform it just days after this devastating event is beyond my comprehension.

The reaction of the black American population to Dr King's death was a series of riots that broke out across the country. Within days, nearly 20,000 people had been arrested, and just under 40 had died. The death of Dr King had brought his policy of non-violence to an end. The years of trying to deal with a volatile situation through non-violent means were over. The anger and bitterness his death caused would reverberate around the world. Despite her pain and heartache, Nina was determined to carry on. Andy had scheduled a series of dates in Europe, and rather than let the momentum being gathered by Nina's career peter out, they went ahead. However, one concert in particular that was to prove too much came at the Montreux Jazz Festival. Still grieving at the loss of her friend and mentor, Nina was forced to leave the stage unable to continue. With tears streaming down her face, she was led away – all in the public glare.

Nina was trying bravely to 'go on with the show', yet none of us could comprehend how hard this time was for her. I had been afraid to ask her how she felt about what had happened, but I knew she was always willing to be open with me about civil rights issues. Even though she'd already let loose at me once during this visit, I decided it was worth the risk and, when a brief moment came for us to be alone, I asked her how could this have happened.

'He was becoming too strong, you know, they couldn't let him live. The people were finally getting the message, and they had to shut him up. But, you know, they can try to kill me – I know they want to – but I'm not going to be quiet, *no way!* I'm not scared of them. They think killing us will stop us, but even if I die someone else will keep on telling them the truth. I'm hurting inside, you understand. You know all the things I told you about – you didn't understand, did you? Now you know. They killed Martin, man, just shot him dead like a dog. This is too hard, sometimes it's just too goddam hard.'

I could see she was very upset and I certainly didn't want to add to her sadness. This was the first time I'd seen her cry, and it hurt. To the public she was a performer, but to me she was so much more, and seeing the pain in her eyes was just too much. I apologised for upsetting her and said I'd leave her to rest. As I turned to leave she looked at me and through the tears said, 'Sylvia, you *need* to keep learning. Don't forget what you know – it's important. The message can't die with Martin; you can keep his memory alive by passing it on. You're young, but you've got an old soul. You understand; you know what's really going on.'

With that I left, but the memory of her face, the pain and anguish her belief in equality and justice had caused, stayed with me. My own crusade continued over the years, and I know when Nina saw me years later wearing my 'Free Angela Davis' badge, she realised that I had listened well.

I still can't understand how she could have recorded the song 'Why?' To listen to it was hard enough, but how she could sing those words without breaking down is a mystery and one I never solved.

7 'Ain't Got No – I Got Life'

The telegram arrived on 16 October 1968. It was one simple sentence: 'JUST THOUGHT YOU WOULD LIKE TO KNOW THAT NINA SIMONE HAS ENTERED THE UK CHARTS AT 45.' It may have entered at 45 but it kept on climbing, and had reached Number Five by the time Nina arrived that December. I guess the incredible chart success of 'Ain't Got No – I Got Life' took us all by surprise, even Nina. Of course to us it was way overdue, as her career had been in full swing since the 1950s and here we were in 1968. Despite the tremendous pressures that constant touring could inflict, Andy was aware that in order to keep Nina's career moving, sacrifices had to be made. As a result, a very short promotional tour had been scheduled.

David was fortunate enough to be able to grab some time with her, which was a minor miracle given her schedule. She was staying at the Mayfair Hotel in London's West End, and over dinner David discussed what was going on with us. Nina was always interested in her Appreciation Society and proceeded to ask David how many fans she now had. 'Oh, it's going great; expanding by leaps and bounds.' That brought a smile to her face. I had remarked to David a few days earlier how much more relaxed she appeared, and that even her physical appearance had altered. It was true. Gone were the wigs, replaced by an afro, and her style of dress was now much more informal. David asked her how the pressures of her escalating fame were affecting her. 'Well you know, man, sometimes it's hard. I don't know if I can keep up the pace, but I have so many people depending on me, I have to do the best I can.' David understood it was hard, but just had to let her know how good she looked. 'Well, Nina, I must say that you look so relaxed no one would know just how hard it can be. I mean, you've changed your whole look – I hardly recognised you.' Nina knew by now when he was applying a certain amount of charm, and responded with a huge grin.

Feeling that his time had come, David decided to revisit a previous question: 'Nina, do you remember a few years ago you asked me if I could dance, and you said if I didn't dance, I had to have sex. Well, I do both now.' With that, Nina began to roar with laughter. 'Oh really! So, man, who is she? You have to tell me.' Uneasily he replied, 'Well, actually, the she's a he.' Not knowing what the reaction might be, he braced himself for the response. Nina sat up very straight in her chair, and with a somewhat serious look replied, 'Oh, well I know those things go on.' I guess being in the entertainment industry, people's sexuality was not an issue and fortunately she was totally unfazed by the revelation. The evening ended way too soon, but he knew just how packed her schedule was.

David was also extremely busy at that time. He had recently been involved in the launch of a record store with two friends, Dave Godin and Robert Blackmore. When David told Nina and Andy about his venture they were both thrilled and, prior to her visit, he had received a great letter from Nina wishing him luck. To put the icing on the cake, Andy arranged for Nina to drop in at David's record store, Soul City, and it was another unforgettable day.

Away from her piano and her lyrics, Nina revealed that despite her celebrity status she was quite shy! Soul City was a small store in the heart of London, on Monmouth Street, WC2. By the time Nina arrived, the place was filled to capacity and everyone wanted to meet her. We had suggested fans bring a photo or an album to be signed, but we had not quite anticipated the response, hence the overflow onto a crowded street. Nina was overwhelmed by the huge crowd – that much was written all over her face. None the less she signed autographs and totally mesmerised everyone with her fabulous smile. Despite the fact that the store was packed with her most ardent fans, she seemed reluctant to engage them. In later years this would be attributed to her acting like a 'diva', however it was simply that she was knocked out by the response she got from people. She wanted her fans to approach her and feel comfortable, and knew barking remarks would not achieve this. Nina always wanted her fans to see her as a person as well as a star.

I gave her a painting I had done and, as a thank you for her visit, we asked her to choose any album from the store. Nina grabbed *Sam And Dave*, smiled and said, 'Do you like them? They're *real* cool, you know!' With that, she was gone, leaving in her wake a mass of satisfied fans.

One of the downsides to her rising success meant that Nina was pursued by the press more than ever, and she laughed when she spoke to me later that night. 'Ha! You know they were waiting for me at my hotel. Now they're fighting to get to me. But I know they just want to dig for stuff, they want to get in my business, but I'm too smart for them. You and David know what I mean – you've been here *all* the time.'

I had to laugh. She was in her own way trying to say how much she appreciated the fact we had been around way before her chart success, and she was right. Nina wasn't just someone we cared about when the hits were coming, it went beyond that, and she knew it.

The press was hounding her, but on one level she enjoyed it. Holding court as the High Priestess of Soul was now becoming a regular occurrence. Much was being made of her hit, and reporters wanted to know why she had chosen the song from the show *Hair*. In several interviews she explained how, having seen the show both on and off Broadway, she had asked for the music to be sent to her. The result was of course her own unique recording of 'Ain't Got No – I Got Life'. While she was here she also managed to squeeze in a visit to the British version of the show, and afterwards commented on how much she loved it and how friendly the cast seemed. Many of the reporters asked how, exactly, she could be described 'musically', and once again Nina had to explain that she didn't have just one category, but switched among genres. To illustrate just how much more relaxed she was on this short trip, her normal response to such questions would be a snap of the tongue and a somewhat terse reply, but this time she was patient.

Following an appearance on *Top Of The Pops*, I had the opportunity for a quick chat, and asked her if having a hit record had been the reason for this change in attitude. With a grin she replied, 'Well it is good to know they finally dig me, but, you know, I just feel more at ease. Even though it means more work, and more travelling I'm having a ball and at least this time I'm getting paid! Yes, honey, RCA are paying me my dues, and it's about time too.'

I knew she had felt ripped off in the past, so this must have been a huge relief. Consequently, the pent-up anger and frustration gave way to a more relaxed attitude. Time alone with her was in short supply, but we managed to spend a few hours laughing and joking about our various experiences, which made a pleasant change from the more intense conversations of the past.

During 1968, English critic Phyl Garland was moved by one of Nina's London performances and wrote the following.

'She cast her spell with the fluid but frequently complex patterns of notes she plays on her piano and with the distinct sound of her richly reedy voice. This voice of hers isn't the finely honed tool of a trained singer but it possesses something that those other voices lack, an earthy naturalness; the compelling coarseness of a home-made instrument that might have been whittled by hand in the fields and then played with consummate artistry...

'She sings with her whole body, with her facial expressions, alternatively wooing and chastizing the audience with her words.'

Before leaving for what would be a 'brief' return to the States, Nina delivered an unbelievable performance on *The David Frost Show*, and she confided later that even she knew how well she'd connected with the television audience. The atmosphere of a television studio can be cold, and it requires a much greater effort to come across as natural. For Nina, all challenges were met head-on and, although it was the 'Frost' show, she created a tremendous warmth inside the walls of that studio!

I guessed that somewhere deep inside she was still grieving. The loss of Dr King, assassinated in 1968, and the subsequent violence played heavily on her heart. There would be brief moments when her façade would slip and I would observe just how deeply affected she was. There were several occasions where her anger would get the better of her, although the outbursts were not intentional. No matter how much adulation she received, she remained like a tiger waiting to pounce. Her strong beliefs were undiminished by fame.

This would be an ongoing subject between us, but we'd often just catch up as regular people. The volume of work with the Appreciation Society had increased tenfold and Andy had arranged for her to return in a couple of months for a much longer tour. I was relieved, as it would give me a chance to catch up on what was fast becoming a huge backlog of letters.

The newsletters had to be written, photographs had to be sent and, of course, letters had to be replied to, so it wasn't just a case of sitting back and relaxing. In truth, though, it was fun. Each month we had to fill the pages of the newsletter and we would share Nina's tour itinerary so as to let everyone know where her concerts were being held. We also had to answer the many questions people posed, and review her records. Looking back, it was rather like having a second job – the more fans she accumulated the more work there was for me to do. But I was so happy to see Nina finally getting recognition, I didn't care about the work.

If I thought then that the increased volume of work was getting a bit unmanageable, you can imagine what it was like once 'To Love Somebody' became a hit. I'm surprised I could be found at all. At times I was literally buried beneath a stack of letters, piled sky high, and I had no choice but to answer them. After all, Nina was creating the music, so my part was easy in comparison.

8 'Times They Are A-Changing'

The year was 1969 and Nina had left the UK at the end of January following her brief promotional tour. David and I had been working hard during that time and were pressuring RCA to build on the momentum that 'Ain't Got No – I Got Life' had created. Having polled the members of the Appreciation Society, we were in no doubt that the natural follow-up should be Nina's beautiful interpretation of The Bee Gees' song 'To Love Somebody'. RCA was not sure if this would be the track to continue Nina's chart reign, and was reluctant to release it. We were convinced that we were right, along with 95 per cent of voters in the Society. To say we put pressure on RCA would be putting it mildly. We bombarded executives daily with calls, and asked the members of the Society to phone as well. The poor receptionist at RCA must have been fed up with the constant barrage, but we knew 'To Love Somebody' was a sure-fire hit and we weren't about to let it go. Andy had agreed, and said that Nina was more than happy to trust our judgement as she knew we had her best interests at heart.

Our perseverance finally paid off, and the subsequent chart success of 'To Love Somebody' justified our efforts. Of course, Nina and Andy were as thrilled as we were. As a show of their appreciation, Andy arranged for a reception at the end of the London tour at the Mayfair Hotel in the West End, to enable Nina's fans to meet her in person. Admission was by ticket only. I co-ordinated the event and soon disappeared under a mountain of ticket requests. The March newsletter gave details and suggested that fans living outside London might want to catch her in concert at the London Palladium the night before the reception and stay for the weekend.

Prior to the concert at the Palladium, she had also scheduled a show at the Royal Festival Hall. With the number of people wanting to see her performances escalating, Nina had little choice but to schedule several major venues at one time.

Nina was in rare form that night. The depth of feeling she conveyed in her performance was incredible and it was without doubt one of the most intense

I'd ever seen. This was all the more remarkable given the circumstances backstage moments before the curtain was due to rise.

I could hear Nina's not-so-soft tones emanating from her dressing room. She was screaming at her husband with a fair amount of vitriol. 'You go out there, go out and tell them *I'm tired*. You think I'm a machine, you're just like all the rest. You just want me to perform, you don't give a damn.' Andy was no stranger to these outbursts, and usually managed to calm her down and avert a crisis. On this occasion, though, Nina was having none of it. The more Andy tried to soothe her, the louder she became. I stayed in the doorway, in case I needed to make a quick getaway, and figured I might as well let her know I was there. I suppose I was becoming less afraid of the outbursts of anger, and I could run fairly fast back then. I looked at Andy and he looked beseechingly back at me as if to say, 'What can I do?'

I turned to Nina and tried to act as if I hadn't heard a thing. 'I'm so looking forward to tonight, there are hundreds of Appreciation Society members out there and I know it's going to be totally amazing.' Nina glared at me, was I mad? She was in the middle of a tirade and all I could mumble was how exciting it was going to be. 'What are you talking about, man, didn't you hear me? I'm tired. I'm not going out there so *you* can go and tell them. I don't give a damn who's out there, I'm not going.'

I was about to remind her about the hundreds of people who had paid to see her when, all of a sudden, she stopped in her tracks. She looked at me and said with a grin, 'How many of my fans are out there? Well, tell me, how many?' I was praying this sudden change meant all was well. 'Oh, you won't believe it Nina, there's got to be hundreds out there. I went outside earlier, and they were lining up all round the block. It's brilliant! They're carrying photos, albums, all sorts of press cuttings on you, and I could hear people talking. They're just so excited.' She looked at me with a mixture of curiosity and slight annoyance. 'Ha! So they've brought my albums. Well, they had better not be those damn bootlegs, you know. I need to get paid!'

I felt the tide had turned, but she had to have one last snipe at Andy, accusing him of being uncaring. Nina was every inch the High Priestess and we were merely her subjects. 'Well, you better let me get ready then if you want me to go out there. But I'm telling you, you better ease off me, man; give me a break real soon. I'm not gonna keep doing this shit for ever, you know. I'm human too.' With that I eased out of the room and minutes later a regally attired Nina appeared, totally serene and seemingly unaware of the scare she had just caused.

Having already performed in Dublin, Holland, Cardiff and Edinburgh, her outburst did seem justified, but I wasn't about to tell her that. As hard as her schedule was, she had to take advantage of the heightened interest her chart success had garnered. Constant touring was the price to pay for having two hit records.

Newsletter No. 5 reviewed the concert, and gives a great account of her performance.

'It's difficult for us to remember all the numbers Nina did that night but amongst them were an amazing performance of the Albert King blues tune 'Born Under A Bad Sign', 'To Love Somebody', 'Four Women', and the show-stopping 'Ain't Got No – I Got Life'. Nina was aided throughout by four of the most capable musicians ever! Gene on bass, Don on drums, Weldon on organ, and Al on guitar, plus Gena and Doris providing some truly memorable harmonies. The whole thing was so good, the sound was so tight, and the electricity that Nina generated was of the highest voltage!! In the second half, when things really seemed to get going audience-wise (our only criticism: the audience took so long to really warm up, and even waited until the very end to show the full extent of their appreciation), Nina moved everyone with her beautiful 'The Other Woman' and got the whole audience together with 'I Wish I Knew' (one of the most magical moments during a spellbinding evening!). Other numbers Nina featured included an old adapted spiritual 'Tossing And Turning' (which featured some truly incredible drumming from Don, who had a solo spot during this number), 'Times They Are A-Changing', 'Compensation' (which included some beautiful harmonies between Nina, Gena, and Doris), and her encore (one of several) was 'Backlash Blues'. Of course, the fitting climax to the evening was the audience response at the end, during which four *very* enthusiastic fans insisted on joining Nina actually on stage! Her final encore was 'I Shall Be Released' during which she wailed to Gena and Doris to hold on to an unbelievably long note! Nina proved that night, as she was to at all her concerts, that she is unequalled and is unquestionably much more than the High Priestess of Soul – she's soul personified.'

This review was written over 30 years ago, yet it captures the magic that continued throughout Nina's career.

Following the Festival Hall concert we slipped backstage for a very brief chat with her. I had told David of the earlier outburst and was more than a little worried about what her mood might be when we saw her. He reminded me that she rarely remembered these tirades and would probably have forgotten all about it. He was right. Having given yet another mind-blowing performance her earlier eruption had been brushed aside and she was in great spirits when we arrived.

I asked her if she'd enjoyed the concert and she was happy to respond, 'It was good, man, but these English people take so damn long to warm up, maybe it's because it's so cold here. Is that it?' I had to think about this for a minute. Where was David when I needed him? Actually he was with Andy, and as usual was discussing business. 'You know what, Nina, you may be right, but I think it's more about the whole British reserve thing. You know, we usually don't get too excited in public – well, let's just say most people don't. I guess David and I may be the exceptions to the rule.' She began to laugh. 'Ha! Yes, that's it, man, you're right, because I sure as hell know it isn't me. But at least when they do warm up they really dig it.' No matter what, she was always able to tap into her audiences and even the most reserved would have no choice but to be moved by her.

We chatted for a while longer and David asked her how she felt about the fact that, although she'd had a huge hit with 'I Loves You, Porgy', it was the subsequent hit singles 'Ain't Got No – I Got Life' and 'To Love Somebody' that were responsible for her escalating popularity. 'Well, David, you know when I did "Porgy" I didn't have anyone handling the business, so I had no idea how to deal with it or what to do next. So I got ripped off, and they just used me and didn't give a damn about what I was going to do next. You know, I had to start all over again, like all those years of hard work, man, they didn't count for anything. That's why I try to find out what's going on now, but Andy takes care of that stuff mostly so I don't have to worry about it. But, you know, you must tell the fans that I do appreciate them buying my records. It's important you tell them.' She had genuine concerns about what her fans thought. It was yet another arena of life for which she took responsibility.

She continued, 'You see, I know you and Sylvia care, and you both work so hard and it's good to have people around me I can trust. You know I do trust you, don't you?' She was referring to the fact that she trusted us enough to let us push RCA into releasing 'To Love Somebody'. David and I accepted that this was a compliment and, as we could see she was tired, we congratulated her on yet another magnificent performance and said we'd see her the following day. She seemed rather puzzled by this: 'I'm seeing you tomorrow? You know it gets so crazy sometimes I don't know one day from the next, or one town from the next, but hey you guys both take care, you hear me.'

The next morning we were trying to decide whether to travel to Manchester with her. Given the pace of her schedule we were beginning to get weary. We were both working at Soul City and also running the Appreciation Society. It was laughable really – she was touring all over Europe and *we* were tired! Finally, after much debate, we decided to stay in London and await her return – and David suggested I let her know we weren't going with her. Although David had known Nina longer, I seemed to have a closer rapport with her. Plus he didn't want to listen to her if she was upset. On the telephone I told her that we really had to catch up on things, both at the shop and with the Society. This seemed a reasonable explanation and for once she accepted it without question. We agreed that we'd see her as soon as she got back from Munich, and wished her well.

Having a few days to try to catch up was a blessing. With Nina's constant touring came added responsibilities to a multitude of loyal fans. We could hardly ignore them, especially given how hard she was working. Not only was she touring, but she had also been back in the studio and RCA had released an album, which despite its lack of commercial success was a masterpiece.

Nina Simone And Piano! captured her remarkable musicianship at its purest. Using no accompaniment other than a tambourine on one track and some vocal doubling on another, the LP was an amazing feat. Nina selected an eclectic mix of songs, ranging from Jonathan King's 'Everyone's Gone To The Moon' to the old spiritual 'Nobody's Fault But Mine'. Some songs reflected her views on life, then there were simple love songs such as Carolyn Franklin's 'Seems Like I'm Never Tired Of Lovin' You'. Although the album won critical acclaim it failed to match the sales figures of the earlier '*Nuff Said!* – only with the passage of time has it been acknowledged as one of her most exceptional recordings.

Later, interviewers would marvel at her interpretation and natural abilities during solo performances. Whether backed by a full orchestra or simply sitting alone at the piano, her timing and delivery were impeccable.

9 'To Love Somebody'

Nina returned triumphant from her brief tour of Europe and we made arrangements to see her next show at the London Palladium. The show had been sold out for weeks, and we both figured we'd have to sit a lot further back than usual. To our surprise Andy had arranged it so that we could watch the whole show from the wings, from a couple of chairs strategically placed so that we wouldn't miss a thing. What a treat! Being this close was as good as it got. Thankfully we had kept notes during the show, and reprinted below is our 'review' of the concert from yet another newsletter. As you can tell, this time the audience was so much warmer and, from the wings, we really got a feel for what was happening on stage.

> 'Nina emerged in a beautiful African robe, and began her concert by informing everyone that this evening's performance was dedicated to the memory of Dr Martin Luther King, who died one year previously. Nina certainly gave her all that night, from the exceptionally moving "When I Was A Young Girl", to the magnificent "Four Women" and "Times They Are A-Changing". The climax came with "Revolution" which exploded on stage! The encores brought Nina back again and again! We really thought the whole place would tumble down with the noise the audience made and Nina's final solo was her amazing reading of the Jacques Brel number "The Desperate Ones" from her new LP.'

What we had not put in the newsletter was the fact that, once again during a major concert, she had risked alienating her audience. David recalls how at one point during the show she stopped, looked out and announced, 'This is for all the black people in the audience.' Given the fact there were only about ten black people in the place and they were miles from the American South, her words seemed irrelevant. Often she called for all the black people in the audience to stand up – sometimes it was as few as two – and said, 'I'm singing only to you. I don't care about the others.' Curiously her white audience would often clap madly, but I wasn't sure how far their liberal tendencies would stretch.

I had already had long discussions about her insistence on making these remarks, but she was a strong-willed woman. She continually reminded me that as a young white girl I could not comprehend the situation, that she had done her best to teach me but there was no substitute for first-hand experience.

Part of my problem was a belief that English audiences were less radical. Of course, people knew about the horrendous discrimination taking place across the water and our history was not exactly 'pure' when it came to our colonial past, but racism was never paraded as blatantly in Britain as it was in America. We had no Deep South and only the occasional race riot. The level of racism never reached the scale it had in America nor was it rooted in an unjust legal system as it was in the States.

I know she understood where I was coming from, but she regarded it as her duty to reinforce her beliefs regardless of the audience in front of her. Over many years we would come back to this point until I finally accepted she had a valid reason for her anger and I let it go.

Following her performance, David and I had to practically fight our way through the crowd of fans waiting to meet the High Priestess. The more famous Nina became, the harder it was to reach her. Having finally battled our way to the door we slipped inside. Dripping with sweat and with a towel draped over her arms, she looked like the reincarnation of a mystical Egyptian queen. Unlike my previous interactions, this time I just stood and looked at Nina with all the love and wonder of a child. How was it possible that this woman had found her way into my soul and touched it with such passion that it left me dazed?

'Well what's wrong with you, honey? You look like you've seen a ghost – speak to me.' I realised I had been standing staring at her and no words had yet managed to pass my young lips. 'Oh, sorry Nina I just can't quite figure out *what* to say. For the first time in my life I'm truly speechless.' Nina, knowing me to be rather chatty, found this totally amusing, and a huge wail of laughter erupted from her lips. 'You mean *you* don't have anything to say, not a word? Come on now, honey, I didn't scare you that much, did I?'

I had known her for several years and had never been this quiet in her presence. I had to say something. 'No, no don't get me wrong. It's not that you scared me, you just got so deep inside me I don't know what I can say. Seriously, there just aren't words to describe what you just did on stage.' Her reply was not typical and I believe that even she was taken aback by what had occurred. 'Yes, man, I know what you mean. The spirits of my African ancestors were there. I could feel them and they really took hold of me. Ha! Even I got a bit scared of what they may do to me. The crowd felt it too. I know they did. I could see them moving about. I *know* they got the spirit this time. Shit, it was everywhere, man. Yes, it was deep, man.'

There was no doubt, that anyone within sight of her that night must have got the spirit. I was convinced that her previous concert at the Festival Hall had been without doubt the most intense I'd ever witnessed, but she had just gone one step further. That was Nina. Just when you thought 'she can't top that', she did, and with such ease it was eerie to witness.

As usual people were shouting 'I love you, Nina' from the door, and with that I smiled and said 'Well, Miss Nina [a term of affection I occasionally used], I guess you'd better let your adoring guests in before they break the door down.' I knew Nina would not be rushed, though. When she was ready she would let them know. 'Honey, they can wait 'til I'm good and ready. I need to get some rest, but you know they won't let me.' With that, she shot Andy a glare, and I prayed it would not spark another outburst. Fortunately the throng of admirers prevented anything like that, and I sat and watched while Nina held court.

My admiration of her as a performer was justified, but to watch her in action with a room full of celebrities was an added bonus. There were times when she would turn on the charm in such a way that to witness it at first hand was both fascinating and, at times, amusing. I also knew that it could be plain hard work. Performing was draining, but to have to put on another show afterwards for the celebrities and record company executives was no easy task. Of course, it could also depend on her mood and sometimes that was nothing less than explosive.

Having witnessed a constant stream of visitors, we were about to leave and let her get some rest. 'Where the hell do you think you're going?' We were by now totally confused. Surely she was tired and wanted to rest? We were wrong. I turned to David, shrugged my shoulders and replied, 'Well, Nina, we thought you'd want to rest, and we'd leave you in peace.' 'No, man, I don't want to rest; I want to party. Shit, man, I've got to get rid of some of this energy or I'll never sleep. We're all going to a club – you guys have to come along.' When Nina commanded we usually obeyed and rarely regretted it.

I was sure older people needed more rest than us 'young folk'. Thank goodness I never voiced that opinion – I dread to think what reaction it would have sparked.

Instead I replied, 'I can't believe how much energy you've got. I thought you'd be worn out with all that performing. You are totally amazing.'

She seemed to take this all in her stride and merely smiled. 'Yeah, I'm tired, but performing creates so much energy, I have to let it out or I'll bust.' A few minutes later, having changed into more appropriate garb, we all left, heading for a club in London's West End.

When Nina said get rid of some energy, I had absolutely no idea that would mean partying 'til the small hours, but that's just what we did. To see her shaking on the dance floor was a rare treat in itself. She sure could move! As for stamina, well she outpaced just about everyone else without breaking a sweat. David was worried, as he knew he'd be in trouble for letting me stay out so late, but he also knew we couldn't just leave. Finally he went over to Nina and said he had to get me home as our mother would probably go mad at me being out so late. 'Oh, yes, man, I keep forgetting, Sylvia's still so young, but if your mother gets mad tell her I was looking out for you guys. I'll call her, you know, and let her know you were with me.'

We could just picture our mother and Nina in conversation. I started to laugh at the thought, and Nina, wondering what the hell was wrong with me, smiled and asked, 'Why you laughing? You don't believe I'd call your mother? I will, you know. Don't you think I won't.' I tried to stop laughing, and managed a garbled reply, 'No it's not that. It's just I had a picture of you on the phone to my mum, and I couldn't help but laugh. You know my mum's a huge fan, and I'm sure if you did call her she'd forget all about the fact I'm out late.' Nina could obviously picture the same scenario and began to laugh too: 'Ha! Yes well that's all right then, but maybe you'd better get home. I don't really want to cause your mother to worry. Mothers do worry you know.' With those words of wisdom ringing in our ears, David smiled, and we left reminding her just how much we were looking forward to the reception the following night.

The reception at the Mayfair Hotel was billed as a way of thanking her growing legion of fans, and of course both of us. Entry was by ticket only, and the invitation stated that the reception would begin at 7pm in the Devon and Landsdowne Suite. Now bear in mind that most British people are fastidious about punctuality and try hard not to be late. By 7:15pm the room was packed to overflowing with fans clutching albums and photographs, all waiting for their idol's signature to be added. Obviously they had no idea we'd been partying 'til all hours, and they were beginning to get a little impatient. At 8pm, and despite a few frantic calls to her room, Nina had still not emerged. Andy assured us she would be down in a minute, and we did our best to entertain the fans with stories. However, even we were beginning to get a bit panicky when 9pm approached and still no Nina! Finally, at 9:30pm and in true diva fashion, Nina swept graciously into the room, beaming at the hordes of die-hard fans. She was bolder with her fans on that occasion.

At one point she came over and, smiling, said, 'Sylvia, do you know they know practically everything there is to know about *me*. They know when I recorded songs that even I had forgotten about. Man, they are some very serious fans. Ha! They even know about those damn bootlegs.' I just had to laugh. 'Well, we did tell you they loved you, so I guess it's no surprise they know so much about you.'

She was obviously shocked to see the level of devotion with which her fans treated her and the amount of knowledge they had. A while later she came back over and asked me why some of them were holding back. 'Do you think they're afraid of me? Ha! I bet I scared the hell out of some of them. That's it, man, they think I'm really going to put a spell on them.' She was having a ball, and all I could say in response was, 'Well, I don't know if they're really afraid [they were probably terrified], but you know we've told you how shy us Brits are, that's probably what it is.' Accepting my explanation, she returned to the crowd, and I sensed she was now determined to break through even the most timid fan's demeanour. Judging by the smiles and laughter, she succeeded brilliantly. I often felt that on some level she really enjoyed a challenge. If you said people were just acting 'cold' she'd try to warm them up; if they were shy, she'd loosen them up with the sight of one of her famous smiles – and all of it done with ease. During this period, and despite her gruelling schedule, she tried not to disappoint her fans and succeeded in style.

In later years it proved harder to keep up with all the demands made upon her and at times she simply couldn't give any more. Sadly, those were the times the media seemed to latch on to. Yes they would acknowledge her unmistakable gift, but most of their attention would be focused on her behaviour rather than her exquisite performance. Even though I experienced many of the highs and lows of her life, I still had respect for her as a person. It was not easy to juggle all the balls she had to keep in the air – performer, wife, mother, human rights campaigner – but she tried her best to keep them all going and, if they fell, she would pick them up and try again. Watching her perform, party and then entertain a room full of fans, I would often be completely baffled as to just how she managed it. I was young, fairly fit and yet even without the physical and emotional drain of performing, I was quickly running out of steam.

Following the reception, she was finally able to get a few days' rest and took her first holiday in England. The press managed to catch her during this time, and showed a smiling Nina cycling through London's Hyde Park. Sadly, the days flew past and before we knew it, it was time for her to leave. I spoke to her very briefly on the phone, and was glad to hear she'd enjoyed her vacation and had been thrilled by the whole visit. I made her a promise to behave myself, as she was worried that my 'hanging out' with her was encouraging me to be slightly rebellious.

In the meantime she had more concerts lined up, and the recording studios were again beckoning. Having faced a commercial failure with the *Nina Simone And Piano!* album, RCA decided to release a further album in 1969. To cash in on the success of The Bee Gees single, the LP was entitled *To Love Somebody*. It contained three Bob Dylan songs, Pete Seeger's 'Turn! Turn! Turn!' and Leonard Cohen's 'Suzanne'. The masterpiece was Nina's own composition, written with keyboard player Weldon Irvine Jr, entitled 'Revolution'. A funky affair, the song bore no resemblance to The Beatles tune of the same name. It did manage to gain some airplay in the USA, making an impression on the R&B charts, but its message may have been too much for her British audiences, who basically ignored it when it was released as a single in the UK.

This lack of interest would fill more than a few pages of the music-press interviews Nina gave, and was a source of great irritation and annoyance to her. Having had two major hit singles in the UK she was surprised by the lukewarm reception 'Revolution' received from the record-buying public.

10 'Revolution'

Against expectations, and as noted at the end of the previous chapter, Nina's single 'Revolution' failed to make a decent impact on the public. It may have been overshadowed by The Beatles' song of the same name. Perhaps the public was also cautious after getting wind of her occasionally irrational behaviour. Certainly her tolerance for sub-standard musicianship was at an all-time low, but, as she explained in an interview in *Melody Maker* at the end of 1968, she was often disappointed by her own performances too: 'Yes, I demand of my musicians what I demand of myself. I set very high standards because I'm a musician myself. Maybe, just once in a while, I might really please myself but more often, I don't. There is always something I could have done better.'

During her visit to Britain Nina had given several press interviews, in which she questioned the public's lack of response to 'Revolution'. Having just had two major hit singles, and played a series of sell-out concerts, she believed her chart reign would continue. I was a little apprehensive about broaching the subject, but had begun to understand that she respected those who spoke their minds, even if she didn't agree with them.

Sitting in her room at the Mayfair Hotel, I decided to ask why she thought the public weren't responding. 'You know, Sylvia, I don't get it. It's about a revolution, man; not just colour, but everything! It's about the barriers being broken down, and they sure as hell need getting rid of. It's time, honey. People are just so hung up about life, age, sex, how much money you've got – it's all just a mess. We need a revolution to sort it all out and get back to God. You know how lost we are, man – it's sad.'

Once again, I was keenly aware of the messages in her music. Nina did not trivialise her craft and it wasn't just the lack of financial reward that affected her. She was more concerned about people who weren't getting 'the message' than she was about the fretful accountants at the record companies. Having listened to the song, I had presumed everyone would understand what she was saying, but the lack of sales proved otherwise.

Nina rarely refused to engage me in my quest for understanding and I am eternally grateful for that. I continued, 'Do you think it's because by really listening, people then have to acknowledge that things aren't balanced?' Nina looked somewhat surprised at my question. 'Ha! You know for someone so young, you seem to know where it's at. Yeah, you know just what I'm saying. Everyone's so hung up on how they look, how much money they've got, they just don't care about what's real. It's sad, people just don't take time to care about each other, and they're just too busy trying to get a piece of the pie. You know, sometimes I wonder why I try so hard but then God blessed me and so I have to pass on the messages. It's what I'm here for, you know.' Yes, I did know. Even at our first meetings I knew that, apart from the gift of music, she had been sent to us with a message, and it was up to us to listen and learn.

Over the years Nina was vilified by the press, taken to task over her beliefs and labelled as everything from 'eccentric' to 'crazy', but the label that most aptly described her was 'messenger'. Through her music she gave the world an opportunity to grow. Fortunately, I was like a sponge and soaked up all she imparted during our little talks. To sit in her presence and know she was passing on some of her very personal insights really changed my outlook on life and humanity. Of course, with Nina you had to take the rough with the smooth, and sometimes it was hard to believe that the woman shouting and screaming abuse at the top of her voice was the same person who could sit quietly and impart wisdom.

As usual Nina's schedule was crazy and she was leaving within days, so our time together was limited. I made the most of those rare occasions when I got her to myself. I had more questions and she remained content to answer them. I'd never really talked about how she felt when she performed, and I was curious. 'Nina, I was wondering, when you're on stage, how does it feel? I mean, knowing there are hundreds of people out there under your spell. It must seem strange.'

'No, honey, it's not what you call strange. I just let the "spirit" move me, and it just takes over. But, you know, I expect people to respect me. It takes so much from me, they should respect what I do. Sometimes I sit at the piano and my hands move across the keys on their own – it's like God has my hands and I just follow. Do you understand me? Do you know what I'm saying?'

I wasn't quite sure that I did, as I had yet to have a truly spiritual experience myself, but the passion with which she was talking conveyed the message. 'You know, Nina, that's probably why I feel so emotional when I see you play or listen to you sing. It's as if God's touching you, and you're passing it on.

Sometimes I watch your hands when you're playing, and I can't understand how you can do what you do. It's as if they have a life of their own.'

She realised that, despite my youth, I had begun to understand what she said and her eyes began to light up as she replied, 'Yes honey, *that's it*, you got it, you really got it. Ha! That's what the audience can feel – it's like electricity going through me and out into the place. They can feel it, man.'

That's why Nina's music was so important. It was not just a means of becoming a celebrity, it was the only way she could express her soul's purpose. Sadly, our time was over once again, and as she got up to leave she gave me one of her magical smiles. 'You know, honey, you sure ask a hell of a lot of questions. But that's all right as you have a lot to learn, a whole lot.' I returned her smile, knowing that she had given me another opportunity to see the real Nina, not just a public face.

Part of my being that close and that honest was to be the cause of a rather uncomfortable incident during this trip. Just prior to her visit, David had been hospitalised with a serious illness. Nina had been told, and she was deeply worried and genuinely upset. She made sure she called him and let him know just how much she cared, and told him that she was looking forward to seeing him real soon. Fortunately, by the time she arrived he was on the road to recovery and was convalescing in the country, but was under strict instructions not to do anything stressful or tiring. That ruled out any Nina activity, so it fell to me to take care of that side of things. Although David was the catalyst for our introduction, it seemed I was more relaxed with Nina during our one-to-one meetings. I often wondered about that, and it took many years for me to fully understand the connection between us.

To boost the sluggish sales of 'Revolution', Nina was to appear on *Top Of The Pops* and it fell to me to accompany her. Andy had been held up at a business meeting, but he assured me she would be fine, and said I should just relax and enjoy the taping. The studio was crowded and the backstage area chaotic. Finally it was time for Nina to go on stage and, dressed in a short black dress, she sat at the piano to begin. Often with a studio taping there are breaks, so it came as no surprise when the word 'Cut!' could be heard. Nina had told me to stand at the front so she could see me and I had duly obliged. As the producer shouted 'Cut!', Nina bellowed, 'Sylvia, Sylvia! Where the hell are you? What's going on?'

I had no clue what was going on until one of the floor managers approached me. He said that as Nina was sitting in a black dress with a black screen behind her they were having trouble picking her out with the camera. All they were getting was basically her eyes and teeth. He asked me if she could change into a lighter dress as this would solve the 'problem'.

I stood and looked at the young man in front of me and replied firmly, 'If you think I'm going to tell Nina that she's showing up too dark for your cameras, you must be mad. No way am I telling her that. Have you lost your mind!' All the while I'm talking, Nina is screaming my name and demanding to know what is going on. I knew she would be incandescent with rage if I told her she was basically too 'dark' for the cameras and, rather than risk an ugly confrontation, I began moving towards the back of the studio. I could still hear her screams, but I kept on walking. By the time I had plucked up courage to return, the problem had been resolved. Rather than braving the wrath of Nina, the floor manager had replaced the black screen with a white one and the taping went ahead with no further delays.

Returning backstage, I knew she would want to know what had happened and, as I wasn't in the mood for a scene, I had to think pretty damn fast. As soon as we sat down she turned on me, 'Where the hell were you, man? I was calling for you and I could see you out front, so where the hell did you go? Have you gone deaf, man? I was calling for you.'

I took a deep breath, 'Oh, Nina I'm so sorry. Just as you began shouting I got the most terrible pains in my stomach and I just had to run to the toilet. I couldn't help it, I had to go.' She was no fool and eyed me suspiciously. 'Ha! You must think I'm stupid. I saw you, man, you were running.' I replied rather quickly, 'Well, Nina, if I hadn't run I dread to think what might have happened! I had really bad pains, you know. I'm sorry, but what else can I say?' She had little choice but to accept my explanation. She wasn't happy, though. 'So what was going on then? Why did they stop the show?' Darn it, she just wasn't giving up on this one. 'Look, Nina, I honestly don't know. By the time I got back you'd finished your song and all I could see was everyone cheering like mad and clapping. No one told me what was wrong so I don't know. All I know is everyone said you were amazing and that's it.'

She let it go at that, but I suspect she knew I was lying. No one had told her why they had stopped taping the show, thank goodness. The last thing she would have appreciated was being told she was too black to be seen! Of course I had to relay the story to David and it reduced both of us to hysterics. He could just picture me desperately trying to move towards the back through a crush of people, all the while hearing Nina screaming my name.

Nina left for a series of concerts in the USA, David continued his recovery and I did my best to keep things going on the Appreciation Society front. Following her return to the States, and with the effects of the poor sales of 'Revolution' still being felt, RCA decided to push ahead with another release, hoping to replicate the chart successes of 'Ain't Got No...' and 'To Love Somebody'. As a result 'In The Morning' was coupled with 'Cherish' as a double A-side, and proved much more commercially viable. Andy called and said he was coming over to London for a few days to set up a further tour for sometime in November, so we were again looking forward to seeing Nina. By now David was almost back to his usual self and, although he was told to rest, a 'royal' visit was looming and he wasn't about to miss it. Unfortunately, I had been involved in a minor accident and as a result we were playing catch-up with the newsletters and with letting the fans know what had been going on.

Nina knew full well that we had both been dealing with the effects of illness and injury, yet on her arrival in November she still demanded to know where all her fans were. (We had been unable to organise a reception for her.) This was not the only time that demands for attention from her fans would be a cause of friction between us.

I was upset about her expectations, given the circumstances, and was about ready to have a Nina-style tantrum myself when Andy intervened. Apparently with the manic pace of her schedule, Nina had forgotten we'd both been out of action until Andy tactfully reminded her. She looked at me and could obviously tell I was angry. 'You know sometimes I don't know what day it is. He's working me to death, man.' I guess that was Nina's way of apologising for her lack of compassion, and blaming Andy at the same time. We didn't stay mad at her for long and, as David and I walked through the lounge of the Mayfair Hotel, we simply smiled at one another.

It was this kind of attitude from Nina that hurt people and it was partly due to hectic tours that blended days into weeks and weeks into months, with no reference to everyday reality. Not that this was always a valid excuse. Sometimes she would just be plain rude. Most of the time it was better to ignore the questionable aspects of her behaviour and we became quite used to it.

Many years later, I discovered that Nina had hidden from both David and me the fact that she was suffering from a medical condition that created an imbalance in her brain. Her mood swings were nothing more than symptoms of this imbalance. Whatever the cause, we still accepted Nina for herself and cared deeply for her regardless.

Nina was again appearing at the London Palladium, and despite our initial encounter we looked forward to watching her genius on stage once more. The tension between her and Andy had escalated, and the angry exchanges were becoming much more frequent. Being around them at this time was becoming increasingly difficult. When Nina was angry it was usually Andy who tried to smooth things over, but as he was more and more the focus of her anger, it became impossible for him to calm her down. As usual, her inner turmoil was pushed to one side during her performances, and I wondered how she could be singing songs of love while clearly suffering the near break-up of her marriage. This was one question I chose not to ask.

It was obvious that she was exhausted, both physically and emotionally, and the outbursts usually centred around her inability to have some time off to rest. The times she treasured, at home in Mount Vernon, USA, with Andy and Lisa, were becoming few and far between. Once again as I entered her dressing room I could hear a sound that was becoming familiar. Nina was angry.

'Goddam it, you don't give a damn, you just want me to be a work horse. Nina sing, Nina play, Nina smile. Well I'm sick of it, you hear me, man? You can't keep working me to death. I've had enough. I need a rest, man, and you better let me rest or you'll be sorry, real sorry. You know I ain't lying, you better back off.'

Having witnessed similar scenes before, I noticed that this time it was different. Usually she would let off steam and a while later all would be calm, but things had turned ugly and the anger was much more intense. I wasn't sure what to do. On the one hand, I did feel sympathy for her: it couldn't have been easy – the constant touring, waking up in strange hotel rooms week after week, performing one-nighters all over the world. Add to this the recording schedules, the interviews, and all while trying to be a wife and mother to boot. No wonder the pressure was beginning to take such a heavy toll. Yet it was this life that she had chosen and Andy was just trying to make it happen for her.

I decided the best course of action was to withdraw. I turned to David and suggested we leave. We were heading towards the door when Nina turned her attention towards us. 'Where the hell do you think you're going, huh? You tell this mother I've had enough. You know he's trying to kill me, don't you? Say something man. He's gonna kill me, work me to death like some kind of field hand.'

Neither of us were prepared for this, and I looked at David, praying he'd know what to do or say. 'Look, Nina, we love you, and it's obvious you're tired and upset, but really it's between you and Andy.' Well, David had tried, but Nina was by now even more furious. 'Ha! You don't care. Why should you? You think he's such a great guy. Well, you don't know what he's doing to me. I'm telling you, man, if you find me dead, he's the one. You better take him outta here or I might just shoot him dead. I mean it, man.'

It was getting out of hand and trying to soothe matters was impossible. Finally, Andy walked over to where we were, and came outside with us. 'Look, guys, I know she's angry, but she's been working back-to-back shows and, yes, she does need a break. It's just hard with the record company screaming for product, trying to keep her in the public eye and taking time out. I'm trying to sort things out, but it's hard.'

Obviously, Andy felt he needed to say something, but this didn't really help. Our loyalty was to Nina, but we also knew Andy had worked hard as her manager – no easy task – in addition to being her husband. However, we were not about to take sides on the matter, and politely excused ourselves.

The journey home was uncomfortable for both of us. We both cared deeply about Nina, not just as an artist but as a person, and it was clear she was very unhappy. To watch her perform earlier had been another of life's highlights, and yet knowing that behind the public glare was a woman in pain was distressing. Sadly, this signalled the end of her marriage to Andy, and the subsequent fallout blighted the rest of her life. Whatever trust she had in men was lost, and would never be properly regained. Years later at Ronnie Scott's, the Soho jazz club in London, she admitted that when Andy went, she resolved never to trust another man with her heart, and I don't believe she ever really did.

Nina was due to leave two days later, and we spoke briefly on the phone. She was still upset, but was sorry she had not had time to see us before she went. I told her we both hoped she could work things out as we just wanted her to be happy. 'Yes, that's what I want, some peace. This life is crazy, man. I just want some peace, to be with Lisa and to be happy. I deserve it, you know. I'm human like everyone else, but people don't know. They don't see me in that way.' I was beginning to choke up inside as I wished her well. There was nothing I could do or say to help.

She could perform in front of hundreds of people shouting and screaming, 'We love you, Nina', and yet she was just as vulnerable as the next woman. She wanted to be loved and although she had people around who cared for her deeply, the relationship she craved proved elusive. I passed the phone to David who wished her all the love in the world and she said goodbye.

For a while we sat and talked about how upsetting this whole situation had become. What had started out as a love of a unique and talented artist, had become much more personal and knowing she was hurting made us both deeply sad. There was little either of us could do but hope and pray that, somehow, she would find a way to work things out.

11 'My Man's Gone Now'

The break-up of Nina's marriage came as no surprise. Having left the UK in November 1969, her schedule had not relented until midway through the following year. During this time, the anger and bitterness had spiralled and eventually Nina split with Andy. She was determined to teach him a lesson. She decided to take a long-deserved break until he agreed to cut down her schedule. Andy had spent years pushing Nina to achieve a set of goals and was unwilling to yield. Years ago, he had pinned a list of goals to a board in their first home and he never lost sight of them. She was fulfilling her destiny and he was helping her to do it, but somewhere along the line the laughter had stopped.

When Nina first met Andy, she described how he had affected her so badly that she was rushed to hospital. The doctors had no idea that what was ailing Nina was a serious case of love sickness. Nina recalled in a *London Evening Standard* interview how she had dreamt about Andy, and that he was her ideal man. She also stated that she had made a pact with God: 'All right, God, if you want me to continue to play this music you had better give me a man. If you don't, I'll drink and go to the dogs. You gave me this talent but that doesn't mean I'm not also a human being. I'm a girl and I have desires like other girls, there's just too much to enjoy out there.' In her view, Andy was heaven-sent.

Andrew Stroud was in fact a New York policeman, When they first met he charmed her and kept his occupation a secret. When she found out soon afterwards, Nina was not deterred. Even though he was considered a 'hard' man, she found him gentle and kind. His enthusiasm for her as a performer was a bonus and he would take over the running of her career as her manager. It is often said that business and pleasure do not mix, and perhaps their relationship is a prime example of the truth of this adage. They loved each other but could not live and work together. Yet with the birth of daughter Lisa Celeste, life was complete. Married, with a career on the upswing and now a mother, Nina was without doubt enjoying a new sense of happiness.

During the course of their marriage, David and I met Andy many times. Strangely, I can honestly say I know very little about him, perhaps because Nina took up most of my time or maybe he was busy handling the business details. He was always polite, and appeared to be courteous and kind, much like my own father. But there was another side to him that only Nina and Lisa would know. Following the tour of England, it came as no great surprise to hear they had divorced. Nina never forgave Andy for what she called his 'betrayal', and years after their split she would rage at how he had abused her trust.

If you listen to Nina singing 'Be My Husband', it will give you an insight into how she regarded honour and trust as being the keystones to a successful and contented marriage. Nina once confided to me that she would have left it all behind for the love and commitment of a happy and stable family life.

I doubted whether this was truly the case. Having struggled for years to be recognised as a classical performer, and then switching gear to attain commercial success had not been easy. Giving it all up for contented domesticity didn't quite gel with the person I knew. I have no doubt she loved Andy, and one of her great regrets was just how much time she spent away from her daughter. However, she was also a realist and it was just not possible to have it all. No matter how many tantrums she threw, she had to choose between the family life she craved and the lure of the business.

It was never easy witnessing the battles between Andy and Nina. On the one hand, I knew Nina could be difficult and, being a strong personality, often made unrealistic demands. However, she was also a woman with feelings and needs like everyone else. The outbursts we had witnessed prior to her leaving the previous year were testament to just how volatile the situation had become. I must admit to being slightly biased in my views, as I felt a fierce loyalty to Nina, and believed Andy was pushing her too hard. The press were only too happy to try to find people who would relay any outbursts they witnessed. While she appeared to weather the storm, and in later years did find some sense of happiness while in Liberia, she would never again fully trust anyone.

Nina believed that leaving would give Andy time to reflect and give in to her demands for more spare time. Andy, though, took her leaving as a signal that their marriage was at an end, and even though their paths would cross again, the spell had been broken. Many years later, I asked her if she would like to be able to change anything in her life. She said, 'Honey, all I ever wanted was really to be loved for me. You know, my first love could have loved me if I'd let him, but I ran. Ha! You see, men are scared of me, they think I'm too strong, and I frighten them. Andy wasn't scared, but he pushed me so damn hard, I had to get away, but we got to have a beautiful daughter, so God blessed me anyway. I just wish he loved me enough to see what he was doing. Man, I don't know where all the good men are, but they better come outta hiding soon.' With that, she gave me one of her smiles. The years had left her badly scarred emotionally, and as a result she had put up a barrier to hide behind. It rarely came down.

Many stories have been written about her marriage, how difficult she was to love, and how Andy must have endured hell trying to handle everything. The only truth I know is that what started as an intensely loving relationship could not survive the trials and tribulations of public life. On her return from her rest, Nina decided she would never again allow a man to get that close, and that from then on she would handle her business. Given her previous attempts at managing the business, she soon came to realise she would need help. With her trust at an all-time low, she turned to the one man she knew she could still trust, her young brother Sam Waymon.

Sam, a fellow musician, took over the day-to-day running of her life, as well as performing with her on stage. She spent a few months reorganising her life, and following a further rest period was back in the public arena. A ten-page spread in *Essence* magazine showed a more relaxed Nina, with her daughter Lisa, and the photographs were among the most beautiful ever taken of her. Sam had begun to line up a series of concerts, all the while knowing Nina would no longer accept being worked too hard or pushed too far. Trying to strike a balance wasn't easy, but as her sibling it was a little easier for Sam to handle Nina's various moods.

He was also aware that she was still raw following the divorce, and resolved to be as gentle as he could. If 1970 had been a milestone in her life it was also the year of another rebirth. From being a wife, mother and performer, she was now adjusting to her new role as a divorced woman with a child and a career to maintain. Back in England, David and I were trying, with great difficulty, to fill the pages of our newsletter. Nina's much deserved rest had left a void, and even though she had been in the recording studio for a while, there had been no concerts to report on. The contents of the last newsletters are a mystery, as they have disappeared from our records.

Although she had been absent from the stage for a while, Nina had recorded one song that would become part of her musical legacy to the world. 'Young, Gifted And Black' was recorded in 1969 and was inspired by Nina's friendship with renowned playwright Lorraine Hansberry. The song, which was co-written by Weldon Irvine Jr, would be one of her last hit singles, climbing into the Top Ten of the US R&B charts. More importantly, it would become the anthem for the civil rights movement, and would be an inspiration for millions around the world. A ten-minute version was recorded live at the Philharmonic Hall in New York in October 1969 and would form the centrepiece for yet another album. *Black Gold*, released by RCA in 1970, included this extended version. A version of the Richie Havens song 'No Opportunity Necessary' was also recorded but not included on the album.

Life had changed dramatically not just for Nina – we had also gone through our own changes and it was becoming increasingly hard to devote so much time to running the Appreciation Society. The public's interest was also beginning to wane. This proved to be a source of much debate, as Nina expected her legion of fans to remain loyal at all times, whether she was in the public eye or not.

12 'You'll Go To Hell'

Fortunately for us, Nina's hiatus from performing was soon at an end. It was January 1971, and Nina's re-emergence included a series of mini-concerts in Europe. David was now working almost full time as a journalist for the British magazine *Blues & Soul*, and I would occasionally write a review of a concert, or sometimes interview one of the myriad of American black artists of the day. David agreed to do a piece for the magazine on Nina. Entitled 'Nina Simone – Superstar For 1971', it discussed her prolonged silence and her plans for the future. David went to Amsterdam to catch up with Nina for the interview.

Before he left, he made arrangements for his stay with Sam. 'I had never been to Amsterdam before. On my arrival I called Sam and he explained where the hotel was and said he'd see me soon. So far so good, I thought, on my way to the hotel, but I guess I should have known when dealing with all things "à la Simone" they can get complicated. This trip was to be no different. I arrived at the hotel only to discover Sam was out, so I decided to find Nina. I was put through to her room and a rather abrupt-sounding girl answered the phone: "Yes, how can I help you?" I told her I was with *Blues & Soul* and also ran Nina's Appreciation Society in England. A few minutes passed and then Nina came on the phone. "Oh, you're here?" I said yes, and that I was trying to work out with Sam where I was going to stay. Nina's reply was a little testy: "Well, you can't stay in my room. Anyway I'm sending down my assistant." With that she hung up the phone.

'I was about to discover just how much she'd changed since our last meeting. I knew the past year had been one of emotional turmoil, and would try my best to accept how it must have affected her. A few minutes later a girl appeared. A rather formidable sight clad entirely in black leather, she walked over and said, "Nina sent me down to find out how we can help you?" I replied that I wasn't sure what to do as I had been unable to find Sam. With what I shall describe as "attitude" she suggested I wait until he returned from wherever he had gone. With that, she left and I went and sat in the lounge hoping Sam would show up sooner rather than later.

'It turned out he had been at the concert hall checking on things prior to a taping of the show. He had not made any arrangements for me, and eventually said I could share his room. My, how things had changed. It didn't seem that long ago that Nina had been more than happy for me to spend the night on her sofa in the luxurious surroundings of her London suite.

'"Oh well", I thought, and proceeded to accompany Sam for something to eat. A few hours later we all went over to the concert hall, only to find that there were a series of delays and a few problems. Things were not looking good. Knowing how important it was for Nina to have things done professionally, this had all the hallmarks of an impending disaster. A Dutch group called Boy Edgar Band was billed to appear and was also backing Nina's act. Unfortunately the band members had not prepared, they hadn't had a proper rehearsal and had no real clue as to what music they were going to play. Originally they had been supposed to play five songs with Nina, but that got cut to only three. Nina was furious and walked off stage. The audience wasn't exactly ecstatic either, and people were beginning to shout and scream abuse. The show was being taped for Dutch Television, but Nina's tantrum brought everything to an abrupt halt.

'I followed Nina backstage and she turned to me: "David I don't know *what* to do. This band is shit man. They didn't rehearse properly with me and they keep fucking up." Nina was genuinely upset – she was a perfectionist and would never intentionally perform below her high standards. "Well, man, what am I going to do, tell me?" I thought about it for a moment. "Well, Nina, why don't you just go to the piano and do 'Strange Fruit'? Just you and the piano: no musicians, just you, solo." She thought about this for a few seconds, and then marched back towards the stage.

'She sat hands poised above the keys, and gave a rendition of "Strange Fruit" that was the most emotionally charged I had ever seen. Each note came to life, the tone of her voice took on a life of its own. Nina proved once again just why I adored her, and what had begun as a minor disaster turned into one of the most unbelievable impromptu performances I'd ever witnessed. The audience went wild, and she followed up with "To Love Somebody". In contrast to the humbled and embarrassed band behind her, she sparkled. I never saw the tape, but I'm sure that anyone who watched this performance must have felt her charisma through the television screen.

'Following the taping we left, and Sam decided he wanted to hang out, so he says to me, "Let's all go to a club." Sounded fine to me, I was ready to let off some steam after watching that amazing performance. Nina, determined not to be left out, declared she was coming with us. We arrived at this rather small club, and she looked around and glared at Sam. "There's only men in here. I told you not to bring me to places like this. I told you I don't want to be seen in places like this. What's wrong with you, man? You can do what the hell you like, but I don't want to be *here*." Sam, who was clearly used to her outbursts, ignored her, but the volume was beginning to get louder by leaps and bounds. Finally, she declared with a somewhat deafening roar. "I'm leaving. You stay if you want. I don't know why *you* go to places like this." With that she flounced out leaving us standing there.

'She was definitely not homophobic but this was her younger brother, and being gay was not the issue. It was the fact that he frequented gay clubs that alarmed her. She had known by our previous conversations that I was comfortable with my own sexuality, and had never once confronted me about it. In fact, we had once had a conversation about the fact that the business was composed of such an eclectic mix of people, that basically everyone was accepted. Added to this there was the fact that her audiences usually included a rather large gay contingent.

'Sam and I stayed for a while, and I refrained from further discussion of what had just happened. I did, however, ask how Nina was doing now that Andy had gone. He explained that, as her brother, he felt very protective towards her but that her working with Andy didn't really go well. He was also aware of how much she loved Andy and it had been tough letting him go. Nina had in fact gone home to North Carolina following her brief vacation, to ask for Sam's help and to tell her family of their break-up. Despite the fact that, initially, her parents weren't thrilled by her choice, they had come to respect Andy, and were sad to learn of their divorce.

'Nina recalled years later that it was during this visit that she had felt the ultimate betrayal by yet another man. This time the man in question was her own father. During her visit she had overheard a conversation with her father, who was bemoaning the fact that it was his hard work that held the family together. This cut Nina to the core. For years she had faithfully sent money home to help maintain the rest of the family, and hearing her father come out with what was to her "the first time I'd ever heard him lie" killed a part of her. From that day forward she refused to have anything to do with him. The one man she had depended on her entire life to always be truthful had shown that he was human like all the rest. Even when he lay in hospital at death's door she could not bring herself to forgive his betrayal of her trust.'

Sam, aware that something major had happened during this visit, felt even more protective of his older sister, and did his best to ensure that he never fell into the category of those whom she felt had betrayed her. He did his utmost to prevent outbursts like the one in the club.

'We never discussed his lifestyle, that was his own business, but I could see that Nina's reaction had deeply upset him. When we left we sat for a while talking about their plans for the future. "Well, David, you know I've only been working with Nina for about six months now, but it's going well. I hope to arrange some dates for her in Europe soon, but I don't want to push her into anything too hard. She's had a rough year and needs to rest still." It was refreshing to know that Nina had someone who genuinely cared about her well-being, and would do their best to see she was happy.'

Nina had depended on Andy to take care of the business, and he had done a successful job of shielding her from the day-to-day running of things. Even after their divorce she respected him for his ability to juggle everything so well. Alas, Nina discovered that, when it came to paying taxes, Andy had not been 100 per cent efficient. Now the Internal Revenue Service in America had focused its attention on Nina. Even though she knew this was serious, she was reluctant to cast blame, and began battling the IRS as best she could. Sam was trying to help her pick up the pieces, but the IRS was threatening to take her home in Mount Vernon and freeze her bank accounts, and it was decided to enlist the help of a tax attorney.

Nina's battles with the IRS continued for years. Having worked constantly, touring the world in first-class style, the harsh realities of her single life were beginning to take their toll. Following the concert in Amsterdam, David said his farewells and Nina flew back to New York to begin work on a new album for RCA. For the first time, Andy Stroud's name did not appear as the producer of the album that resulted from these sessions. Instead, *Here Comes The Sun*, which was considered by many to be one of Nina's finest recordings, was produced by well-known arranger Harold Wheeler with Nat Shapiro, a respected author and producer. Nina was credited with all the arrangements on this album, and chose a picture of herself as the much younger Eunice Waymon as part of the artwork for the cover. She also chose to reach back in time and pulled out a quote she had written at the age of 12: 'All music is what awakens within us when we are reminded by the instruments; it is not the violins or the clarinets; it is not the beating of the drums – nor the score of the baritone singing his sweet romanza; nor that of the men's chorus, nor that of the women's chorus – it is nearer and farther than they.'

Here Comes The Sun was yet another diverse mixture of moods and artistry, and included songs such as the George Harrison track, 'O-O-H Child' (an upbeat song of hope and inspiration that had been a hit for R&B family group The Five Stairsteps), 'Angel Of The Morning' (a UK hit for former Ikette PP Arnold) and Bob Dylan's 'Just Like A Woman'. The recording sessions spanned a week, and many years later, when RCA was doing some research for the 1998 CD reissue *Sugar In My Bowl: The Very Best Of Nina Simone*, tapes were uncovered of Nina's version of the Aaron Neville song 'Tell It Like It Is' and a nine-minute masterpiece entitled '22nd Century', highlighting Nina at her musical best.

One of the songs from these sessions would go on to be used on a later release. George Harrison's 'Isn't It A Pity' would be used on Nina's 1972 album for RCA entitled *Emergency Ward*. It was possibly the fact that *Emergency Ward* only contained four tracks that determined the use of this earlier work on the album. (One of the tracks was an 18-minute version of George Harrison's 'My Sweet Lord', which more than made up for the lack of titles.) Another track on this album, 'Poppies', was recorded live at Fort Dix, a New Jersey army camp, before an audience mainly comprised of black GIs, and included her daughter Lisa and brother Sam, together with a junior choir from a New York Baptist church. It will always remain one of Nina's most unforgettable recordings and the whole album was, in essence, Nina's personal statement about the Vietnam War. Years later, many would compare Nina's *Emergency Ward* to the Marvin Gaye classic *What's Going On*, as both albums highlighted the issues surrounding war, peace and survival that were confronting the American public.

Nina's life may have been personally challenging at that time, but when it came to her music she refused to compromise. Some of her most prolific statements concerning the war, the need to find peaceful solutions to life's problems and the search for love were to be found on these recordings. It was also during this time that she received news that her father was ill. By now Nina had cut all ties to her father, and even though she knew he was ill, her sense of betrayal prevented her from visiting him. Her family was totally bewildered. What could have happened? They had always been so close and yet now, as he clung to life in the local hospital in North Carolina, she refused to budge.

Nina continued with a series of concerts that were already booked, although she was plagued by financial problems as well as the emotional devastation of divorce and her father's illness. Booked to perform at the Kennedy Center in Washington, and with her attention focused on rehearsals, she was told her father had died. The man she had held up as her hero had passed into the next realm without one last glance from his adoring daughter. Nina went ahead with the performance, and would later say that she couldn't understand how she sat and performed in front of a room packed with thousands of people, feeling nothing. Perhaps she had simply buried her feelings too deep. She had cried for her fellow crusaders in the war against bigotry and oppression, written passionately about the injustices of man's inhumanity to man, yet she could not express her emotions for her own father.

As if this was not a heavy enough burden for her to carry, within a week of her father's death, her sister Lucille died of cancer. With that death, an even bigger part of Nina was extinguished. On one level she was now utterly devoid of human emotion. With the passage of time she would heal and begin to feel emotions again, but at this particular moment she was numb.

Nina chose to seal a doorway to her heart, and there would be few who could ever prise it open again. Her daughter, Lisa, was the one remaining object of unconditional love and they went off to Barbados in 1974 to make up for the many years Nina's career had stolen from them. This was a shaft of light in what seemed to be a never-ending tunnel of darkness and they shared a holiday filled with much-needed laughter. Nina had certainly lived out the title of one of her songs, 'You'll Go To Hell', and yet she was not about to give up on life completely. Fortunately, she would emerge from this time a stronger person, if somewhat changed.

During the years that followed, I would occasionally catch her in what I would call a 'reflective' mood, and I often wonder if it was at these times that she was allowing herself to feel again. I know that this period of her life was when she was labelled 'cold' by the media. One thing Nina could never be was cold, but she wore a mask that shielded her inner torment. If at times she was dismissive, it was a safety mechanism brought about by pain, and even though being on the receiving end of some of her serious 'attitude' could be upsetting, it was never done with calculation or cruelty. If she thought she could get away with acting up, she would. Having seen her in action over several years, my response was usually laughter or, in rare cases, to simply walk away with a dignified air. I had been shown how by the ultimate master, and I had learned my lesson well.

13 'Here Comes The Sun'

David and I were aware that Nina had been through an extremely difficult time at the start of the 1970s and, although we had let the Society lie dormant for a while, our personal interest in Nina remained constant. There were telephone updates and I recall one phone call in particular. It was a chilly Saturday afternoon in 1974 when my mother announced that a woman called 'Nina' was on the phone for me. (At that time our mother was in the early stages of Alzheimer's and her memory wasn't always sharp.) I reminded her who the 'Nina' person was and grabbed the phone.

'So, where are all my fans then?' I was more than a little taken aback. What was she talking about, was she planning a visit or what? I began mumbling some sort of pathetic excuse, when all of a sudden this huge bellow of laughter emanated from the phone, 'Ha! I got you real good that time, didn't I honey? Okay, so Nina was playing. It had been a while since I'd heard that fabulous sound, and it was very refreshing. I quickly replied, 'Yes, Nina, as usual, you got me good. Where are you? What are you doing? Are you coming over?' She continued to laugh, 'Slow down, honey, you sound just like David – a million questions all the time.

'I'm in Barbados and I just might be in love. I'm having a ball and he's not just any guy *he's the damn prime minister*!' I burst out laughing. This was great as Nina was beginning to sound a lot like her old self again. She continued, 'But you know you can't tell *anyone* – well, you can tell David. I think I may just retire here and just live here with Lisa and enjoy life and lie in the sun and have some fun. No more travelling honey. Well you know it's about time *daaarling.*'

I wasn't too sure I liked the sound of this. While I accepted that she deserved a life and some personal happiness, I was still a bit selfish when it came to her music. 'Oh, so you're giving everything up to lay in the sun with a gorgeous man and Lisa? Well, what can I say except it's bloody freezing here, and it's not fair.' Once again the phone erupted with her laughter, 'Well, if I didn't have to make money, you know I would stay here for ever, and even though he's rich man, I can't have him keep me, honey. I have to have my freedom you know, but who knows, man. Right now it's good: Lisa's having a good time and we're getting a chance to be together swimming, dancing and hanging out. Hell, it's been so long since I just had some good old-fashioned fun, I'm not giving it up without a fight, honey.' We talked for a while longer; I let her know I was glad that everything seemed to be working out for her and that I appreciated her letting me know what was going on.

Being in Barbados was just the tonic she needed. Having met someone who respected her as a person and as an artist was the icing on the cake. Despite this she still had to think hard about the practicalities of raising her daughter and the ongoing fight with the IRS. Everything had changed, and the music was no exception. The public were beginning to wonder what had happened to her. She had gone from being on top of the charts to virtual obscurity within a few short years.

Not that she had completely forgotten about her career. She had in fact recorded three albums since the release of *To Love Somebody*. The previously discussed *Here Comes The Sun* and *Emergency Ward* were followed by a final album for RCA called *It Is Finished*. Taped in July 1973 at the Philharmonic Hall in New York, *It Is Finished* captured all the intensity of a live concert. She had chosen a selection of songs, some of which had been included on previous albums, but performing them live lent them a whole new feel. From the classic 'Mr Bojangles' to the erotic 'I Want A Little Sugar In My Bowl' she launched into a foot-stomping version of the spiritual 'Come By Here Good Lord', and 'Dambala' (with long-time guitarist Al Schackman on sitar), finishing up with 'Obeah Woman'.

The album was not released immediately and when it was finally put out in 1974, it included some additional songs from a previously recorded studio session, one of which was appropriately entitled 'Let It Be Me'. It seemed a fitting end to her eight-year association with RCA. They had begun their working relationship back in the 1960s and now, more than ten years later, 'it was finished'.

However, the ending of her long-term relationship with RCA would create a fresh set of problems for Nina. She was used to working with high-calibre musicians and producers, and in some of the top studios around. Having now left the fold at RCA, she had to face the realities of the ever-changing music scene. While her music had always been a reflection of the times, the business side of the industry had been one she had not dealt with personally for many years. Now the same executives who had once promised her the moon were no longer willing to spend money on an artist who refused to join the growing ranks of 'disco queens'. Nina was a serious artist and her music mirrored who she was. She was never flippant with her messages. For her it was far too important and she knew that the music she created affected people. If she sang about inequality people listened, and if she sang about her faith in God, people knew what 'faith' meant.

Reclining on a beach in Barbados was without doubt a much more appealing option, but one she would ultimately refuse. How easy it would have been to simply allow this man to take care of her, as long as she accepted he was married and that her role would be defined as 'mistress'. She could have lain in the sun and let all her troubles fade into the sunset, but she had been given a mission by God and wasn't about to let it go.

I heard nothing from her for a while and then, out of the blue, I received yet another call, this time not quite as upbeat. Nina was back in the States, and things were not going too well. 'Shit, man, those record companies: they just want to use me, they think I'll record any piece of shit. Well, they don't know who they're dealing with.' I was a little reluctant to ask what had happened since our last conversation, but being a few thousand miles away gave me confidence. 'Nina, I'm a bit confused. I thought you were in Barbados having a ball. What happened?' Her reply was filled with anger, 'Ha! You know he was just like all the rest, like all the men I've known he just wanted to use me. You know I was going to live with him. I took everything over there and he thinks he can treat me like shit. Well he messed with the wrong one, honey. I ain't about to let no man treat me that way ever again and you know that's the truth. So now I'm back in the goddam States and now these record company guys think they can get me to sing any shit. I've had enough of this crap, man. It seems like I always have to struggle, and no one gives a damn. You tell David I need him to call me, man. He knows these people; he can talk to them.'

Nina was without doubt way beyond furious. To be honest I wasn't at all sure what to say, but figured I had to say something: 'Look, Nina, I'll have David call, but I don't know what he can do. I'm really so sorry to hear things didn't work out. I thought everything was going great. But no matter what's happened, I care and so does David. Believe me, there are lots of people who love you and care about you.' All of which was true but failed to soothe her. I'd learnt years ago that when Nina was this angry nothing would calm those turbulent waters.

Perhaps the years of eroded trust had scarred her so deeply that even when someone showed they genuinely cared she never quite believed it. This would not be the last time I would tell her how much I cared, only to sense her disbelief. I accepted long ago that it was not about me, but was a result of her inner pain.

After a few more angry outbursts Nina hung up, with me promising faithfully to have David call her. He was not at all happy as I relayed our conversation. He felt her music warranted a level of respect from the record companies. He was also disturbed that she had been emotionally damaged by another failed relationship. We would often discuss how sad it seemed that, for all her talent, her quest for love always seemed to end in vain.

Yes, she could be difficult at times but no more than anyone else. Just because she was a public figure didn't mean she didn't have feelings. One thing Nina had in abundance was a truly wicked sense of humour. She was a very warm and loving person, and it seemed that her search shouldn't have been that hard. Admittedly, she could play the 'celebrity' at times. Had I been a man I may have been a little afraid to be in a relationship with her. But I believed that if she could just meet someone strong enough to deal with her forceful personality, she'd finally be happy.

David did call her back but it was a very strained conversation. She was insisting that he talk to the record company executives and sort them out. He tried very tactfully to explain it was not something he could get involved with as he really didn't have that sort of influence. Eventually the phone went down. David was upset. I asked him what was the bottom line and he explained that Nina was still angry with Andy, the record companies...in fact it seemed to him she was angry with the whole world. Back then, David was aware that trying to 'baby' Nina would do no good, and was very matter-of-fact in his approach. I figured the softer and gentler I was with her, the quicker she'd calm down and be at peace again. Somewhere in the middle was possibly the right approach, but this time neither of us could solve Nina's dilemma.

Time passed, and once again Nina was dealing with some very unpleasant realities. Even though she had the love of family and friends, it was not enough to sustain her. Her life was never straightforward and it was often a case of just when one part seemed to be working, another fell apart. Yes, there had been times when she managed to find the right balance, but then all too often something would happen to tip the scales.

A new relationship had to be balanced with a career, and not all men could handle the competition. Often it would be her refusal to be 'kept' by men that would see them off. They figured that if they controlled the purse strings, they then controlled the woman, but Nina was far too independent for that and refused to be held hostage by anyone.

14 'I'm Going Back Home'

With the situation in America unresolved, Nina had once again to accept that her legal battles would be ongoing for many years. For whatever reason (and there were many), just being on American soil affected her in a negative way. I always believed it was some sort of karmic influence and that one day she might be able to resolve whatever issues were blocking her. However, divorce had highlighted her financial difficulties and they had to be dealt with at some stage.

Her troubles were briefly put to one side when she found she would be the recipient of an award at a forthcoming celebration in Washington DC to mark Human Kindness Day. On 11 May 1974, Nina stood in front of a crowd of over 10,000 people, all of whom were there to pay tribute to her work and commitment to humanity. Human Kindness Day honoured Nina for her work, and a review of the day published in *Blues & Soul* is testament to her status as a humanitarian.

A wealth of talent was flown in for the occasion. For Nina, though, it was the sight of her mother pushing her way through a crowd of people that was the highlight of the day. The direction she had taken with her music had not won the approval of her mother, yet now there seemed a hitherto unknown understanding. Not that her mother ever felt anything but love for her daughter – it was the strict adherence to her faith that had caused a rift between them, as her mother had always believed Nina's music was a gift from God and should be used exclusively in His service. Over the years Nina had in fact responded by singing and recording many songs with traditional gospel roots, and many were directly influenced by her faith.

David managed to set up a very brief interview with her two days after this event, and recalled how happy she was at the honour. 'It makes some of the hard times worthwhile, you know. You understand, man – you know what I've been through – but seeing all those people, I mean thousands, it's a true blessing.' She went on to tell David that at the moment she had no plans for any major tours and, given their earlier conversations, was in no great rush to get back to recording, but really just wanted to take some time off to rest. David was well aware of how difficult the past few years had been, and even though it might mean the loss of her music for a while, he also knew she deserved a complete break to rejuvenate herself.

Having ended her association with RCA and returned to the States, Nina entered a further period of isolation from the world of music. The loss of her home in Mount Vernon had indeed caused a great deal of upheaval. It had for a long time been a place where a certain amount of stability could be guaranteed for her and her family, and her daughter Lisa felt the impact fairly heavily.

Everything Nina owned had been impounded in Barbados following the end of her relationship with the Prime Minister, Earl Barrow. She and Lisa arrived back in New York with only the clothes they stood up in. Despite having no home, no manager and no man, and with an uneasy financial situation, Nina would not be beaten. Her friendship over the years with a fellow performer, South African singer Miriam Makeba, would transform this seemingly dark period into one of love and light. Invited to go to Liberia, she took what few possessions she still had, and boarded a plane heading for her 'spiritual' home: Africa.

She would always have a close affinity with Africa, as she felt her roots were intertwined with this extraordinary continent. Her passionate belief in equality, combined with the troubled history of her ancestors, made Africa the true core of her being. It was from these far-distant shores that her great grandparents had been abducted and forced to live as slaves in America. It was from here that her very lifeblood came. Her anger and frustration at the ever prevalent racism of the country of her birth was directly connected to her heritage in Africa. Even when the civil rights movement all but disintegrated, she held true to her beliefs that one day those who had enslaved her ancestors would repent and not only admit to their wrongdoings, but work to heal the wounds they had inflicted on an entire race. Landing in Africa with the soil of her mother country beneath her feet, she was optimistic that she would find some much needed peace.

Following the recent disturbing episode with Earl Barrow, the one thing she was not looking for was yet another romantic entanglement. That didn't mean she was about to become a nun, though. After all, she was still a passionate woman, and even though her experiences with men had proved none too successful, she still loved their company.

The press had been tipped off about her arrival in Liberia, so it was splashed across the front page of the local newspaper. The people of Liberia respected her, and unlike the foreign press would not aim to invade her privacy or tarnish her name. They did, however, report the fact that a few days after her arrival she had succumbed to a combination of sheer joy and perhaps a little too much of the local wine, and danced naked in a club in town. It was true. She had been so intoxicated by her surroundings that she had peeled off layers of clothing to dance naked in the crowded room! Liberia without doubt liberated her in a surprising ways.

Her antics did not go unnoticed and one very prominent member of Liberian society in particular had been informed of her impromptu performance. Nina somehow seemed to draw very high-profile men into her life. Perhaps her reputation scared a lot of 'regular' guys as she was often regarded as larger than life. Influential businessman CC Dennis had fallen under Nina's 'spell'. Nina had to return to the States very briefly to sort out her finances and clear up a few loose ends, but she was determined to return to Liberia as quickly as possible. She had no idea how long she would stay in Africa, but she knew that Liberia held a special place in her heart, and she was going to try her best to make it her new home.

Within a matter of weeks, she had been invited by CC Dennis to visit him at his home. It turned out to be a mansion, and despite the fact Nina was used to luxurious surroundings, she was impressed. Not a young man, Dennis was none the less handsome and exuded an air of authority. This was combined with an elegance of character that appealed to Nina. In her autobiography, *I Put A Spell On You*, she described him as a 'black Rhett Butler'. One thing was perfectly clear – the two were more than a match for each other. CC was respected and, like Nina, was used to getting his own way. The combination of their respective strengths and positions made for some interesting and amusing interactions between them. Usually a temper tantrum from Nina would elicit a somewhat subdued reaction, but CC was not just any man and he would give as good as he got. If Nina screamed he simply screamed louder. It must have been a sight to behold.

Things were beginning to get serious and, rather than act on impulse this time, Nina decided to go home to Tryon, and discuss the situation with her mother. As usual, being in the States was never straightforward and she ended up going back to Liberia by way of New York. What was supposed to be a brief visit had taken longer than expected, and she lived to regret having left for so long. On her return things had changed. A rival for CC's affections had made her move and usurped the absent chanteuse. Nina was distraught to find that he refused to even speak to her, let alone see her. The full impact of what had occurred didn't hit her straight away. She appeared resilient on the surface but deep down she was shattered. Another 'betrayal' by a man, yet this time she felt that her rival's influence had more to do with the break-up. How many more times would she have to endure this scenario? It would be easy to catalogue this series of events as sheer bad luck, but that would be too simple. Nina never fully appreciated that in some way she was responsible for her choices and her actions.

Despite the break-up of her relationship with CC she decided to stay in Liberia in the short term. Even though it was hard (as some of the doors that had opened as a consequence of their association were now very firmly shut), Liberia still felt like home.

She also had another opportunity to spend quality time with Lisa, now aged 14. The years of touring had separated them for long enough and, with the divorce, she wanted to ensure that Lisa never felt neglected. Although life in Liberia was on the whole happy and stable, Nina still needed to deal with Lisa's education. Despite Lisa's loud protestations, she decided to send her to school in Switzerland. In order not to be separated from her daughter, she knew her only course of action would be to leave her adopted home in Liberia and join Lisa there.

On returning to Europe, word soon got out that she was back, and offers started to come in for her to return to work. She was still having to deal with the mountain of issues her divorce from Andy had created, and was bombarded by calls from lawyers and accountants, all of whom claimed she owed them money. They were circling like jackals with the scent of unpaid studio bills and the like in their nostrils. Nina had spent countless years making vast fortunes in the music industry. Unfortunately, she had never taken an interest in the business itself and had no idea how the money was spent. Her split from Andy highlighted how little she knew about her grass-roots finances and her ever-growing mistrust of people did nothing to help matters. Shortly after her return to Europe she accepted an offer of help from a businessman called Winfred Gibson. He offered to straighten things out, and invited her to London where he assured her that he would set up a series of tours and recordings.

Once again she permitted herself to believe all she heard. Within days of arriving in London it was clear all was not as it should be and, following an encounter with the hotel manager, Nina decided to confront Winfred about the unpaid hotel bill. The result was shocking and would be yet another low point in her life. With Nina screaming accusations at him, his response was to physically assault her and run. She managed to call for help, but following a painkilling injection that knocked her out, she awoke to the sight of her room in a state of disarray and all her money gone. The resulting press coverage spoke in barely veiled terms of an attempted suicide bid.

At this time David lived in Los Angeles and I was trying my best to keep the Society from total collapse. With barely sight nor sound of Nina, the public had turned their attentions elsewhere, save for a few die-hard fans. I had heard nothing from Nina since her arrival, and my shock at her predicament as reported in the papers left me horrified and deeply saddened. Surely this couldn't be true? The Nina I knew was a fighter, a survivor of injustice, not a woman I could ever imagine trying to kill herself. Determined to find out what was going on, I managed to track her down at the clinic where she was recuperating.

Having known Nina for much of my life, this was for me the most upsetting time I could recall since we'd met. With her neck in a brace and her face slightly puffy, the sight before me was totally shocking. I sat in her room and began to speak. 'Nina, I'm just so sorry. What on earth happened? Why didn't you call me? You know I'd have been there for you. This is absolutely dreadful, I'm just so deeply sorry seeing you this way.' She looked at me with a combination of pain and disillusionment. 'He beat me up, the motherfucker – beat *me* up. Can you believe this shit? Who the hell did he think he was messing with, just tell me, man?'

I was more than a little confused, as I had no idea as to what had preceded this dreadful incident, and didn't want to put any additional pressure on her by interrogating her. 'Nina, I don't know who did this to you, but they should be locked up. I just wish I'd known what was going on.' Trying hard to sit up she continued, 'Look Sylvia, it's not your fault. I could have called but I wasn't sure where you were and there was just so much shit going on. Yeah, he needs locking up, but you know the police here, man, they just don't want to know. They think I'm the crazy one. I'm the one beaten, and yet they say there's nothing they can do. I'm so sick of all this shit, man. It just never seems to stop.' I could see she was both tired and upset, and even though I volunteered to stay, she wanted to be alone, so I agreed to return early the following day.

Following her release from the clinic, she decided to rest at a health farm in the country and I had several phone conversations with her during that time. She told me a lot of what had happened since she'd gone to Liberia, and what stood out most was how much she'd loved living there. 'You know Africa's my home, don't you? Yes, that's where I belong. I was happier there than in such a long time. If only I hadn't gone back to America it would have worked out. Ha! I should have known, every time I go back to the States, shit always happens. I guess I should know better, but I keep on believing one day they'll really get it over there, but they just want to pretend all the time. You know what I'm saying, don't you? You remember the things I told you about how they treated me and my people. Well nothing's changed, nothing. Man, why did I go back to the States?'

Even though America was a land of great opportunity, that was only true as long as you didn't make waves – and Nina didn't make waves so much as floods of biblical proportions. The problem of just where she was going to live had resurfaced. Having been in Barbados, Liberia and Switzerland, finding a 'home' was once again a priority.

The conversation was one we would revisit more than once: 'I don't know where the hell I'm going, man. I hate living in America, it's always the same old garbage, and Switzerland's so boring. If I stay there I'll go crazy. But I've got to live some damn place!' I suggested she stay in England for a while as she had had a fairly relaxed time here, but she wasn't exactly enthusiastic about that idea either. 'Look, man, you know what the press are like here. Hell, they're nearly as bad as in the States. They sure as hell won't give me any peace now, man, and I need to rest and feel better. I'm still in pain, you know: my neck's still really bad and I can't sleep because of it. Shit, I can't seem to find any peace, no damn peace.'

In some way she was right. The media did have a penchant for hounding her and showed little mercy despite her obvious pain. I didn't know what else to suggest, but let her know that whatever she chose to do I'd be around to help her.

She decided to rest for a while and then return to performing with a series of shows at Ronnie Scott's. The club always welcomed her with open arms, and would not put her under undue pressure. No matter how upset she was, and how much physical pain she was in, she was still one of the world's greatest performers, and no matter what had happened over the past few years she would always rise above it on stage. Maybe she was right and a series of concerts would be just the tonic she needed. I was still worried about her health and well-being, however, and insisted that she keep in touch while she was recuperating.

I received several intermittent calls and she finally declared she was ready to return for a concert at Ronnie Scott's, much to my great joy. I offered to help her as much as my own work schedule would permit, and promised I'd see her before the show. Backstage she was in poor spirits. She had hired a nurse to travel with her, as she was obviously still suffering the effects of her assault. I brought her a huge bouquet of white roses (I knew they were her favourites) and she seemed to perk up at the sight of me peering out from behind them. 'See, she knows how to treat me. She knows what makes me smile. You should watch and learn.' She had turned her attention to her nurse, and a man who was apparently taking care of her business affairs. I had to laugh, it seemed nothing would ever dampen her spirits – even a great deal of pain.

'So, Miss Nina, are you feeling any better? Only you certainly look good.' I had learned over many years that a few well-phrased compliments would never be refused, but still she was not happy. 'Ha! You think I look *good*? I look like shit, man. My neck still hurts and I'm in pain. It never healed right, you know. Now these people [looking again at her assistants], they don't care, all they want is the money. It's still the same shit. I miss Liberia, my people. Ha! At least there I was treated right. Not like now – it's just the same damn stuff all over again.' This time I could see she was hurt, not just the physical pain, but remembering the time she had spent in Liberia obviously brought bitter memories sharply back into focus.

Rather than make some flippant remark, I stayed silent. She went on stage, and despite the pain from her neck injury, gave an outstanding performance. I have no idea how she managed it, but whatever demons she was dealing with, when she sat at the piano she laid everything to rest for the duration of the performance. It was as if she went somewhere deep within her, to a place only she could find, that was an area of tranquillity. Having seen her perform countless times over the years, I never saw her allow anything to mute her musical abilities.

There are few that could lay claim to such a majestic accomplishment, and even she would not refer to herself as anything but a performer who had been blessed by God. Despite the media spotlight on her, the one area they chose to focus on most was not her ability as a performer, but her personal life. Yes, there were many superb reviews, but none could capture the true essence of who she was. It was probably due to the fact that mere words could never truly encompass her creative gift – it went far beyond simply being a classically trained and talented performer and into a realm of its own.

The audience response to her at Ronnie Scott's was always enthusiastic but, given how much the press had delighted in highlighting her personal low points, those watching seemed to have an added empathy towards her this particular night. Unlike previous occasions when her performance had moved me to the point of total and utter silence, I was extremely vocal in my praise: 'Wow, you just don't let *anything* stop you from being totally and utterly mind-blowing. God, I wish I had even a tenth of your talent. It's truly something else.' Nina knew I was always genuine in my praise and, despite her obvious exhaustion and pain, managed a smile. 'That was such a good audience man, they really dug it didn't they? It makes me feel good when they get what I'm doing – you know, when they get lost in everything – it really feels good.'

For just a few moments she had felt the sense of love and affection that her British audiences would always emit. Despite the label of us being a rather 'cold' nation, when confronted with such genius it was impossible to retain the proverbial stiff upper lip. I was thrilled that she had been touched by the audience, especially at this time as she was clearly in need of a huge dose of love.

A few days later she left, and even though I'd had to confess to not having done much work on her behalf with her fans, she was willing to let it go, and simply reminded me that they were important and I had to promise to get back on the case. I'll say one thing for Nina: she would never forget her fans, and if she thought they were being ignored, she would let me know in no uncertain terms.

15 'Backlash Blues'

Having returned to Europe and a series of concerts, Nina was trying to move on with her life. With no full-time management, it was increasingly hard to deal with the day-to-day affairs that burden a professional entertainer. Even the slightest mishap can throw off a schedule completely. Andy used to deal with the business and tried to ensure that everything went according to plan. Nina was often angered by the seemingly inept way those around her handled things. Years of being on the road meant she knew just what she wanted, and she expected things to run smoothly. No longer willing to accept inferior dressing rooms or late arrivals by promoters, she was becoming aware of just how much work Andy had put into managing her life.

Her decision to leave him had not been pre-planned. It was almost a spur-of-the-moment thing, with Nina simply trying to teach Andy a lesson. All she had ever wanted was to make him see how much she needed a rest. Alas, as a consequence of her haste she now had to deal with everything, business included.

Touring around Europe only highlighted the disadvantages an artist has when trying to 'do it all'. Promoters and managers rarely show respect for an artist without representation, and Nina was no exception. If they thought they could get away with paying her less than agreed, they would, regardless of how angry she got. After all, didn't the press describe her as 'difficult'? They were quick to justify their actions with this monster reputation. If they were confronted, they claimed Nina was acting like a diva, making unreasonable demands and false claims. Her open dislike for this side of the industry began to show up in reviews of concerts in the form of her attitude to certain audiences. The media had vilified her for a show in France, during which the industry-filled audience had booed her. Nina's response was to storm off stage in disgust. Fortunately, the British press sympathised with her and her views for once, and suggested that it was the industry's desire to see Nina fall that was behind their unkind treatment of her. Sadly, her goal to secure a manager who had her well-being rather than his own bank balance at heart proved elusive.

During this period, Nina began a series of talks with Andy and he persuaded her that, despite their personal situation, he could once again take care of the business side of her life. Misguidedly, she agreed to a series of concerts in the States, with him acting as her manager.

Yet again, Nina was besieged by American reporters, this time asking whether she thought she might go to prison. She was completely baffled. What in the hell were they talking about? On meeting Andy she soon became aware that he had made arrangements for her to attend a court proceeding relating to the IRS, the tax authority. The court hearing had been set up to resolve years of wrangling with the IRS. Andy had agreed to go with her to straighten the whole mess up but, at the last minute, left her to face the wrath of the US Internal Revenue Service alone. She was a true fighter, but also knew when to cuss or charm. On this occasion she resorted to the latter and escaped being sent to prison for failing to pay her back-taxes. She did, however, receive a hefty fine.

Andy had booked several high-profile dates, including Carnegie Hall and the Newport Jazz Festival, but by the time she was due to perform Nina was close to breaking point. Whereas in the past Andy had shielded her from many of the details that running a tour involved, this time around he was less punctilious and it was Nina who had to deal with them. Realising her mistake in trying to recreate her business relationship with Andy, and still not feeling 100 per cent well, she decided to leave the States before the tour ended. Knowing she had disappointed her fans was never an easy thing for her to accept. In addition, she was upset at having to let down the promoter. The press again had a field day, claiming she was unreliable and was on the verge of a breakdown. With headlines declaring her 'crazy', she fled the country.

Back in Europe, Nina agreed to several concerts, one of which was at the Royal Festival Hall. She called me on her arrival and, as I was now working for *Blues & Soul* as a writer, I asked if she'd mind my doing an interview. This was a first for me as David had usually been the one responsible for any interviews, and I felt a little uncomfortable at the thought of writing about her as she was by now, first and foremost, a friend. On meeting up with her I could tell that she was far from over her physical injuries and was still suffering the effects of the beating. I told her I just got angrier and angrier when I thought about what had happened, and that it inspired hitherto unknown violent tendencies in me. 'Now, Sylvia, don't let it get you crazy. I know you care but beating up on that piece of shit won't help, man. It'll land you in jail and I don't want to come get you, you hear!'

Yes, I heard but I was still mad. We spoke for a moment and I told her how uncomfortable I was at interviewing her. 'That's okay, honey. I'll try to behave.' Finally, I was able to see that magical smile reappear. Given all she had been through, I was relieved to see that, once again, she was able to briefly put it aside and let the light in.

The article in *Blues & Soul* detailed briefly what had happened on her previous visit: the attack, and how being alone without a manager had affected her and her current project. Following what seemed like an eternity, she had finally agreed to sign a contract with CTI and had gone into the studio to record *Baltimore*. I loved it: It was a new sound and the songs seemed to have a different feel to them. I told her I really liked the album, but she wasn't exactly ecstatic. 'Ha! Well I'm not at all happy with it. You know how important my music is. I told them I had to have control over it, man. I don't want people messing with my music, but they just did what the hell they wanted.'

I asked her what was wrong? 'Have you seen the cover? I hate it, it's not who I am, and they never even bothered to ask *me* what songs should go on to the damn record. I should be the one to say what they put on my album, it's my work, my sweat that goes into it. Hell, they just took over, never even asked me what I wanted, before I knew it, it was done. You know how mad that makes me after all these years and still I have to let some fat cat record producer decide what he thinks should be done? It's the same shit that I've been dealing with all my life and here we are twentysomething years later and nothing's changed.'

With everything that had happened the new contract was to be a fresh start, but again it had not turned out as she had envisaged. I didn't want to portray her as a victim then, and I don't now, but her life seemed a series of events that would challenge even the strongest soul. No matter how difficult some of her decisions seemed, she would always find a way back from any despair she felt and prove once more how determined she was not just to get through life but to embrace it.

Despite the fact that Nina had not been over-enthusiastic about *Baltimore* it became a firm favourite with her fans, and a welcome end to almost four years of silence. The album had been recorded for CTI, which was owned by jazz veteran Creed Taylor. Taylor had seen Nina at a Drury Lane show she had done in 1977 and was so mesmerised that he convinced Nina to record the album a month later. Nina was in Brussels at Studio Katy, surrounded by some of New York's top session players (including arranger/keyboardist David

Matthews, bass player Will Lee, guitarist Eric Gale and drummer Andy Newmark). The selection of songs ran the gamut from Hall And Oates' 'Rich Girl' and the Quincy Jones classic 'Everything Must Change', to Judy Collins' 'My Father' and, of course, Randy Newman's 'Baltimore'.

In spite of her claims that she had not been consulted about the choice of material, it was in fact Nina who had chosen 'Balm In Gilead', 'My Father', 'If You Pray Right' and 'Music For Lovers'. The polished production and beautiful arrangements would see *Baltimore* become a classic and, even now, it is as fresh as the day she recorded it.

Sometimes Nina's quest for true perfection would cause her to dismiss aspects of her work that others viewed as masterpieces. Even though she had been slightly 'down' on this particular album, she was in fact quite happy with the quality of the recording. Interestingly, one of the tracks, 'My Father', was one that she had tried to record while she was still with RCA, but during the session had broken down and had been unable to finish it due to the recent loss of her own father.

With a further concert scheduled, I said my goodbyes and agreed to catch up with her within a day or two. Despite her pain, she walked slowly but regally on stage at the Festival Hall to the deafening sound of thousands, and began yet another astonishing performance. The only part of the show that let me know how she was truly feeling came with her rendition of 'Backlash Blues' – it was as if she was feeling each and every word. Instead of it being about the injustices of the 'system' it was as if all the hurt she was feeling poured into that song and that she truly knew who 'Mr Backlash' was.

Following the show I fought my way backstage. (Nothing much had changed there: I was still, all these years, later having to battle the crowds of well-wishers and celebrities to get to her.) Backstage she was sitting looking weary. I was again concerned that she was ignoring her pain and exhaustion in order to maintain her high standards. 'Nina, are you okay? Is there anything I can get you or do for you? You look so tired.' 'Hell, yes I'm tired, but what can you do? You can't do a damn thing about it, man. I have to do it myself. You think it's easy being me? Ha! Let me tell you honey, if God hadn't blessed me I'd say he's cursed me, but I know better than to take it out on God.'

I was so used to her anger by now that it had no impact, but I was still worried as I thought she should be resting, and suggested she go back to her hotel. 'You think so, and what about all those people outside? You think I can just *leave*? They're my fans, man. You should understand I can't just walk out

'Mom dear': Picture taken by Maurice Seymour in 1957. Nina scribbled over the name 'Eunice' and replaced it with 'Dr Nina Simone'

A standing ovation at Carnegie Hall in New York, circa 1963

Nina during the civil rights march in Washington, 1963

Nina shares a joke with writer James Baldwin in 1964

Nina helps two-year-old Lisa cut her birthday cake, September 1964

Nina gives a stirring performance on *American Bandstand* in the mid 1960s

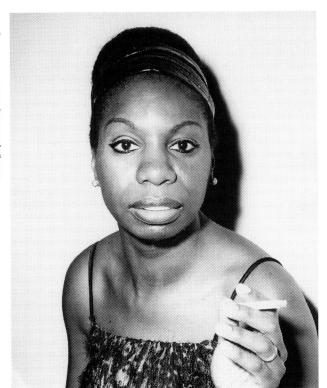

An early shot of Nina in a more relaxed mood, circa 1964

Nina in carefree times, circa 1965

Nina entertains party goers during a visit to Holland in 1967

Nina sings at the
opening night of the
Newport Jazz
Festival, 1968

The 'spirit' moves Nina during
a live concert in 1968

BBC tv LIGHT ENTERTAINMENT PRESENTS

SHOW
OF THE WEEK
DICK GREGORY
ENTERTAINS
with
NINA SIMONE

Nina shows her striking elegance and power in a 1969 fashion shot

Nina receives a gold disc to commemorate sales of 'To Love Somebody' in 1969

Nina works on a project based on the poetry of black children

on them, no matter how I feel.' I was hoping the subject of her 'fans' wouldn't come up again as she had already given me a hard time about the fact I hadn't been sending out news on her. What she had failed to realise was that while she had been away, either in Barbados or Liberia or Switzerland or America, the public didn't sit waiting for news, they moved on. Given how she was feeling and not wanting to upset her further, I simply accepted her wishes and sat quietly while people filed through the door. Finally, the last person left, shouting, 'Don't forget we love you, Nina!'

With so many people declaring their undying love and devotion, she would still find a way to push those closest to her away. Several times over the years she had tried to push both David and I away from her, but being stubborn creatures we had simply stayed put. Not that it was always easy. When someone you care about refuses to accept your feelings are genuine it can hurt, but that was the case with Nina and you either accepted it or let it tear you apart. For now I was more than happy to hang around and hoped that one day she would truly believe it when I said I cared, and even if she never again let me know what she felt, somewhere within me I knew she understood.

Despite her complaints over the choice of material and cover of *Baltimore*, she was fully aware how difficult securing a new record deal had been. David saw her a few years before her death when he had been visiting Elliot Horn, a publicist for RCA in LA. David had himself begun recording and had sent Elliot a copy of a demo tape he had done. On the way back from Elliot's office, who should be walking along but Nina. They spent a while chatting and Nina seemed genuinely pleased to see David, and even more happy to know that he had recorded a demo. David recalled one statement she made that continues to inspire him to this day. 'Well, man, you did learn from the best, so they better take notice of you or I'll have to let them hear from *me*.' David had to laugh. Yes, it was true: his music had been greatly influenced by Nina.

Meanwhile, Nina had been at RCA to discuss a possible new deal with them, but as Elliot would later tell David, it never went through. Unfortunately, although she had provided the company with a string of hits in the late '60s, her insistence on total control, plus some other rather colourful tales of her antics in the studio, had caused them to pass on a further opportunity to have Nina back in the RCA fold.

Sometimes she could be her own worst enemy, and this would be yet a further example of how her inability to bend had an impact. Added to this was the fact that a whole slew of lawyers from various record companies were claiming she owed them money. It was as if she was right back where she had begun, her first dealings with the record industry being with Bethlehem Records.

It was the end of 1979 and Nina was still determined to continue her career, come what may. Following her tour of Europe and our meeting in London, she returned to the States, and David got yet another chance to catch up with her. He reviewed her concert at Avery Fisher Hall, New York, for *Blues & Soul* and described how she had performed songs from *Baltimore* accompanied by only one of her long-standing musicians, guitarist Al Schackman. Her moving performance of 'Everything Must Change' had an obvious effect on both Nina and her audience. Given everything she had endured it was an appropriate choice of song. As usual, her personal situation was left at the stage door and despite the fact she had arrived nearly two hours late, her comments to the audience summed it up adequately. Standing in a regal costume she declared, 'I understand you had to wait in line for 12 hours for these tickets. Well, I'm worth every penny of it!'

Nina was in fine form and treated her audience to a couple of songs a cappella. The range of material spanned several years and she ended the show with a rather strange combination of 'Close Encounters Of The Third Kind' and the old blues tune 'Going Down Slow', explaining to the roaring crowd, 'Well, you've always wondered what kind of person I am – well, I'm one of the third kind.' With the audience in rapture she left the stage and David was able to spend a few moments with her.

She had proved to her New York audiences that no matter how long she was gone, when she re-emerged she was always ready to show them a good time. She told David that even though she had had to deal with more than her fair share of 'bullshit' during her years in the States, she was glad she had performed once more in New York, and that her audiences there always knew how to show their appreciation. She told David that she was feeling a lot better following a recent visit to Israel, her first tour of the country, and that this had proved to be a spiritually uplifting event. The people of Israel had shown her a wealth of love that she had not really felt since leaving behind her beloved Africa. They treated her like a true queen, and she left that country feeling refreshed and renewed. Following the concert in New York she was again being hounded by a variety of lawyers and accountants, and with Andy now out of the picture once more, she decided the time had come for her to leave.

She had, however, committed to yet another concert, at a very chic New York club known as Grand Finale, and refused to cancel. David went along to see her again, hoping for yet another inspiring performance such as the one at Avery Fisher Hall. However, for the first time in his life – and possibly Nina's – she was not on good form. Her voice was hoarse and she barely sang a lot of her tunes, but spoke them. Her behaviour bordered on erratic, but once again her audience accepted her without question. As David wrote in a subsequent review, despite her obvious vocal problems she miraculously created a magic in the room and her audience responded. She sang a variety of songs and skipped through many, such as 'Pirate Jenny', 'No Woman, No Cry' and 'Young, Gifted And Black' without drawing breath. She ended the night with her 1959 hit 'I Loves You, Porgy', and despite the problems David recalled how all those years later it still sent chills down his spine. His review ended with the hope that despite this below-par performance, her best years were definitely not behind her. Unlike previous shows, he was unable to catch up with her backstage and as he felt she was obviously not feeling great he decided not to pursue it.

He called me the following day and recounted the previous night's performance. I had told him how concerned I'd been, having last seen her a few months ago. For us seeing her during this time was painful, knowing she had given her life to the struggles of her people, and time and time again had felt betrayed by those she loved. We both had genuine feelings for her, and had found just how difficult it was to convince her that our motives were completely innocent. During the course of our lives, we had watched her grow as a performer and seen her battle injustice, prejudice and hostility with dignity and strength. We both admired and loved her, as a person, and had never asked for anything other than the return of our friendship.

I explained to David that having her trust eroded over the years by a variety of people was bound to have an impact on her as a person and, deep down, we both knew she held us in a place of affection, even if this was not always obvious. It was to be her daughter Lisa who relayed to us just how much she had cared, and she told us that, 'Mommy always said how much she loved you.'

We agreed that no matter what happened we would always maintain our respect and affection for Nina, and we both believed that would be the case regardless of the situation. I was to discover several years later that I did, however, have a breaking point and she finally brought me to it, much to my distress. Nina was never intentionally cruel, but would sometimes be so caught up in whatever was going on that she would react without a thought for the impact. Accepting her life was going through yet another incarnation,

I did not see her for a couple of years, during which time she moved to France. As we often kept in touch by phone it was never that difficult to know what was going on.

She had left the States and headed to Europe. This time she decided to forego England and Switzerland, and landed at Paris airport for what was to be yet another fresh start. The first thing on her agenda was to find a place to live. She rented a small apartment and began learning French. (Although she had sung several songs in French, she had not fully mastered the language.) Within a short while she was speaking French almost fluently. The French had always admired her, but that was back in the days when she was a 'star'. Now she was living alone in an apartment in a none-too-glamorous part of the city. After several encounters with so-called managers and promoters, she finally found herself work at a local club in Paris. It was a case of déjà vu – having started out in a small-town bar in Atlantic City, here she was nearly 20 years later, singing in a similar club in Paris. Having paid a lifetime of dues only to find herself practically back to square one left her feeling that, somewhere along the way, she must have offended God or at the very least those she cared for, and this was payback time.

Having to start over must have made her feel that she was being punished for her behaviour or choices. Lisa had by now finished school in Switzerland and went to live in the States with her father. For Nina this was not how she had planned things, and she missed her daughter dreadfully. Leaving her in school in Switzerland had been hard, but knowing that Lisa had decided to live in the States felt worse. It was to come as a complete and utter shock to discover that instead of enrolling in college, Lisa decided to join the Army. Nina's objections duly noted, Lisa began what would be a nine-year stint in the US Army. At least Nina could breathe a sigh of relief that she had not chosen the music industry as her vocation. Little did she know that that was yet to come!

Their relationship had been complicated by Nina's choice of career, and while she was without doubt fiercely protective and always loving towards Lisa, their relationship was never what most people would describe as normal. Worlds apart, they were both following differing paths: Lisa's took her to a career in the military, while Nina was once again having to reinvent her life as a performer. Time had passed and it was now the 1980s. Having climbed a mountain and slipped a few times, she was ready to start the journey back to the top.

One of Nina's most endearing personal qualities was her ability to love. Even though there were times when the wall she had built got in the way, those who really knew her saw a warm, funny and passionate woman. Even during this period, with all that had happened, she would break into that magical smile and show her capacity to embrace life. Years of broken promises and some shattered dreams had not prevented her from expressing love, although she had erected a high barrier that few could penetrate. To the public she would always show love, and respect, and would expect it in return. Woe betide them if they forgot. Even the French audiences would finally admire and respect her genius, even if she had not quite re-emerged as they had expected.

16 'Go Limp'

Following a series of shows in Paris, Nina's audiences began to expand once more and things seemed to be picking up. She decided she would once again look to the United States for a record deal. Part of her agreement with CTI had included making a videotape to promote the *Baltimore* album. Armed with a copy of the tape she headed to Los Angeles determined to 'take care of business'. When she got there she found the doors to the executive offices seemingly impenetrable, but she wasn't about to give up this time.

Within days of her arrival, she had managed to track down David, and he was happy to know she was once again seeking a new record deal. He felt it was time the industry paid their dues to her. He suggested a number of companies he felt would be responsive, and wished her luck as she began yet another phase of her life. She seemed to have conquered many of her demons and was trying to maintain a positive outlook on what lie ahead. Being a strong-willed black woman had often brought trouble to her door, but she was not yet ready to quit. Somehow she would make the industry listen. With the major record companies refusing even to return her calls, she finally found a smaller company whose main focus was marketing music videos.

The president of the company, Anthony Sannucci, had at least offered to sit down with her and listen to what she had to say. He suggested taking over as her manager and said he could use his influence to sort out many of her outstanding issues. Yet for now Nina refused to accept his advice and was even angry that after all her years of hard work, she was being told the only option open to her was to hire a manager. She was determined never to let anyone take control of her life again, and if she couldn't do things her way she would wait until the time came when she could. Returning to Paris she was approached to record a new album for French label, Carrère, called *Fodder On My Wings*. It had by now been almost three years since *Baltimore* and she knew she had to have product to reach a larger audience.

Following the recording she agreed to a series of dates back at Ronnie Scott's in London. No matter what was going on in her life, Ronnie Scott's always welcomed her with open arms. The people there were used to her occasional temper tantrums, and she knew that she would always be greeted with a packed audience, whether she had new material or not. On her arrival in the UK she discovered that I had moved and it took her a while to track me down. I never discovered how she found me. Even when I asked her later, she would merely grin and remain silent.

She called and told me to come to her hotel. It was almost comical how, even now as a grown woman, all she had to do was call and I'd drop whatever I was doing and rush to her side. Fortunately I found her in much better spirits this time around. Having spoken to her a few times on the phone in the previous couple of years, it was a joy to behold her in person. She told me that she had just finished *Fodder On My Wings* and was feeling a lot more positive about the future. Her only complaint was the lack of someone to share the burden that touring could bring. She had tried several times over the years to convince me to try to take on the job, but I knew better. The friendship we had forged only survived because I knew the boundaries and avoided crossing them.

Working for Nina was one offer I refused point blank and I'm thankful that, despite her charm offences, I held firm. I knew it wasn't easy for her to deal with the business as well as the performing, but I told her that I would always be there should she need someone to talk to, and that I really wasn't cut out for life as a manager. If she thought the industry was difficult with her, I was sure they would have had a field day with me!

With no management protection, she was vulnerable to media intrusion. After a Ronnie Scott's performance, I saw her unleash a torrent of abuse at a reporter who had dared invade her space. The journalist in question had waited until everyone had left before confronting Nina. She was not amused. Having decided to return to her hotel to get some much needed rest, the last thing she wanted was to face a barrage of unwanted questions. I tried to place myself between her and the eager reporter, to no avail. He simply shouted his questions over my head. I could sense Nina's anger was beginning to rise. 'Who the hell are you, man? Get out of the way. Sylvia, just tell him to leave right now. I'm tired and want to rest. I don't need this shit, man. I've just given all I'm going to give for one night, you hear me?'

He must have been deaf or just plain stupid to ignore her, but that's just what he did. He continued hurling questions at her and now even I was beginning to get angry. Hadn't she just spent nearly two hours giving her all to a packed room? How dare he assume he could impose on her now? I turned to the reporter and told him in no uncertain terms that Nina was leaving and he better get out of the way or else. I figured if he hadn't been scared by Nina he was probably going to ignore me, but for some strange reason he looked straight at me, stammered an apology and left. Nina was cracking up. She had stood slightly back watching me 'in action' and was laughing hysterically at what I'd done. I turned to her and said, 'Well, he deserved it. Hell, you asked him politely to leave; he must have been deaf or something.' Still laughing, she replied, 'I didn't know you had such a fiery temper. Where the hell did that come from?' 'I'll give you two guesses, Miss Nina.' She was almost crying with laughter and although the reporter's intrusion had been unwanted, the hilarity it created was worth the inconvenience.

Somehow we managed to stop laughing long enough to get back to the hotel and once I'd made sure she was comfortable I left, the sound of her laughter ringing in my mind. When Nina was in a playful mood, or just plain happy, her laughter was truly infectious. There were times it became painful and I'd beg her to stop as my sides would be hurting so much that I couldn't move.

Nina had agreed to a week's worth of engagements at Ronnie Scott's and despite her more relaxed attitude, by the end of the week she'd had enough. She decided not to finish her last show and ended the engagement a day early. Journalists were already intrigued by her eccentricities, which included turning up for a show in a fur coat and trainers, clutching a carrier bag. I knew this sort of action would result in more bad press and tried to talk her out of it, but she just would not listen.

'Nina, look it's only one more date, why can't you just finish tomorrow as planned? After all, you always tell me how much your fans deserve respect. If you leave now you know how upset they'll be.' I was certainly getting bolder as the years passed, and was no longer afraid to say what I thought. As was to be expected Nina's reply was terse: 'Hell, *you* don't have to sing night after night, how do you know what I'm feeling? I'm tired and I've had enough. I'm going back to France and there's nothing you can say that will change my mind, so you may as well quit now. You don't own me, you know – nobody does, I'm *Nina Simone* for God's sake. Do you hear me?' I figured half of London could hear her by now, but she was, like me, stubborn and if she said no she meant it. We were sitting in her hotel suite, and with that, she walked into her bedroom and slammed the door. I presumed I had been dismissed so I left.

What she had failed to tell me was that she had just been told of the death of Earl Barrow. Even though their relationship had ended years before, she always had happy memories of their time together. With his death, all the sadness returned and it also brought back to the surface unresolved feelings about her father. I had no idea what had happened, as Nina would rarely discuss such personal and intimate situations. When I found out following her departure, I was upset that she didn't feel comfortable enough to share with me how she was feeling. I had a chance to ask her about this during what, sadly, would be our last ever meeting, and her answer came as a surprise.

Having met me as a child she felt it was not appropriate to discuss such deeply private issues with me; even as I became a grown woman it was not something that she felt comfortable with. Part of that whole mindset was, I believe, generational. My own parents rarely discussed emotionally charged issues with me, as they felt it was not appropriate to bare their soul to their children. Also, their parents had never been that open and I figured it was a belief handed down from one generation to the next. My generation had for some reason developed a different take on the matter. I felt that those closest to me were the very people I would share my most intimate feelings with. It was almost as if I had learned that by being willing to open my heart, even if it might increase the chances of getting hurt, it was well worth the risk to be able to work through my issues.

Not being willing or able to share such intimate secrets caused Nina to close down, and carrying everything inside was painful. Although I could do nothing to ease the pain she was feeling about the death of Earl Barrow, I did think that my knowing about it might have enabled me to be much more supportive. Having bade me farewell, she left for Paris. Once there the overwhelming sense of loss burned, and she decided to call Anthony Sannucci to accept his offer. He flew to Paris and took her back to Los Angeles.

During her battles with the IRS the restrictions imposed on her served as a barrier to her performing and she had kept concert appearances to a bare minimum. Sannucci set about clearing up the situation with the IRS, leaving her free to once again tour the States without fear of arrest or financial persecution.

With him assuming the role of manager she set about relaunching her career and, despite her loathing of the country's politics, she began to see a resurgence of interest in her music. One event in particular would provide her with the means to start over, and it came from the most unlikely source. Given that 'My

Baby Just Cares For Me' had been the cause of so much of her anger and outrage at the industry, and had cost her a small fortune in lost royalties, it would be this song that would catapult her into the spotlight again. It was chosen as the song that would be used to promote world-famous perfume Chanel No 5. One of Nina's loves was expensive perfume and when she heard that Chanel was using the song she was over the moon. Suddenly offers were flooding in from all over Europe. She had left Paris at an all-time low and was to return in style. Gone were the grubby dressing rooms, replaced with fresh rooms filled with her favourite white roses and, of course, the obligatory bottle or two of champagne. This was the life she had worked for and fought for, and she was ready to enjoy it once more.

During the next few years she would undertake several tours of Europe, and despite her somewhat hasty retreat from London, again Ronnie Scott's welcomed her back. We got a chance to see one another, and I was ecstatic to see a more relaxed Nina sitting in front of me. We laughed at how ironic it was that it should be 'My Baby Just Cares' that would propel her back into the spotlight. 'Yeah, it blew me away. All those years I'd cursed and screamed about that damn song, and it finally paid off. It's funny how life turns on a circle. Hey, it didn't hurt any that Chanel picked it, man. You know how much I love French perfume, *daaarling*.'

Yes, I knew, and of course there was also the inevitable champagne. A recent documentary following her death highlighted this fact when fellow performer Patti Labelle recounted how Nina had told her years ago that she must insist on a decent dressing room and at least one bottle of bubbly. Patti's reply was that she didn't drink alcohol, but Nina simply explained that in order to be treated as a star one had to act as a star. That was her mantra and she had earned it through hard work and determination.

We continued talking and she explained how her situation had changed with the appearance of Sannucci. 'He's okay, man. He knows how to get my money, and he doesn't mess with me. Not like some of those swindlers and crooks I've known. It's a nice change to be able to forget the business and let someone else handle it without worrying if they're ripping me off.'

I'd heard her say this so many times over the years and I knew it was something that deeply disturbed her. There's no doubt she had been ripped off during her career – there were so many bootleg albums, had she been paid for just a third of them she could have retired years ago to live a life of luxury. We carried on our conversation: 'I'm so glad to know you've got someone on your side again. It's about time and you know you deserve it after all these years. I'm just thrilled that everything seems to be working out for you.' I figured that, as she was so upbeat and had been laughing so much during our conversation, all was well. I would quickly see that this was not quite the case. Within minutes she approached the subject of her fans. 'So, honey, what's happening with the fan club? You are keeping things going aren't you?' Nina had always referred to the Nina Simone Appreciation Society as the 'fan club', despite us having changed the name nearly 20 years earlier.

I was well and truly cornered. I could no longer pretend her fan base was as extensive as it had been during the 'hit' years. Even though I'd explained the situation on a previous visit, I knew she wasn't going to accept anything other than the whole truth. 'Look, Nina, I have to be honest. It's not the same as it was back in the '60s. People don't seem to bother with fan clubs so much any more. They buy the albums, go to the concerts, but they don't seem to be as committed to the artists themselves… I'm not sure what you want me to do?' She gave me a look that said 'beware'. 'Why are you asking me? It's your job. You're supposed to be running the damn thing, don't expect me to figure it out. Shit, Sylvia, don't you think I have enough to do with performing, running around all over the world and making music. What the hell have you been doing all this time. Well you better sort it out, man. My fans need to know what I'm doing. It's up to *you* to let them know. You wanted to run the fan club so you better run it, or I'll find someone who does. You hear me!'

I was more than a little angry. After all the years and all the work both myself and David had committed to on her behalf, she still wasn't happy. What did she expect me to do: hijack people at her shows and force them to sign up to the Society? What we had begun back in 1965 had undergone many changes. We had started with a fan base of fewer than 20 people and had seen it grow to several thousand members worldwide. However, as with everything in life, times change, as do people's desires and wishes. During her hit years we would be inundated with requests for photographs, and news of her travels and recordings – in fact even the most minor news was greeted with enthusiasm, but that was nearly 20 years ago.

Add to this the fact that I was now a grown woman with a job and personal life, and that left little time to deal with running the Society. Not that I had ever considered disbanding it, but the number of people willing to send even the most modest fee for being a member had almost completely evaporated. I knew this would be an issue and my question had been genuine. If she had any suggestions,

I was more than happy to take them on board. Also I felt at this point that our friendship was more important than the Society, and if one ended surely it shouldn't affect the other? I would find out the answer to that question the following year.

Right now I was more than a little upset. While I appreciated her outbursts came from years of believing everyone wanted something from her, I was definitely not in this category and it had, in fact, been costing me money to keep things running. I had never considered asking Nina for financial assistance with the costs of running the Society. If the number of members didn't cover the cost of mailing out newsletters and photos, then I simply used my own money, it was as simple as that. Whereas I was fully aware that some of the more high-profile fan clubs employed people to run them and were set up with help from the artists, I had never considered this an option. No, I had taken over running the Society when David left for the States, and wasn't about to give up now, even if it was becoming a burden. Nina's artistry was beyond reproach and she deserved all the recognition that having a fan club provided. I remembered the days when I would sit buried beneath a mountain of mail, all with requests for photos, news of her tours and virtually anything associated with Nina. At times it was sheer hard work.

I realised, however, that getting angry or upset would do nothing to resolve the current crisis, and I resolved to try and smooth things over. 'Look, Nina, you're probably right, I know I should be doing more to keep the membership numbers up, and I promise when I leave I'll take some time to figure out the best way to revitalise the Society. It's not that I don't care – I genuinely do – but with working and my own personal stuff I know I've let things slide a bit, but I'll sort it out.' She looked me straight in the eyes and very slowly I could see the beginnings of a grin. '*Daaarling*, I don't mean to get mad with you, but you know, no matter what's going on I care about my fans. They're always there for me, man, and I don't want them thinking I don't give a damn – that's not right. Even in Paris when I was having a hard time, my "real" fans came to see me. They tracked me down, honey, and it made me feel like I could go on. You should understand what I'm saying: after all these years I can't just forget about them, they haven't forgotten me. Ha! Not that anyone could forget me, could they, honey?' Crisis over, she had finally had to give in and smile, and I thanked God, Allah – in fact every spiritual entity that had ever before heard my thanks – in that moment.

Nina was playing Ronnie Scott's the rest of the week, and following her performances we would sit backstage for a while and talk about a whole range of things. It was great to hear her laugh again. She had a wicked sense of humour, and on more than one occasion I would witness her mischief-making schemes backfire, only to be followed by the most ear-splitting laughter. She was also a terrible flirt, and loved to 'play' with the various suitors that tried to get close to her. Any opportunity to watch her in action was always a treat and one such scenario was looming.

Nina had long since decided that a long-term relationship with a man was taboo, but that didn't mean she couldn't have fun. The problem would often be that the men she liked were scared of her. It was understandable given her fearsome reputation, but she had many sides to her character, and if only she had allowed her softer side to appear more frequently, the myth would have been shattered. She did have a very sensual nature, though. If you're in any doubt, just listen to some of her songs. From 'Sugar In My Bowl', 'Don't Take All Night' and 'Gimme Some', right through to 'Take Care Of Business', all had one central theme: sex! Pure and simple, she had recorded so many sexually explicit songs over the years, it was no wonder men went crazy. It took me a few years before I understood what many of her songs were about, but once I did I saw her in a whole new light. If you really want to capture just a tiny part of who Nina was, I suggest you listen to 'Go Limp' on the Philips *Nina Simone In Concert* album. That one track highlights her sense of humour and her intense sensuality.

On this particular day she knew that a certain young man had been trying to catch her eye, and she was quite happy to allow him a glimpse of her 'charm'. Unfortunately, he hadn't quite figured out how to approach her and each time he appeared she would grab my arm: 'See, *daaarling*, I told you he's trying to get to me. Ha! He's so cute I think I'll have some fun.' What was she up to? Well, she was right about one thing: he was definitely cute, and even though he was only about 20 years old, I knew Nina wasn't looking for anything serious, but was just playing. Suddenly she got him in her sights. 'Hey, man, what you doing over there? Why don't you come over here so I can see you?' I was desperately trying not to laugh as I knew she was being mischievous. The guy was clearly shy, and took for ever to reach her side. Finally he turned to her. 'Hello Miss Simone. My name's Jonathan and I just wanted to say how amazing I think you are.' I could see the gleam in her eyes getting bigger with each moment. 'Ha! So you think I'm amazing. So where's my flowers, man; you know I must have flowers. White roses are my favourites but if you can't buy me roses that's okay, as long as what you buy me are cute.' The poor guy didn't stand a chance. Nina was giving him her full-on charm assault.

As she talked, her voice changed, and it began to take on a much more sultry feel. 'Oh, Miss Simone, I'm so terribly sorry. I should have brought you flowers, but I wasn't sure you'd see me and I was a little nervous anyway.' He was making it far too easy for her, but she was loving it. 'Well, honey, if you want to spend time with me you *must* get me some flowers. Oh, and I just love French perfume, you know. Why don't you go and then you can come back after the show tonight? I can see you then, man.' He was caught, hook, line and sinker. She had ensnared him with the ease of a spider who'd just seen dinner. I was having a really hard time sitting quietly throughout this performance and as soon as he left I almost exploded with laughter: 'Oh, Nina, you are bad! He's so shy. The poor thing. I bet he's running all the way to the florist – and as for the perfume, you could at least have given him a hint as to what you like.' She was in hysterics. She was all too aware of how she could affect people, especially men, but it was done in fun and there was never any intention of upsetting this unsuspecting man. 'It's okay, honey, when he gets back I'll just charm the socks right off of him, and he'll be just fine. Don't worry, I won't eat him – well at least not right away.'

How could I not admire this majestic woman? Musical genius, mother, lover, fighter, survivor, and so much more. I hoped the guy had not spent a fortune trying to please Nina, but felt okay as I knew even if he had returned empty-handed she would have treated him well. After the show, sure enough there he was, waiting patiently by the dressing room door. If we thought he looked cute earlier, by now he'd gone completely over the top and was wearing a white tuxedo jacket, shirt and red bow tie – totally gorgeous and carrying a huge bouquet of white roses and a gold wrapped box. Well, Nina had certainly picked the right man to play with. I asked him to wait a moment and ran back inside.

I ran into the room so fast she looked at me as if I'd gone mad. 'Nina, you are never going to believe it. Not only has he brought you gifts, but, honey, when you *see* him you may want to do more than have some fun!' She was beaming like a contented Cheshire cat. 'Oh, so he looks good, does he? Well, I may have to see about him. Don't worry, honey, you know I'm only messing. I wouldn't do *that*, even if he is cute. He's a baby and I've had my share of that for now. But hell, man, you'd better let him in before he runs off again.' She was referring to the fact that during the week he'd tried so hard to be cool, but the closer he got the more he seemed to lose his nerve, and we both saw him turn quickly when he knew we had spotted him. Nina adjusted her beautiful gold-coloured gown and sat bolt upright. The Queen was ready to receive her guest. I don't know how I kept a straight face as I watched her in action; I wanted to cry with laughter as she cajoled and purred her way through the next 20 minutes.

It turned out he was the son of a fairly prominent businessman, and had been a fan of her music from a very young age. His father had given him tickets to see her years ago and he had fallen in love at that moment. Even though this started out with Nina simply having 'fun', by the time he left he had earned her respect and she had promised that if she had time, yes she would visit him at his father's home in the country.

I had to admire her. 'Well, Miss Simone, that was a bit of a turnaround wasn't it?' Nina was still grinning and I was grateful to see her in such high spirits. She really did deserve to have fun just like everyone else. 'Honey, he was just way too cute. Ha! And what a nice guy. You know he knows all my music and his father has *all* my albums. Mind you, he was getting a bit too "excited" if you know what I mean, but, hell, I am a High Priestess!' I was quite sure that the reference to his 'excitement' was true and there was no doubt he certainly brought a glow to her face and a sparkle to her eyes. I'm not sure if she ever saw him again, but for that one brief moment the room was filled with laughter and all was right with the world.

With the week nearly over, I was sad that she was leaving as we had spent most of the time laughing and just enjoying each other's company. Despite the years of our friendship, stuff always seemed to get in the way, but this time – apart from the odd moment – we'd had a ball. Sensing I was a little down, she turned to me as I was about to leave: 'Hey, you know we'll see each other real soon, man. I'm coming back in a couple of weeks. So, you better do some damn work; I can't have you lazing about the entire time, can I?' I gave her one of my own special grins. 'Okay, Nina, here's the deal: you keep smiling and enjoying life, and I promise to get on the case and make sure I get all your fans lined up for your return. Is that a deal?' 'Ha! You'd better make sure you do. I don't want to come back and not see my fans waiting for me, you hear me?' With that, she gave me a huge hug and I left.

The only problem I had now was what on earth had made me make such a stupid promise. Where was I going to find all these imaginary fans? Oh well, I wasn't going to worry about it now. I'd deal with it before she returned. At least that was the plan.

17 'Young, Gifted And Black'

True to her word, she returned two weeks later. I decided the best thing to do was relax, pray and hope that the word 'fans' never issued forth from her lips. Fortunately I had been granted a temporary reprieve. Nina's usual line-up of musicians had changed, and unlike her previous trip, this time she was working with just one musician: drummer Paul Robinson. Paul would work with Nina for almost 20 years, and I was fortunate to be able to talk to him about their relationship and get an insight into the more technical aspects of her career.

Paul's first encounter with Nina began almost accidentally. He had been working at Ronnie Scott's the week prior to her last visit as part of a big band ensemble known as Superjazz. Martin Drew, who was the resident drummer with Ronnie Scott's house band, was unable to work with Nina as he had a prior engagement working with Oscar Peterson. A few days later, Paul received a call from Ronnie Scott's asking him if he was interested in playing with Nina. That night he went along to watch Nina's set and check out her music. The following night he joined the band, and began his long association with her. That first night went well, although he never actually spoke to Nina. His first encounter with her came during her next visit.

As for Nina, she had hired percussionist Leopoldo Fleming to accompany her. However, in typically chaotic fashion, no one had remembered to apply for his work permit, and on arrival in the UK he was refused entry. Paul received a frantic phone call from Pete King at Ronnie Scott's asking if he could go down to Oxford and pick Nina up. Climbing into his father's Audi, with his drums packed tightly in the back, he set off to meet her. She had decided to go to a health farm in Oxford before starting her engagement at Ronnie's. Paul arrived, Nina and Sannucci greeted him, and they all squeezed into the car. This was the start of their relationship, with the three of them squashed into an old Audi, its gearbox practically hanging off and Paul's drum kit almost poking them in the ribs. They finally arrived at Ronnie's, and both Nina and Sannucci got out leaving Paul to struggle with his equipment.

So, this was his new 'boss'. Having driven from London to Oxford and back again, he was now left blocking the street outside Ronnie's while trying to unload his gear, with just minutes to spare before going on stage. He finally dragged everything inside and, a few gin and tonics later, joined Nina on stage. It was then she first realised that as well as being able to play, he was not the sort of person that was easily intimidated! Unlike some of her previous musicians, Paul (a typical down-to-earth northerner) would not be bullied by her, and after several performances together she began to show her appreciation.

During this visit they began to talk, and their relationship evolved. Musically they discovered they were a perfect match. Despite the fact that Nina was a classically trained musician, Paul had no trouble working alongside her, and stated that as far as he was concerned a good musician was just that. He had himself been trained for almost 14 years and had performed a lot of jazz-orientated music prior to meeting Nina. The two connected almost immediately and even though Nina would often change gear during the course of a show, Paul enjoyed the chance to work with someone who would change the musical environment during a performance.

Unlike some of the musicians she worked with, who would simply try to recreate the sound of one of Nina's records, Paul had an ability to reinvent any song and that proved most rewarding for both of them. Nina loved the fact that he could keep up with her, and that he did not try to imitate what had gone before, but would make it sound fresh. I never actually met Paul until Nina's death brought us together in France, and despite the fact that we had probably seen each other more than once or twice over the years, we had never spoken. It was the case that, just as their relationship was beginning, mine and Nina's was about to be torn apart.

Prior to that fateful event, we had several opportunities to talk during this trip, as her schedule seemed to have been worked out to allow her the maximum amount of downtime. I took advantage of this as it had always been difficult to get 'alone' time with her in the past, and I had some burning questions that I wanted to discuss with her. These were not light-hearted matters, but having been around her long enough by now, I knew she was willing to talk about serious subjects if she detected genuine interest.

One conversation in particular stood out, and I remember thinking just how articulate Nina was. I'd decided to ask her how she felt at the disbanding of the civil rights movement after all the years of struggle and the deaths of so many. Years after radical action by blacks began, America still seemed in a state of denial about its race dilemma.

'You know, they can pretend everything's fine, and try to forget what we went through, but one day they'll have to face it all over again. My people will see how they've tried to fool them and will rise up again. I don't mean riots and violence – no, man – this time they'll use their minds to force change. When I think about all those brilliant people who died for the chance to be considered equal, it makes me sick, physically sick, man. It hurts, you know, that even now being a black woman is a curse. Yes, honey, it may be the '80s but the man is still trying to keep us down. They may have taken off the white sheets but, hell, they don't need them now; they just own everything and use their money to hold us back. But, you wait, the day *will* come – I hope I live to see it. Who knows, one day my people may…wake up and know they have the power and, hell, we may even see a black man running the place. Wouldn't that be a real killer? All these years they've tried to stop us moving on, but we will win because we have to win. I don't want my grandchildren to suffer what I did. Hell! I didn't want Lisa to go through the shit I went through. You can't imagine how it feels to see a black man or woman hanging from a tree just for the colour of their skin; it makes you hate so much it never goes away, *never*!'

I never tired of discussing such a serious issue with her. I had never really quizzed her regarding the links between her beliefs and her music, and felt it was time I did. 'Nina, I do have to ask: when you sing "Young, Gifted And Black" do you believe it makes a difference? I mean, when I first heard it, even though I'm white, it made me really believe I could do something special with my life, and I wondered if that's what you planned?'

'That song is just so powerful, man. I prayed, yes I really did pray, that people would really listen and know that after all the years of being told you're no good, you're just another nigger trying to get by, they would realise that it was a lie. White people lie, Sylvia. I know you understand I'm not accusing *you*, but for so long whites have lied about us, and you know I ain't lying about that one. So when I sing "Young, Gifted And Black", it's my way of telling the truth. If you were a young black kid and you'd been told that the colour of your skin would affect your whole life and that no matter what you did you'd never amount to anything much. To hear someone tell you that isn't so, is powerful, man, really powerful.'

She was 100 per cent right, and had explained how she felt with such clarity and grace I knew it would always be a subject we could revisit, and one that she knew I understood. Tentatively I continued, 'When they decided to use "Young, Gifted And Black" as an anthem for the civil rights movement and paid tribute to you for recording it, how did you feel?'

'Ha! That's a good one, man. You know I never planned for any of it. I was totally amazed when Andy told me what they were doing and that my song was going to be their anthem. It felt good, man, to know that after all the years of struggle and seeing people beaten and murdered by the system, that now I could sing a song that gave people hope and courage. The words say it all – being black was not going to hold us back ever again, no way, man. Being proud of who you are sets up a whole new way of thinking and believing, and that's what I wanted them to know. Be proud of being black; don't let anyone try to tell you you were dirty. Ha! I've known white people whose skin may have been light but their hearts were black – deep, dark and black. I just hope that when I'm gone people will keep the fight going and sing that song and be proud. Hell, we died so that the children today can have a voice. That's deep, and they better know that even though Martin's gone, and Malcolm's gone, even Lorraine – she was such a beautiful spirit, man [her eyes were beginning to mist over at this point]. Hell, they can never forget.

'I won't ever forget no, man, no matter what they do to me, and they've tried. You know the FBI tried to shut me up, I mean they would have killed me if they could, but I was too smart for those mothers! I've told Lisa so she will tell her children, and you know what I've been saying all these years is true, and the fact you're white doesn't change things. Some of my people are so light they could pass as white, but even they have to either hide their identity or accept who they are. I get mad when I see people trying to be white. Hell, if they were supposed to be white, God would have made them that way. But I've said all I'm going to say. I've told you for years how I feel and nothing's changed, nothing's really changed, man.'

With that, she seemed to go into a place within her that held all the memories of her years of struggle for the rights of 'her' people, and I respected the fact that just talking about these issues caused her emotional pain. I thanked her again for opening up to me.

Throughout the many years of our friendship, the times I treasured most were ones when Nina would drop her guard slightly and let me see just a glimpse of who lay beneath. The years will never diminish the impact these very intense conversations had on me. I'm proud to know that what she told me shaped my beliefs, and encouraged me to always seek out truth and rail against injustice.

Nothing makes me angrier than bigotry and hatred, whether it's on an overwhelming scale or just the actions and words of individuals. I became a very militant person during the 1960s, and had I not decided to find a more loving way to express my opinions, I'm sure I would still be as radical now as I was back then. My beliefs are the same – my way of expressing them is the part of me that has changed.

I owe a lot to Nina as a humanitarian and a woman of courage, with her fierce determination to stay true to her beliefs. It takes a hell of a lot of strength to spend a lifetime battling a system that would, if allowed, bury you without a second thought. Nina was that and so much more, and these conversations merely highlighted just a small insight into her inner self.

I was not the only one who was aware of how hard it had been for Nina. Paul Robinson explained his views to me, saying, 'She had come from a period in time when being black was not easy. She carried all these things around with her: being a star, a black woman growing up in America in the '50s, and, yes, sometimes I'd get a piece of it from her. Obviously being a successful black woman – and an outspoken one – at a time when black people still had to sit at the back of the bus had a tremendous effect on her. If she had been starting out in the '70s or even '80s she wouldn't have had such a hard time being so vocal.'

Nina not only influenced and touched my life, she left a deep impression on all who entered her realm. With her Ronnie Scott's engagement over, she was preparing to leave again. I'd spent the last few weeks laughing, learning and treasuring our time together, and had managed to escape an in-depth probe into the affairs of the 'fan club'. In fact, whether it was her mood or just my prayers being answered, the topic had not come up once during this visit. Little did I know that it was just a case of the inevitable being delayed, and that the whole issue would escalate into one giant blow-up sooner rather than later...

18 'I Wish I Knew'

Nina's previous visit had left me feeling she had finally reached a place of contentment. Her career had seen a revival due in part to Chanel and its use of 'My Baby Just Cares For Me', and she had the added bonus of having a manager in the form of Anthony Sannucci, who seemed well equipped to handle her and the business.

All that came to an abrupt end with her split from Sannucci. He had joined a long line of managers who stopped asking her opinion on matters and tried to assume total control. The final straw had come as a result of his refusal to discuss an upcoming tour of England, during which she was to again perform at Ronnie Scott's. Although she had a great affinity with the well-known jazz club, Sannucci had insisted on extending her original engagement from two weeks to three without consulting her. She was furious about being committed to such a long engagement. The end result was that she fired him and was once more alone. He would be reinstated a while later, but until then Nina had yet again to handle everything on her own.

Even though I hadn't heard from her, I knew she was in town as I had seen an ad in the newspaper for tickets for her Ronnie Scott's shows. By now I had gone through a major personal upheaval, and had taken a job in the City of London, working for a firm of solicitors. My life was without doubt far more stable than it had been for several years. I had also moved again and figured that was why I hadn't heard from her, but once again Nina finally managed to track me down. She insisted I meet her at her hotel, and I gave her my word I'd get there as soon as I could.

She was staying at the Grosvenor House Hotel in London's West End, and I made my way there with a serious amount of trepidation. I had been unable to keep my promise and had not worked out how to increase the almost non-existent membership of the Society. I just had to hope that, once again, the subject wouldn't come up. I found her in a somewhat edgy mood and felt a certain amount of compassion for her assistant, who looked worn down by the series of commands thrown at her by Nina. 'Shit, girl, just do what I say. You know I have to have my clothes unpacked straight away. I can't go on stage wearing wrinkled clothes, damn it. Why can't you use your head, man?' Things were obviously not going well, and I hoped – well, prayed – that she wouldn't turn her obvious anger in my direction. I was wrong.

Within minutes she was grilling me. 'So, where the hell were you? Why didn't you meet me at the airport, and where were all my fans? What the hell's going on, Sylvia?' I knew it was bound to happen and so, trying to think as quickly as possible, I managed what I considered a brilliant response: 'Nina, I'm not trying to make excuses but you did arrive rather early, and I had no idea when you were coming as no one had called me. As for your fans, well most of them have to work and can't just take off when they feel like it.' 'Ha! What do you mean no one called you? I told them to call you before I left. See, I can't trust anybody. No one knows what the fuck to do. Well my fans better be there for my show!' With that, she declared that she was going to get some rest and I should wait for her to wake up and then we'd go for dinner. Gone was the previously happy and relaxed Nina; in her place was a distinctly moody woman.

I sat talking to her assistant for a while, trying to find out what had been going on, but she was too busy getting everything unpacked and generally sorting out Nina's clothes to focus on me. I sat watching the television for a while, and before too long a rather groggy Nina appeared in the doorway. 'We need some food, girl. I'm hungry. What are we doing about eating?' Having been around her for long enough I knew this was not an unusual request, more a response to the growling of her stomach. Following a brief discussion it was decided we would eat downstairs in the hotel's restaurant.

The atmosphere over dinner was fairly calm due in part to the fact that everyone was busy eating, but it didn't last. With the business of eating done, she began to hurl yet another series of questions at me. 'So, Sylvia where are all my fans? How many do we have now – it must be a few thousand? Where are they all?' I knew she wasn't going to let it go, but I wasn't ready for a full-scale row in public. I also knew that she was getting bored, and having all-female company was never something she really enjoyed. Had I managed to summon up a couple of her adoring male fans all would have been fine, but that wasn't about to happen and so I had to figure something else out. I explained to her that while I loved being around her it was getting late (nearly 1am) and I had to work the following day. I suggested we talk about this some other time, and I promised I'd call her the following day and see her at Ronnie

Scott's before the show began. Grudgingly she agreed and, before letting me go, let me know in no uncertain terms that there better be a few hundred fans at her show or else! I didn't want to know what the 'or else' was, but I was sure it would not be pleasant.

Once home, I began to reflect on what was obviously going to be a problem. The fact was that she had not had a major UK hit for several years now, and the public had a very short memory. That's not to say she didn't have a large following – there were without doubt a number of die-hard fans who stayed loyal no matter what. The problem was that they were in short supply. Add to this the fact that most of her followers were older and more apt to show their appreciation by attending her performances or buying her records, than flinging their bodies out of bed at 5am to wait at an airport, and you have the truth of the matter.

It was late and I was tired, but I decided to call David. Maybe he would have a solution to my dilemma. I relayed the conversation and my immediate problem, but he could think of no other way of dealing with it than to tell Nina the truth. He knew this would result in a major upset, but reminded me that the truth was really the only option. I agreed, but was dreading the coming days. Following an exceptionally restless night, I got up and began getting ready to go to work. The phone rang. It was Nina. She wanted to remind me that she was expecting to see me early the next day and was looking forward to seeing all her fans. I put down the phone feeling like I was carrying the weight of the world on my shoulders.

I could not conjure fans out of thin air and I arrived at work very down. Fortunately I was working with a long-term friend, Michael Critchley, who sensed something was wrong. Michael had met Nina several times over the years and knew what I was talking about when I said she would go completely mad if she felt I had failed her. He told me not to worry as he would give it some thought and between us we would find a solution. I attempted to put it out of my mind and at least give the appearance of doing some work when the phone rang. Michael was shouting down the phone that he'd had a brainwave. I rushed downstairs to find out what he'd come up with. His idea was absolutely brilliant and even now I am grateful for his lifesaving plan.

The lawyers we worked for were a mixed group, but for some strange reason they had a common link: they all adored Nina. When they first found out I knew her they were thrilled and were always eager to hear any news I had on her. With this in mind, Michael's suggestion was that I ask everyone at work to come, and also to bring their wives, etc. That way I could gather up a reasonable amount of 'fans', and taking time off wouldn't be a problem either. I looked at him and wondered if his brilliant suggestion could work. I thought it was worth a try. I started making the rounds of the various partners, clerks and accountants, and by midday all was going to plan. I had encountered a slight amount of resistance as they realised it would leave virtually no one in the office, but the chance to attend a 'private' taping of her show was far too tempting to be ignored.

The next part of the plan involved calling everyone we knew – friends, family, even friends of friends, no one was spared. By the end of the day we had triumphed and with nearly 200 people confirmed I could finally relax. The added bonus was that everyone who had been invited genuinely loved Nina, and was thrilled at the prospect of seeing her up close. I was eternally grateful to Michael, and also thanked God for smoothing the path for me.

That night when Nina called I was so upbeat she asked me if I was on drugs? 'No, I've given all that stuff up.' In fact she had given me a major lecture on the subject of drugs during a previous visit. I had been asked to review her concert at the Drury Lane Theatre for *Blues & Soul* and had gone to the show somewhat stoned, for want of a better word. Following the concert I'd gone backstage and had mumbled something about how much I'd enjoyed 'Arm The Gillians' (I was, of course, referring to 'Balm In Gilead'). Nina looked at me as if I'd gone mad. 'What the hell are you talking about?' I again mumbled some nonsense, and she looked me straight in the eye: 'Sylvia, are you doing drugs, only you are acting very strange, honey? Tell me the truth now!' I informed her that yes I had taken a few puffs and a couple of pills to liven me up but it was no big deal. She didn't agree. 'Listen, you need to promise me that you'll stay off that shit, man. It's no good for you and will send you crazy. I hate drugs, man. They've messed up so many people and I don't want to ever see you like this again. Do you hear me? I'm serious – don't do that shit.'

I was surprised as I would have thought that, being in the industry, she had probably indulged in the odd substance or two, but I was wrong. I promised to stop, but it would be several years before the pleasure of my drug-taking became pain, and I almost died as a result. I did, however, finally learn my lesson and have been drug and alcohol free for over ten years now, thank God.

Having finally convinced her I was fine and had stopped messing about with drugs, I arranged to see her early the next day. She was still a little unsure as to my honesty regarding the drugs issue, but managed a curt reply: 'Ha! Well, you better make sure you do get their early. I want to see you before the show. I need you to be there to sort things out, so you make sure you're sober man. I don't want it to be no half-assed shit; it's being taped by the BBC, you know.' Yes, I knew, BBC2 had arranged to do a special on Nina at Ronnie Scott's, and it was important that it went well. It was her first television special for a number of years and she wanted it to go well, and so did I. It was a great opportunity to revive the public's interest in her and to remind them what a truly amazing artist she was.

No matter what twists and turns her private life took, her music was the one thing upon which she never compromised. She knew it was vital to keep herself in the public eye if she wanted to maintain her status as the High Priestess of Soul. Given her music was better defined as a fusion of jazz, blues and gospel, the label had always been an interesting one.

I went to bed that night knowing everything was on track and slept like a baby. The following day was hectic to say the least. Everyone was trying to work at double speed in order to leave early for the show. I didn't bother trying to work, and left to go to Ronnie Scott's armed with a large bouquet on behalf of the entire firm. My only regret is that, back then, I didn't have a camcorder or anything like that. If only I had, I could have captured the sight of lawyers, bankers, accountants, City men and women, and their spouses all walking down the street towards the door of Ronnie Scott's. My only lingering fear was that not enough of them would turn up. I could relax on that score as not only did enough people turn up, but so many came some had to stand at the back of the club!

I was feeling fairly pleased with myself as I headed for the dressing room door, but my good mood was to be shattered quite abruptly. Nina was not in a good mood. She was again aiming her anger at her assistant and generally being difficult. She waited until I had both feet in the door before unleashing her temper in my direction. 'Shit, man, what the hell time do you call this? I told you to get here early. Anyway I need you to go out front and check everything's okay and all the tables are set up right, and find out where Paul is as I need to talk to him, you hear?' Of course I'd heard but I decided to put my foot down once and for all. 'First of all, Nina, I'm not running around chasing your musicians. Second, I don't know what the arrangements are for the place and I'm not interfering and, finally, I came as early as I could given that I do have a job!'

I knew my reply would not go down well, but I'd had enough. I'd let her bully me for many years and now, as a grown woman, I felt enough was enough. She glared at me as if she was weighing me up, and I was expecting a full-on backlash. 'Ha! Well, if you're not going to help me I guess I'll have to do it myself. I thought you were going to help me, man, not just stand around.' My normal response would have been to back down and apologise, and basically do her bidding, but not this time. I knew if I didn't stand my ground then I never would. I handed her the bouquet of flowers and hoped that this offering might just diffuse the situation. Fortunately, I was right.

Whether it was the flowers or the realisation that I was no longer happy to be treated as some sort of underling, she accepted them with a smile. When she read the message her whole face lit up. The card was signed from her legion of 'adoring' fans. 'That's nice, man, and they got me my favourite flowers. Ha! Well I guess I may forgive you being late then.' With a huge sigh of relief I sat down and watched her deliver several admonitions to those around before finally sitting down to apply her make-up. Rather than tempt fate I kept relatively quiet and, before I knew it, she was heading towards the stage. 'Oh, by the way, I've reserved a table for *you* at the front, so you make sure you sit there, okay!' Hey, that was fine with me, as I knew that no matter how upset she'd been she was sure to deliver a sparkling performance.

The room was full to capacity and people kept coming up and saying how thrilled they were and to thank me. I sat where I had been told, a little puzzled by her request – normally she never made a point of telling me where to sit – but I gave it no more thought. I would soon discover why she had made the request, to my absolute horror.

The set was going well – the audience were treating her with the required respect and generally having a ball. Switching from 'Black Is The Color', to 'See-Line Woman' and then into 'Wild Is The Wind' without pausing for breath, she had the place in the palm of her exquisite hands. Each table had been supplied with a bottle of wine to give the atmosphere of it being a nightclub, and despite it being late afternoon it worked. The only downside was that my nerves had got the better of me and I consumed practically an entire bottle on my own without realising it. I was without doubt a wee bit drunk, and was having a ball, when all of a sudden she started talking to the audience: 'Oh, yes, and the president of my fan club is here, you know. Sylvia, stand up let them see you.' I wanted to crawl under the table and I'm sure, had I not consumed a large amount of wine, I would have. Not only did I hate public attention, but I was wearing a ghastly dress (far too straight-laced for my usual style) as I had come straight from work. People began clapping and screaming, most of them knew me and I was sure they were deliberately trying to embarrass me, and I sat down as if I was on fire. Nina just laughed and winked. 'Huh!' I thought, 'I'll give you winking.' However, I had no choice but to see the funny side and, after a few more glasses of wine, let it go. My only prayer was that the BBC would edit that part out. Alas, it didn't.

She ended the set with 'My Baby Just Cares For Me' and those usually staid lawyers went completely wild, shouting and yelling, 'More, Nina! We want more! We love you!' In the end she did at least three encores before finally leaving the stage. I talked to a few people and thanked Michael once again for saving my life, before heading backstage. He came with me and had a few words with Nina before leaving us alone. 'Nina you are so bad. You know I hate being public. Why did you do that?' She was grinning from ear to ear. 'Well, you are the president of the fan club and people should know and show their appreciation. But honey, what the hell is with that dress? I thought you were going to change. You look so straight, man, it's not you at all.' Fortunately, I knew she was just messing with me, but she was right – I looked far too normal.

I asked her what she thought about the audience and she was overjoyed. 'You know, *daaarling*, when those English guys loosen up they really let it out. Ha! They were great man, they knew all my songs. I need to find me one of those English guys. They know how to treat you.'

I was pleased to see her in such good spirits. The people from the BBC came and thanked her for a truly remarkable performance and promised to let her have a copy of the tape as soon as possible. 'You make sure I get that tape now, you hear me!' She was laughing and joking with them as they packed up their equipment, and I was glad she had finally loosened up.

We had by now moved into the main area of the club and she had asked me to order her a taxi to take her back to the hotel. I was standing at the door looking to see where the taxi was when out of nowhere she began shouting at me, 'I need a man. You need to find me a man, Sylvia. I'm sick of going back to hotels alone. Get me a man now, damn it!' I wasn't sure if she was being serious or not and without thinking turned to her and declared, 'Look, Nina, I can't find you a man – in fact there's no point asking me as I'm not really into men. They aren't exactly high on my list of priorities.' With that, the cat was out of the bag. I hadn't planned to tell her I was gay, as I felt it was private and nothing to do with her, but it was too late now. Whether it was my slight irritation at her demand or what, I don't remember, but I'll never forget the look on her face or her reply. 'What the hell are you talking about? What do you mean you don't like men? What's wrong with men?'

Oh well, I thought, I may as well explain properly: 'Look Nina, there's nothing wrong with men. In fact I like men, I just prefer women that's all, and it's not really your business what I like or don't like, and I'm *not* finding you a man, okay?' My trying a 'defensive attack' wasn't going to stop her questions in the least. 'Shit, Sylvia! What did your mother say, man? Did you tell her? What about David? What does he think about it? I guess he's okay with that. I don't understand it. You're good-looking; you can find a man.'

I knew there was no point in even trying to reply. For whatever reason she simply didn't want to accept what I'd said, and I had already had to deal with my mother's reaction a few years earlier, so I didn't feel like another in-depth probing of my personal choices. Thank God the taxi pulled up at that moment as I was sure that things would turn quite nasty had this continued. It was not that Nina had a problem with gay people – as I've already said, she was fine – but I believe when it came to people she knew personally it got more complicated. As she got into the taxi, I promised to call her later and we'd have a talk.

One of the most profound things about this particular incident was not my confession, it was the sight of her getting into the taxi alone. It had been less than an hour since she had played to a room packed to capacity with adoring fans, and yet here she was asking me to find her some male company. I was sad as I went home. Why couldn't God let her have the one thing she really wanted – true love? Yes, she had a loving family, and friends, but she wanted what we all want, to have the love and intimacy only a certain kind of relationship brings. I wished I had a magic wand and could make the perfect person appear for her. I knew a lot of her anger stemmed from this loneliness. It wasn't so much a physical thing as a need to be loved as a woman, not just as Nina Simone International Star. However, I was a realist and no matter what I wished for, she would have to continue her quest without my assistance.

Another part of her problem with relationships was fear. I've said before how she could intimidate people, and nowhere was this more visible than in her private life. Being larger than life has its downside, and her reputation did not help in her search for love. Having long ago erected a barrier to keep out heartache, it also kept people at a distance, and she couldn't have it both ways. If you want to shut people out to avoid pain, you can't expect them to come rushing into your life. Not everyone wanted to fight for love.

Years later I would understand what a dilemma that could be as I had been in a very volatile long-term relationship, and when it ended I too erected a barrier to avoid a repeat performance. I quickly discovered that by doing this no one could get through, and it meant I'd either have to trust again or accept being alone. The fact that I had dealt with this allowed me to see what she was going through. Years of disappointment had eroded her trust in human beings, and nothing anyone said would change her opinion of love.

There have been so many celebrities over the years who have alluded to the dilemma that being famous creates. You can stand on a stage in front of thousands, and yet if you aren't willing to trust and allow people to touch you, you end up alone or lonely. I had prayed that one day Nina might banish her demons and allow people to get close enough to show their love, without wondering what the hell they wanted from her. Sadly, it just wasn't to be, and though she had the love of her daughter, family and a very few close friends, she never found that heart-stopping love she sought.

19 'Break Down And Let It All Out'

Nina was staying in the UK for at least a week following the taping, and she became increasingly demanding during this time. She was starting to wear me out, both physically and mentally. A showdown between us was looming, one that would separate us for several years. I had spent most of the week working, rushing home, running back to her hotel and hanging out 'til the wee small hours of the night, and it was affecting me badly. On this particular evening, we had arranged to have dinner and once again I dashed home, bathed and dressed, and flew back out the door. I arrived only to be kept waiting for over an hour while she decided what to wear. 'Look, Nina, we're only going for dinner. You don't have to get that dressed up.' A typical Nina reply came from the bedroom: 'Hell, you don't think I'm going out looking anyhow. I have to think of my fans, and I might see someone cute, so you just wait 'til I'm done!'

I was tired, hungry and fed up, and sitting in the living room I decided I'd had enough of all this nonsense and would tell her at dinner that I was taking a break. Dinner was nothing special and I was desperate to leave as it was fast approaching 11pm. I had to get home, sleep and get up again by 6am. Several times I said I had to go, but as usual as soon as I announced my intentions she would change the subject. Finally at just past midnight I said my goodbyes and left. I was completely worn out and the sight of my bed was heavenly. But all too soon my well-earned rest was shattered by the ringing of the telephone.

At first I thought I must be dreaming but, no, I could definitely hear a ringing sound in my ears. I opened one eye and saw that the clock read 3:15am. Instinctively I was gripped with fear when I grabbed the telephone. With relief and indignation, I discovered Nina was on the other end. She was screaming that I had to get some of her fans to come to the hotel right now. The barked orders were so insane they were almost laughable, but instead of chuckling, I lost my rag. 'You must have seriously lost your mind. How dare you call me up in the middle of the night demanding I send people over? Do you really believe that your fans have nothing else to do but run over in the middle of the night to hang out with you? I can't believe you've got the nerve to call me when you knew I was tired.'

The battle had begun. She wasn't about to let this go, but neither was I. With round one over, Nina began round two: 'Hell, what's wrong with you? You can get *someone* over here; surely with all my fans one of them can come. I'm sick of being alone, you hear me? I've had enough. Other people have someone, why haven't I?' I was getting angrier by the minute. 'Nina, you know what, I really don't give a damn about other people right now. I'm tired and you're being ridiculous. Why would anyone get out of bed to come over to your hotel?'

By now Nina was screaming. 'Do you know who the hell you're talking to? How dare you yell at me like that. You need to come over here now. I mean it. I'm not messing with you. Damn it, I don't want to stay here on my own, you know I hate being alone. Why can't you come over, you don't have a man or a woman or whatever the hell you do!' At that moment the years of friendship, the joy at seeing her perform, wanting to see her happy – everything – just flew out the window and I let go with a torrent of anger that later made me wince. 'You know what, Nina, I've had enough. All the years I've known you, whenever you've called me I've been there. I've *never* asked you for a single solitary thing. I've run after you and cared about you since I was a child – well, no more. You keep telling me how people don't respect *you*, but why the hell should they? You don't respect them, and you definitely don't respect me. You know I have to work, you know I've run around with you all week with no complaint, and yet you still aren't satisfied. No, you have to push the boundaries. Well, you've pushed them too far. It's nearly 4 o'clock in the morning, I'm in a nice warm bed and if you think for one damn minute I'm getting out of it to rush out into the freezing cold to keep you company, you're wrong.'

Hearing this uncharacteristic outburst from me was too much. She slammed the phone down with such force I wondered if she'd broken it. I was beyond fury, literally shaking with rage. Although I accepted the fact she was lonely, she had pushed me beyond the bounds of reason and I had lost it. I eventually went back to sleep and the following day at work relayed the previous night's drama to Michael, and told him how upset and hurt I was at what had happened. He tried to calm me down and said that, knowing Nina, she'd probably forget all about it and I should too.

He was wrong, and she left a few days later without contacting me. The bond of friendship that had begun in 1964 ended without another word. Over 20 years of warmth and accord vanished in the few moments it took to make that early-morning call. It was as if all the years of our friendship meant nothing. I was devastated, and decided to call David and tell him what had happened. I relayed the whole story to him and he listened quietly as I let out all my anger and pain. 'Look, Sylvia, I don't know what to tell you. You know Nina can be difficult, but she doesn't mean to hurt you deliberately; she just doesn't always think how it affects others.' I knew he was right, and I was by now feeling guilty. Had I been unreasonable? Maybe I should have just tried to calm her down. But I hadn't and I couldn't turn the clock back. I couldn't imagine never seeing her again, and I prayed that somehow, with time, we might just repair the damage. For now all I could do was accept what I'd done and move on.

With hindsight I'm not overjoyed at how I behaved. While I may have felt justified at the time, it was not a very loving thing to do, and it became a learning experience through which I found new ways of dealing with situations through love instead of anger. Without knowing it, Nina had again had a major influence on my personal development and for that I'm grateful. Although it was several years before we spoke again, when we finally did it was as if nothing had happened. When I saw her again she never mentioned this episode, and neither did I, it was as if we'd never been apart and there had been no problem between us.

For now, though, I had to deal with the present, and the fact that this woman who had been such a major influence on my life was gone. I think I always knew deep down that we'd see each other again. There are some relationships that are bound by a deep and powerful force, and this was one of them. I carried on with life but made sure that I kept up with Nina's comings and goings, even if from a distance. She continued touring Europe and the States, and it was with a heavy heart that I went to see her perform once again at Ronnie Scott's. We had not spoken for a little over six months and, for the first time since we'd met, I really prayed she'd call me. However, I knew she was stubborn and the chances were pretty slim. I'd seen the ads for the show and decided even if we weren't on speaking terms, I still loved to see her perform. Sitting in my seat towards the back, watching her give a remarkable performance was one of the saddest moments of my life. To see her on stage and know I could no longer simply go to her afterwards and hang out hurt me deeply. David suggested that I should do just that, believing that Nina would probably have either forgotten all about our previous exchange, or would forgive me. I wasn't willing to chance her lingering wrath. At least if I stayed away, I'd never know.

I knew one of *Blues & Soul*'s reporters was there and he said he was surprised to see me sitting so far back, and asked if I was going backstage to see her. I explained that I was tired and left it at that. I read his review of the show a few weeks later, and it was hard to see someone else filling my shoes, but to his credit Philip Watson did an excellent job. I often wonder what would have happened if I had gone backstage. Maybe our rift would have been healed swiftly, but I had not yet processed my feelings towards her.

I went home and reflected on the years that had passed. Yes, she could drive you crazy with her demands, but she could also have you clutching your sides with laughter. There were so many sides to Nina. She was young, gifted and black, defiant and very militant, a loving compassionate and sensitive woman, and sometimes bitter about her often volatile love life. The woman I knew was all of these things and more. I had to accept the choice I had made, and move on. Living with regrets would do me no good and if I was meant to see her again, and regain our friendship, I would.

20 'Either Way I Lose'

Having finished her Ronnie Scott's engagements, Nina left the UK at the end of December 1984 and went to Holland. David called me to say he was coming over to England for a visit and I looked forward to seeing him. It was 1985 and I was feeling fairly optimistic. During David's visit he received a call from Bob Kilbourn of *Blues & Soul* magazine saying that Nina was trying to find him. Boy, did that one hurt. I was living in England, but Nina was trying to find David not me. I tried to remain upbeat when David announced he was going to meet her, but he knew how sad I was over the whole affair. 'Don't worry, child. I'm sure she'll have forgotten all about it, and I'll talk to her and see what she says.' I asked him to leave it alone as I felt sure she didn't want my name being brought up. If she had forgiven me or forgotten our dispute she would have spoken to me when she had called, but alas she hadn't.

David went to see her and arrived at a house in northwest London. Nina was staying with a couple who had given her a room in what was a rather small apartment. They seemed genuinely concerned about her, and asked him what they could do to help as she was going through a hard time. Nina and David began talking and David told her he'd thought about her during a recent trip to Egypt. She looked amazed. 'Oh, I can't believe it, man. I was there too.' It turned out they were both there at the same time, which in itself was rather eerie. She asked where he'd been staying and David replied that he had been staying in some small hotel in Cairo. 'I was staying at the Hilton, you know,' she told him. David was startled by this. 'Oh, that's so strange, I was literally walking distance from you. Talk about coincidences!' Nina smiled.

She was sitting there wrapped up in a huge fur coat and he wasn't sure, but he had a feeling she was wearing nothing underneath it (a scene later repeated in public). Suddenly she sprang up. 'Look, man, look at my feet.' Without thought he stared down and was confronted by ten perfectly painted silver toenails. 'See, they're painted silver.' He was beginning to feel a little confused but decided to humour her. 'Oh yes, so they are.' With that she declared, 'Just like Nefertiti did.

You know, she was a queen in Egypt?' He was desperately trying to suppress a giggle when she again shouted, 'You know, I was Nefertiti. I was a great queen.' Of course, the last thing to say to a gay man is that you are a great queen! David could no longer hold back the laughter and rushed to the bathroom. Having composed himself, he returned. 'Sorry Nina, I just had to go.'

'Listen, man,' she said, 'I'm not joking, I *was* Nefertiti.' David had spent several years studying Egyptian history, including the period in which the Pharaoh Ahkenaten had ruled with his wife Nefertiti, and he was hard pressed to believe that the woman sitting in front of him was a reincarnation of the Pharaoh's wife. Sensing her mood, he simply looked at her and replied, 'Oh, okay' as if it were no big deal. He went on to explain how he'd been to visit the site of the ancient city built by Ahkenaten, where he had lived with Nefertiti. They continued talking about Egypt for a while, and he was pleased to see Nina smile more than once during their talk. Suddenly, she stood up. 'Oh, *daaarling*, I've got to put some clothes on; I've got nothing on underneath this coat, you know.' To say he was embarrassed would be a major understatement, but rather than let her know, he simply acknowledged her remark and sat still while she went and got dressed. A while later she re-emerged fully clothed and smiling.

They talked for a while longer and David informed her that he had to go. 'Well, man, you better stay in touch. I'm working on some things here and I don't know where I'm going to next. So *you* better keep in touch, man, you hear me?' Yes, he had heard. Just before leaving he decided to bring my name into the conversation and told her how I sent her my love and best wishes. 'Oh well, that's all right but you know I'm still mad with her. She disrespected me, you know, and I won't take that shit from anyone, man.' Oh well, he had brought up what he knew was a sensitive subject so it was only fair to expect a reaction. If he had thought she had either forgotten or forgiven me, he was wrong. He said farewell and left, promising to keep in touch.

I was waiting impatiently for his return as I wanted to know how she was doing and if she was okay. He relayed most of the conversation and I had to laugh at the thought of Nina talking about being a great queen with him. 'I wish I could have seen that – it must have been hysterical.' 'Yes,' he replied, 'it was one of those unforgettable moments in life, I must admit.' When he had reported the rest of the conversation I realised Nina was obviously going through some major turmoil, and I was more than a little worried. 'David, are you sure there isn't anything we can do. I mean it sounds as if she's losing her sense of reality [sadly this was a direct result of her illness, of which we were still unaware]. Why would she sit dressed in just a fur coat?' David, who as I've said is much more down to earth than me, agreed that something was definitely wrong, but we really couldn't get involved. 'Look, Sylvia, we can't just stop everything we're doing and run around the world with Nina. She's a grown woman, and she does have other people around her; she's not entirely alone you know.'

I knew deep down he was right, but it didn't make me feel any less guilty. Yes, I felt enormous guilt at our fallout and felt sure if I could redeem our friendship if I could assist in her present crisis.

That illusion was firmly shattered when David relayed the end of their conversation – the bit where he had brought up my name. So, she was still unable or unwilling to forgive my outburst. Part of me was angry – after all, it was her fault we'd argued in the first place. Surely she could see I was merely trying to get some rest and her behaviour had been inappropriate. But she chose to believe I was being disrespectful. Given how David had voiced concern about her well-being I decided it was more important to ensure she was cared for than to continue rehashing old arguments.

Before we could install anyone to watch over Nina she had disappeared back to Holland. David left for the States and I was once again alone. I was worried about Nina, but felt powerless. Surely I could do something, but my own life was turbulent enough. In the light of my own problems I forgot all about Nina's. David would call from time to time, and if he had any news about Nina he would let me know. He found out that she had settled in Amsterdam, and although things had gone quiet on the recording front, he had been informed via a friend that she was still touring occasionally.

While living in Amsterdam she stayed with her long-time friend Gerrit De Bruin and his wife, and agreed to be their daughter's godmother. (The child is appropriately called Nina.) Regardless of her own anguish and inner turmoil, her capacity to love was intact. It may seem odd that she could love so greatly and yet push people away at the same time, but she was a complex woman, and she never stopped loving people and life. Her way of expressing those feelings sometimes gave the impression she was a hostile person, but those who really knew her saw a woman who had lost a lot of trust in people but was still willing to give love a try. She stayed in Amsterdam and slowly rebuilt her life. Enjoying the freedoms of a city that was so relaxed suited her. She was able to come and go as she pleased, and was able to fill each and every venue she played.

Inevitably, though, she became disenchanted with her life in Amsterdam, and again headed for the States. Despite all the troubles she had had with the IRS, record companies and so-called managers, she again believed that she could work everything out.

Once back in America, Nina hooked up with former Motown executive Eddie Singleton, who owned an independent record company called VPI. He somehow managed to cajole her back into the studio and the result was *Nina's Back!*. Recorded in a Los Angeles studio (Rock Steady in Hollywood), it brought together a team of talented musicians including George Bohannon and Arthur Adams, with the famous Waters Singers on background vocals.

It had originally been released under the title *It's Cold Out Here*, after a track co-written by Eddie Singleton and Arthur Adams especially for Nina. Another track written by Adams, 'You Must Have Another Lover', was also included, along with a song written by Nina's brother Sam, called 'Saratoga'. Two songs written by Nina and recorded on her *Fodder On My Wings* album, namely the title track and 'I Sing Just To Know That I'm Alive' also appeared.

The cover of the album was without doubt a reflection of Nina's wry sense of humour in that it showed her bare back, a flower in her hair and a towel strategically placed over her derriere! A reworked version of 'I Loves You, Porgy' also featured on the album, but due to distribution problems sales were relatively poor. Much like the hundreds of bootleg albums that were reissued over the years, *Nina's Back!* saw several different incarnations in numerous countries throughout the world.

Nina may have been back in the studio, but whatever problems had beset the distribution did not enhance her career. Despite this, she agreed to a further release on Singleton's VPI label. This time it would be a live album, *Live & Kickin'*, released some two years after *Nina's Back!*. It included live performances across Europe and the Caribbean, with material ranging from 'My Baby Just Cares For Me' to 'Do What You Gotta Do'. Also included were live versions of several songs that were rarely heard during her concerts, one of which was 'Pirate Jenny', and another the infamous 'Backlash Blues'. Nina had the benefit of musical accompaniment from Al Schackman on guitar, Leopoldo Fleming on percussion and Cornell McFadden on drums.

The album was not the only live release during this period. Two further live albums saw the light of day at the same time, one showcasing her recent performances at Ronnie Scott's: *Live At Ronnie Scott's*, released by Hendring-Wadham, and including performances with Nina and drummer Paul Robinson.

Paul recalled how during one of their many concerts he witnessed a musical feat from Nina that would render him near speechless: 'I can't quite remember exactly which show it was, but I do remember the performance. It was one that stood out from many of the others for its sheer artistry. We were playing a fairly mid-tempo blues number when I looked over at Nina and was blown away. She had a fairly strong left hand anyway, and as she was playing the bass line with her left hand, she was soloing with her right hand. The solo was a quarter of a second to the right of the beat, and it was just fantastic! To be able to play with that sort of time with the left hand was incredible. I mean we were both closing in on one another, looking straight at each other. I was just keeping straight time and she was playing the solo to the right and the bass line to the left, it was just awesome. To me it was the best blues solo piano I'd ever seen or worked with. Nina was just so in tune, it was as if she had split her body totally in two... One half was keeping time and the other half soloing off the beat, which is an incredibly difficult thing to do, but she did it as if it were the most natural thing in the world.'

Given Paul's own musical ability, the praise he lavished on Nina showed just how much of an impact she had on music and fellow musicians. Fortunately, the album was also captured on video and was released in 2003 by Quantum Leap, which enabled everyone to see her artistry. It also included a rather hilarious interview with Nina that in some ways captured a part of her essence for posterity.

The third live album to be released was *Let It Be Me*. It was Nina's first on a major record label (Verve) since she had left CTI. It was a mixture of old and new and included 'Baltimore', 'Balm In Gilead', and 'If You Pray Right'. Whether it was by chance or planned, Nina was making sure that everyone knew she was still 'Live' and definitely still 'Kickin''.

21 'Wild Is The Wind'

David was to discover for himself just how 'alive' Nina was before too long. He had continued to live and work in the States and kept in fairly regular contact with her via the telephone. It was then with a certain degree of shock that he picked up the phone one day to hear her say, 'Hey, man, I'm in LA. I've bought a condo. What are you doing? I need to see you. I need some help, man. Can you find me an assistant?' David said he'd think about it and would see her later that week. It was 1986 and he hadn't set eyes on her for nearly a year, but as always when she requested a visit, he was happy to oblige.

David arrived at her new condo to find her in some chaos. Clothes were scattered all over the place, CDs and books littered the tables, and it all gave the air of a somewhat transient lifestyle. Following the usual hugs and kisses Nina turned to him: 'Well, *daaarling*, have you found me some help? You know I can't do everything myself, and I need someone to take care of things so I can work.' David had indeed given it some thought and had come up with what he thought was a great solution to Nina's problem.

Having by now lived in LA for several years, David had formed a close friendship with a fellow performer called Byron Motley. Byron was a talented singer and had been making a living doing background vocals for several well-known stars. David was sure he could handle Nina, as he had been in the business for a while and was aware of the many demands being a performer could entail. He decided to call Byron and run the idea by him – after all, he would have the opportunity to be around a musical genius and earn a few extra dollars at the same time. Byron agreed and David arranged for him to talk to Nina on the phone. They talked for a while and agreed to meet. Following their meeting she hired Byron as her new assistant. Sadly, it was not to be a match made in heaven. It was during this period, while she was working with Eddie Singleton on the *Nina's Back!* album, that David described her as being in a very strange place.

Byron was meant to be the solution to at least one problem, but Nina's demands would again push someone away. Byron recalled how he tried to be patient in the face of her moodiness, but that she quickly found his breaking point. At first things seemed to be going well. They had discovered a common bond: a really unusual sense of humour. During one of Nina's tirades, Byron had started laughing and no matter how angry Nina got he just kept laughing. Eventually she could take it no longer and collapsed on the bed roaring with laughter. He recalled that on more than one occasion this worked. He would point out how ridiculous she was being and, after a few more outbursts, she would agree and begin laughing herself. Byron made no secret of the fact he was gay, and Nina merely shrugged her shoulders and declared, 'I guess I should've known. Damn, I'm beginning to wonder if there are any straight men left in the world!' In fact his sexuality was not an issue, but her unreasonable demands would be.

Nina had stopped driving a few years earlier and one of Byron's jobs was to drive her around in his car whenever she wanted to go out shopping or to the bank. Usually it was no big deal, and despite the fact that she would insist on him announcing her arrival before she would enter the bank, he was happy to accommodate her somewhat unusual conditions. On one fateful day, however, he finally snapped.

It was pouring with rain – unusual for southern California – and she was insisting that he get out of the car and announce her arrival at the local bank. Feeling somewhat annoyed he ran to the bank, trying his best not to get soaking wet. He entered the bank and to a small number of customers announced that 'Dr Nina Simone is coming into the bank.' The guards were a little puzzled and wondered if Byron may be a little crazy, and began to approach him, when the doors opened and in swept Nina. She was wrapped in her full-length fur coat, and demanded to see the manager. Having finalised her business she returned to the car and told Byron to get out in the rain to open the door for her.

Now, she was happy for Byron to handle her business, drive her around and do her bidding, but whenever she went to the bank she would hide whatever money she had withdrawn in a money belt fastened round her waist. She expected Byron to stand in the pouring rain holding an umbrella over her head while she did so. As the raindrops smacked his skin a heated exchange began. He had had enough. He was furious, and screamed that he wasn't standing in the rain for anyone. The security guards were heading towards them at the sound of their raised voices. As they reached the car they could hear the pair locked in battle. 'Listen, Nina, I'm not standing here like some house slave getting soaked because you're afraid I'll steal your money. I don't want your damn money, okay?'

Nina was beyond reason and began hurling abuse at Byron as if he were a child. 'How dare you! I'm Dr Nina Simone and you better show me some respect, man. You want to take my money, that's what it is. Don't think I'm crazy. I know you want my money.' In fact, he hadn't been paid since he started and had made no complaints at all. 'You know what, Nina, I've had it with you. I don't want your money and I don't want you in my car, so find your own way home, I'm leaving!' With that, he yelled at the security guards, 'Get Dr Simone a taxi now, okay!'

Despite his anger he still worried about her, and watched as she got into the taxi before he drove off. As a result of this scene, David received a call the following day after Byron had already relayed the events to him. Nina screamed down the phone, 'Where is he? Where is he, man? He didn't show up for work today.' Attempting to act surprised and sensing he was walking a rather thin line, David simply said he had no idea where Byron was. She would not be placated and continued screaming, 'Well, you better find him, man. I'm here alone, nobody's here. I'm on my own. Can you come over?' Trying to be polite David explained how he was really busy at that moment but would try to see her later. It seemed to calm things down and he promised to call her in a while to see that she was all right. Having learned from experience, he decided not to relay Byron's position – that it would have to be a very cold day in hell before he would work for her again – yet David felt torn. On the one hand, he knew Nina could be difficult, but she needed help. However, he had known Byron for many years and as a result was convinced that it must have been very bad to make him quit without even seeking back-pay.

The following day, Nina rang several times and he had no choice but to hear her out. 'Listen, man, I'm going to work on my autobiography and I want you to come to Morocco.' David was sure he was hearing things and thought the whole thing completely over the top. 'Well, Nina, I can't just take off – I have to work.' She was obviously determined and continued shouting at him. 'I'm leaving in a few days. I can get you a ticket. I've got money, man, I'll pay you.' By now he was feeling upset as he realised that part of her request was for his company and she seemed to think she had to pay him in order to persuade him to come. Waiting a few moments to compose himself, he told her, 'Look, Nina, I'd really love to come with you but I really can't take time off. It's nothing to do with money. I've made commitments and I have to keep them.' David recalled how she was not happy, but the thought of running off with her on an adventure that could be fraught with drama, plus the fact that he had work to do, made it impossible. A few days later she left, and David was given the same silent treatment that I'd had. It seemed that we were both out of favour and, after our previously strong friendship with her, that was hard to accept.

A few years later, we both saw evidence of Nina's exclusion policy. As a music journalist, David had been sent an advance copy of her autobiography, *I Put A Spell On You*, and was bitterly hurt to find that neither of us had been mentioned. Not one line. It was as if we didn't exist, and I remember asking how he felt. 'Well, Sylvia, what can I say? It could be the fact I refused to go to Morocco to work on the book, I just don't know. I mean if you read it she hardly mentions anyone really. Apart from a few music people and civil rights people, there's not a whole lot about anyone so don't get too upset, I'm sure it wasn't intentional.' But I was upset. Surely more than 20 years of friendship was worth a sentence? No, I had proof that to Nina it simply wasn't.

When we subsequently made up our differences I never asked her why we were sidelined, as I thought that if she really wanted me to know she would have told me, and I came to realise it was probably not meant as a personal slight. David came to the conclusion that our absence from the book was simply a case of her writing what was real for her at the time, and very little else. The fact that her brother Sam worked with her for a number of years yet barely received a mention either seemed to bear this out.

Following the 'Moroccan affair', Nina returned to LA briefly and was due to appear at a local club there, the Vine Street Bar & Grill. Byron had rung David to see if he wanted to go and see her perform. David was not surprised that she had not called him and was in two minds whether to go or not, but decided that, no matter what, Nina was still one of the greatest performers he knew. They arranged to meet outside the club, and for once he got there early. Standing by the front door, he saw Nina arrive in a taxi with a young man, and decided to speak to her. As he approached her she pushed the guy in front of him declaring loudly, 'There's some strange people out here you know', and walked in.

David was totally dumbstruck, he couldn't believe she would say such a thing after all the years they had shared. He turned to Byron, who had witnessed the incident: 'Oh, well I guess I'm still out of favour.' He figured it was either his refusal to help with the book or the fact he was standing with Byron – also *persona non grata* – that had led to the comment. Byron was never one to shrink in the face of adversity, though, and made sure that, when Nina came on stage, he made eye contact with her. David was not feeling quite so brave and tried his best to hide from her glare. As the show ended Byron asked David if he was going to see her backstage. Given the hostility prior to the show, David figured there was no point and he really didn't want to totally ruin the pleasure her performance had given.

The show had been recorded and was released as one of the three live albums she made during this period. She had again delivered one of her most spine-tingling performances and David didn't want to spoil that magic. He also knew that being with Byron would only make matters worse. Still, Byron was adamant that he was going backstage and, the following day, he relayed to David the events that transpired.

'I managed to push myself into the room,' began his blow-by-blow account, 'which wasn't easy as the guy who was with her tried to stop me, but I wasn't having any of that shit. So, Nina's sitting looking regal as usual, and looks straight at me. "Have you come for your pay? Is that what you want: money? Well, man, I'm not giving you a dime, you walked out on me. How dare you come in here like you own me?"'

Byron had suppressed his laughter. Trying to be as polite as he could he simply turned to her and said, 'Nina, I just came by to say the show was absolutely brilliant, and how amazing you are, that's all.' She was having none of it. 'You must think I'm stupid, man. I know why you came: you want *money, man.*' Byron realised there would be no reasoning with her and turned to the door. 'Yes, man, you better leave. You don't want me to get real mad with you, you hear me?' Byron quickly closed the door on a torrent of abuse.

When David related the story to me a few weeks later I remember my response as if it were yesterday: 'Well, at this rate we'll be able to start a "Former Friends of Nina Simone" club. First me, then you, now Byron. I wonder who's going to be next?' David had to laugh and said that, no matter what, we had some really great memories and had shared a lot of good times over the years. It was true, despite the many turbulent times, there were as many, if not more, extremely special occasions. Nina was no angel, but neither was she a devil. I also had to admit that my behaviour over the years left a lot to be desired, but I was trying my best to learn from previous mistakes.

Almost three years passed before either of us saw her again. During this time the press had again highlighted her 'eccentricities' and one particular article caught my eye. Nina had apparently turned up for an interview in a rather high-class restaurant wearing the infamous fur coat and, yes, nothing underneath it. The journalist had come to this conclusion when Nina gave him a flash of bare flesh before flouncing out of the place. Had David not previously told me a similar story I would never have believed it possible. What I couldn't understand was why she did it. Again, all I can do is surmise that it was one of those days when she had forgotten to take her medication. It annoyed me that the press continually highlighted her somewhat unusual behaviour rather than her unique and God-given talent. However, I knew they had to sell papers and it seemed that Nina displayed her eccentricities for all to see.

I had briefly gone to live in Jamaica and David had returned to the UK for a holiday. With some detective work, Nina found a telephone number and left a message for David to call her back. Happy to be back in the fold, he duly returned her call only to be greeted with an all too familiar outburst: 'I've got no money, there's no one here and I'm lonely. I don't know what to do, man. I'm having a very hard time, David. I need your help to get me out of here.' David was shocked and alarmed. The call upset him deeply as he hated the thought of her anguish. They traded calls for several more days and he finally came up with what he thought would be a solution to her problems. He called her to relay this news only to be told that she had checked out of her hotel, leaving neither a forwarding address nor number. She had called and asked for help but, just when a solution had been found, she had disappeared.

'One of the things I had learned being around Nina,' said David, recalling his dilemma, 'was that when she called you were supposed to drop everything and run to her side, and at times that was just not possible.' Having watched me struggle with my own feelings over this, he now understood what it felt like. Just when you figured out how to help, she was gone. It was hard to treat Nina as just another friend. With most friendships there are boundaries that you try not to cross out of respect for the friendship. With Nina she was either unaware of those boundaries or chose to ignore them, often at the risk of her relationships.

Despite being an international artist, she was still a human being. Knowing this and trying to deal with her demands was akin to walking a tightrope. Part of you wanted to help, but the other part wanted to run. It was not easy, but it was the price to pay for being around sheer genius. Perhaps the idea that real genius generates a form of madness is true, and that madness takes many forms. Whether it was the constant need for attention or just a sense that being 'special' allowed you to cross the line, neither of us really knew. However, Nina wanted instant relief from whatever pain she was feeling, and it wasn't always possible to find a cure that quickly.

David called me a few days after this episode and said he now understood how I felt. When he had been unable to rush to her side, Nina had simply vanished without a word. There's no doubt, though, that it left a sense of guilt and sadness, and a feeling of impotence that no matter how much you cared, it just wasn't enough. Just like the wind, she had breezed in, shared her burdens and, before you could help, blown straight out again; this wind was certainly 'wild'.

22 'Feeling Good'

Time continued to fly by, but whenever Nina re-emerged it seemed as if the clock had stood still. Such was the case in 1992. While she was out of contact with us Nina had been living and working in Amsterdam and then moved on to the South of France. Her old friend Gerrit De Bruin recalls this time saying, 'Nina had left Paris having hit a very low ebb and had contacted Raymond Gonzalez, who agreed to help her. She had promised to behave as "normally" as possible and he arranged for a series of concerts in Holland. She was booked for eight concerts in total and she kept her part of the bargain, behaving in an almost graceful manner throughout her stay. It was decided that something had to be done on a more permanent basis to help Nina with her everyday life. Finally, it was agreed that myself, Al Schackman and Raymond Gonzalez would become Nina's support team. We were renamed the "A-Team" and set about stabilising her life.

'Between us we saw to it that she kept to her medical regime, and she finally decided the time was right for her to move from the small town of Nijmegen to Amsterdam, where she bought an apartment in the house of the Born family at the Jan van Goyenkade. Nina seemed to be much happier living there and the members of the A-Team were joined by another friend, Bobby Hamilton, who lived with Nina in her new home. Sadly, without telling her A-Team, Nina decided to buy a house in Bouc Bel Air in the South of France. This was the beginning of yet another damaging phase for her. The house was away from the life of the town, and Nina soon began slipping back into her old ways, forgetting her medication and lapsing back into a fantasy world. Even though we all tried hard to help, Nina was very stubborn, refused more and more to work, and became very aggressive towards Raymond and pushed him away. Following several run-ins with the law, she was again in a position where she had to rethink things. By this time the members of her A-Team were increasingly unable to take control of the situation and Nina, not wanting to live alone, enlisted the help of Clifton Henderson, who would go on to become her manager as well as looking after her everyday affairs.'

Although it had been almost two years since David or I had heard anything either from or about Nina, she returned to LA and David was fortunate enough to catch up with her. I had been living in LA for almost a year and was getting ready to return to England. I had been keeping busy, having designed and made a series of pillows in the shape of Africa. I had begun selling them at a festival held in LA known as the African Marketplace. When news arrived that Nina was in town and appearing at the Hollywood Bowl, I was sick that it was the one weekend I was working and couldn't miss. Oh well, I knew David would relay the event as best he could. Not only was he going to the concert, but he had made arrangements via *Blues & Soul* to conduct an interview with her during the week.

Darn it, I would miss the show and, as I was leaving that week, would probably miss the interview. I decided (even though we were still not on speaking terms) to give David a set of pillows for Nina and told him to wish her much love and happiness on my behalf. I was no longer tormented by what her reaction might be, and figured as long as I let her know I still cared then no matter how she responded, I'd done my best.

David had arranged to interview her and was looking forward to catching up with her after such a long time. Unfortunately, traffic in LA can derail even the best-laid plans, and realising he was going to be late, he called her. She was not exactly amused but told him to get a move on as she didn't like being kept waiting. Following several more calls he decided that the only way to apologise for his tardiness was to buy her some of her favourite flowers. Finally arriving at his destination he hid the flowers behind his back and as her then-assistant opened the door, he was greeted by a roar: 'David, you're late.' Sensing this was not a great start for their interview he suddenly withdrew the flowers from behind his back and handed them to her. 'Nina, I'm really sorry.' As if on cue that magical grin appeared and he was summoned for the customary hug. All was right with the world, the ice had been broken and it was like stepping back in time.

He had been fortunate enough to see her at the Hollywood Bowl and asked how after all these years she could still perform as if she were a young woman. 'Ha! Well, honey, I am a High Priestess. You know we have certain magical powers that keep us eternally young.' David began to smile. Nina was on great form and the interview was one of the best he'd ever done with her. He asked her how she felt about the fact she drove critics and the media crazy because they couldn't pigeonhole her. 'That's something I've had to deal with all my life. They want me to be a jazz singer or a blues singer; they can't just get that I don't have a category, I just sing what I feel and if it crosses the line then that's all right with me. I never want to be stuck in one place musically – it's not who I am. You know my roots, man: I began believing I'd be performing classical music and when they rejected me [a reference to the Curtis Institute] I had to change direction, and I realised there were no boundaries.'

The tour saw her performing across the United States and David wondered how the audiences had been reacting after such a long absence. 'You know, I was really surprised how much they remember. Even the young ones seem to know my songs, man, and that's something else. Last night really inspired me, knowing that I've not been forgotten and being in Hollywood you know how quickly people forget.' David had to ask how she felt about her British audiences as he knew she had a certain affinity with them. 'I've always loved England, man. You should know – you were there back when no one knew who the hell I was. You and Sylvia, you knew everything. But I dig England. The audiences always seem so cool and so enthusiastic no matter how I feel, they seem to just go with me. You know I just did a television special over there with Paul McCartney. That was a blast. There was a 102-piece orchestra and although I've sung with orchestras before, this was the biggest. That was definitely one of the happiest times I've had musically.'

The interview went on to discuss her 30-year career and the answers were fascinating. 'I can't seem to realise how much I've done sometimes. To be honest, I'm very happy about my career but sometimes it's not *real* to me. I mean…God gave me a talent and although there have been times I've had a love/hate relationship with music, I find that I still get excited about music when I'm on stage. In fact even though I'm interested in everyday living and doing everyday things like swimming and playing tennis, as I grow older I find myself wanting to be on stage more and more.

'You know for years it was all about work, and I never had time to enjoy life. Always being on the road gets old after a while. But now I've found a way to deal with it. I refuse to work every night now, but when I do I enjoy it even more. Also I just bought a home in France in Aix-en-Provence just near the mountains. So now I've nearly got three homes. I bought some land in Ghana and I'm building a beach home there and of course I still have a condo in Hollywood. It's strange how life turns out. From having nowhere to call home, I've now got a choice and that's good because I hate feeling tied down. I need to be able to move around so I don't get bored.'

The balance of the interview discussed how she had lived in numerous countries and had published her autobiography. She was, she conceded, generally happy with life. She went on to tell David how a French company had filmed a documentary based on her book and how there had been talk of a film being made with Whoopi Goldberg in the lead role. Sadly, that didn't come to fruition back then, but as for the future, who knows? As Nina always said, anything is possible.

The interview was drawing to a close and David wanted to ask just a few more questions having waited quite a while for such an in-depth conversation. 'So, Nina, what do you believe it is that keeps you going?' She paused for a moment to reflect on the question before replying, 'Let me see. Well I believe in Africa and I'm dedicated to my people around the world, wherever they are – whether they're Maori, Aborigine, or here in the States. I believe in music, in love and relationships...in the loyalty of good people you keep around you...although I don't know about romantic love any more! I used to want to get married again but' – the wicked smile began to appear at this point – 'these days, people don't know what to do in bed!'

Again, he had been witness to a truly outrageous comment regarding her views on men. Knowing Nina the way he did, he had no choice but to fall about laughing at this statement. Off the record he recalled what followed. 'Nina, you are so bad! How could you say something like that?' Sensing it was playtime, she responded, 'Ha! Well, man, if they knew what the hell they were doing, I'd have snagged at least one by now, but you know how *hard* it is, or should be?' Nina loved to play with David on this subject as she knew that despite his worldly knowledge, she could still cause a blush or two.

David concluded the interview with a few more questions and the last one really summed up the artistry of Dr Nina Simone. 'Why do you think that people are still enjoying such songs as "I Loves You, Porgy" and "My Baby Just Cares" after nearly 30 years?' Smiling broadly she gave her reply: 'Well, I guess my music is timeless...'

The interview over, they sat and talked for a while. 'So, how is your sister, then?' she enquired. Knowing how delicate a subject this might be, he had refrained from bringing it up but was more than a little relieved and happy to know I was no longer a taboo subject. 'Oh, she's doing great. She's here at the moment and sends all her love and best wishes.' She smiled and replied, 'That's good, man. I'm glad she's doing well, you tell her from me okay?' He promised to relay the message, knowing that it was, in fact, her way of saying everything was cool between us and knowing just how pleased I'd be to receive it. He left a smiling Nina, with the promise to return for a more informal chat in a few days' time.

True to his word he relayed the conversation to me on the phone later that day. I felt as if a huge weight had finally been lifted. I had been tortured by her absence for long enough and knew in my heart that one day we would meet again. I was just relieved to know that day had come, even though it would be a few more years before I actually saw her in person.

A few days later David returned and gave her a demo tape he'd been working on, which included a version of 'Strange Mood', a song he thought rather appropriate. She took the tape and promised to listen to it later. He also handed her the set of African pillows I had made especially for her. She was excited at seeing them. 'So, where is she then, and what the hell is she doing, man?' He explained that I had been designing and making sets of African-themed pillows, and selling them at the African Marketplace. 'Ha! She has so many talents, I never know what she's going to do next. You tell her I love them. You know I love Africa and they even have genuine African fabric. She's gifted you know…but then she would be, she's an old soul you know.' David laughed. 'Yes, you're right, she's always doing something creative. I never know what she's going to do next, but I know she really wanted to see you before she leaves and is mad that she's having to work.' 'You tell her I understand, man. I know sometimes work gets in the way of what you want. Shit, I should know. Look how many years it's been and only now can I take a break. But you better tell her what I said, because you know it's been a while since we've spoken but she's still special to me, so don't you forget, you know what happens when I get upset, man.' If she hadn't been smiling it might have been a little threatening, but David knew what she was saying and how important it was to tell me what she'd said.

During their conversation the subject of recording had come up and Nina was happy to report that she was about to sign with Elektra. This was a big event as, aside from the live album she had done with Verve in 1987, she hadn't been signed to a major US label since 1978. One of Elektra's executives, Michael Alago, had seen Nina in concert at Carnegie Hall in New York, and begun negotiations with her. She was excited about doing a new album and told David, 'I just can't wait to start recording again. If we could start tomorrow that would be fine with me. We've already been discussing the songs, and so far I plan to do Prince's "Sign O' The Times", "Papa Can You Hear Me?"

[from the Barbra Streisand film *Yentl*], "I Know It Was The Blood" [a traditional spiritual] and Harold Melvin And The Bluenotes' "Wake Up Everybody". I'm going to be meeting with the producers in October, and hopefully, we can start recording by the end of the year.'

One of the things that stuck in his mind about this particular visit was just how relaxed she seemed. It was as if the years of upheaval had vanished, and all the pain and sadness had melted. She looked incredible and genuinely happy, and he had to tell her how good it was seeing her this way. 'You know, Nina, it's just great to see you looking so radiant.' This was not just a case of flattery – he meant every word and she knew it.

The sound of her laughter echoed around the room as she replied, 'You know, honey, I've always wanted to be happy and most of the time it's been that way. I'm not always angry and sad, man. It's just a lot of times you would catch me when things weren't going right and you know I wasn't about to smile if shit was wrong. But you're right, I feel good: I'm not killing myself working, people seem to appreciate what I do and show me respect, and that's important, man. You must have respect. I've lived in some amazing places and seen things most people could never imagine, some of it good and some bad enough to make you scream with pain, but I've got God and a beautiful daughter and finally people who I can depend on and that's important. You know, after years of being mistreated, ripped off and taken for granted, I finally feel that I can relax. God knows how long it might last but today I feel content and blessed. I'm a survivor and even though there's been times I didn't think I'd make it, I'm still here and it's because I believe and have faith. You know, without faith you may as well forget it. You have to believe in God and have faith, man.' How strange that almost 20 years after she and David had first met, and after all she had been through, Nina would once again reinforce her belief in God.

They said farewell and he left, smiling the whole way home. Having seen her go through the tough times, he was happy to know she had finally overcome the challenges to emerge stronger, more content and full of life. Having relayed the conversation to me, I too was ecstatic, knowing she loved the pillows and, more importantly, still held me in a special place in her life. The world seemed much brighter that day, and I was even more delighted when I received a card several weeks later thanking me for the gift and sending much love.

David also received praise from Nina but in a slightly different form. Returning home one day he picked up the phone to check his messages when to his sheer and utter delight there was a message from her. 'David, I just listened to your tape. You can sing, man – it's excellent, really good! I love the songs and you know you sound very bluesy!' David wasn't quite sure if he was dreaming. Could it really be the one and only Dr Nina Simone telling him he could sing? He kept that message and even to this day a huge smile spreads across his face when he talks about it. To earn praise from a performer of her calibre was mind-blowing, especially as it was only a rough demo tape.

Nina's message continued to inspire him, but sadly she would never get to hear his latest CD, *Reinvention*, as it wasn't completed until after her death. Grateful for her encouragement he dedicated the CD to her memory.

We had both come full circle with Nina. Despite having had to deal with several years' absence, normal service had been resumed. Finally we knew she had come through the hard times, survived the bad times and was at last enjoying a period of peace. She had given so much to her public, sacrificed her own happiness at times and often had to choose between her family and her career, but for now was enjoying life to the full.

Nina did in fact start recording at the beginning of 1993, working with producer André Fischer. The album, *A Single Woman*, featured both Al Schackman and Paul Robinson. Paul had been flown out to LA to work with Nina on the album, but ended up only being used on one track. Nevertheless, he recalled how amazed he was at her versatility. 'One of the things I discovered over the years with Nina was just how contemporary she was. She was never stuck in just one groove or period. *A Single Woman* highlighted this especially the choice of material. Even though I spent most of the time sitting in the hotel room instead of the studio, on the days I worked it was incredible to watch Nina in action. I think that's why I enjoyed being on stage with her so much. She never approached a song the same way, and I'd play my version of what I heard her playing, not what was on a record. In fact, a lot of her "older" material, I had never even heard the originals, and it wasn't until we did a tribute special that I became familiar with songs such as "Plain Gold Ring" and "Wild Is The Wind".'

Even though she had discussed with David which songs she wanted to record, as it turned out some of those original choices were never released. She did record 'Sign O' The Times', but it was not included in the final cut of the album. Released in 1993, *A Single Woman* won much critical acclaim even if the sales were not all that Elektra had hoped for. However, the praise was more than worthy as 'The Folks Who Live On The Hill' and Nina's own composition, 'Marry Me', were outstanding. The lack of commercial success left Elektra feeling less than enthusiastic, but the company arranged for a spot on *The Tonight Show* to promote the album. Sadly, some backstage drama at the taping of the show meant that Nina was squeezed in at the very end to do just one song and her 'attitude' left Elektra reluctant to continue promoting her.

Never one to linger in a musical rut, Nina nevertheless had criticisms about the shift in musical style relating to rap and hip-hop. During an interview in 1994, she revealed how this was one musical genre that 'just didn't quite do it for me'. In fact, asked what she thought about the new-style protest songs, she said that she felt a lot of the messages were getting lost in their delivery. Her feelings on gangsta rap were even more militant: 'I hate that shit, man. They're just falling into a trap, letting people believe that women are second class, and calling them bitches and stuff like that. It's not music, man – its just a whole lot of noise about nothing. I hate to talk about how we used music to get out a message, as if "we" had all the answers, but the kids today are getting messed up with all this stuff, and it's wrong. Hell, Martin and Malcolm would turn in their graves if they heard some of this crazy shit. How in the hell are people going to learn if they can't understand the messages. It makes me mad sometimes. Maybe I just have to accept it's a whole new groove, but that doesn't mean I have to like it!'

Nina was happy to acknowledge that there were some great new artists and said that she loved listening to Lauryn Hill, Erykah Badu and a whole range of contemporary artists. However, almost 40 years since she had first begun singing 'popular' music, she felt that delivering a message was far more important than simply being a performer. It was what she had spent a lifetime doing, and would do so until the very end of her career.

Not only did she deliver 'messages', but one of her compositions, '22nd Century', seemed almost prophetic. If you listen to the words of this song – which, incidentally, was written and recorded in 1971 (although subsequently lost) – it is beyond eerie. In it, Nina predicts such events as a 'plague' (AIDS?), a relaxed attitude towards people's sexuality, and the advent of a whole range of other more recent issues. Nina could see far into the future, it seems. Perhaps the same condition that created such an imbalance in her mind also gave her glimpses of the future. Many of the world's greatest visionaries were considered crazy when they were often just ahead of their time.

23 'Cherish'

Nina continued touring for the next few years and we kept in touch by phone. Her lighter mood had been replaced by a more edgy one, and she seemed tired. I wondered why she kept touring when surely she didn't have to? However, I was also aware of the major battles she had gone through, first with unscrupulous promoters, managers and record companies and then, of course, with the IRS. No doubt this had an impact on her financial stability. I also knew she toured because she enjoyed the interaction with her audiences. Her anger at the record industry was well known and well documented. One incident in particular was splashed across several newspapers. It related to a well-known executive whom she had threatened with a knife over alleged unpaid royalties.

Nina was never one to beg for what was rightfully hers, but would let everyone within earshot know that she had been 'ripped off' in her life. The vast number of Nina Simone bootleg albums in circulation is a living testament to that fact, and while they may have included some unusual and interesting material, the fact remains that she was never paid for them. That's one reason why I have declined to mention them. Indeed, I felt as angry as she did that record companies would release material without her consent or knowledge. On the few occasions I was within hearing distance of her outbursts I would simply agree with her, and let her know I was nearly as mad as she was about the situation.

Nina had never been given an award for her contribution to music – an issue that rankled with David and me. Her doctorates in music and humanities aside, she had gone virtually unrecognised within the industry. She was, of course, too controversial for the music industry's conservative tastes. David had long been associated with the Rhythm & Blues Foundation, an organisation that both honoured and assisted artists who had contributed to music in that sphere. In this capacity he decided it was high time that Nina receive the recognition she so richly deserved. A new millennium had begun and what could be more appropriate for the 21st century than to give thanks to a performer whose music was indeed timeless.

On hearing that she was due in the States for a tour, David contacted the Foundation with a view to it honouring her, but alas the timing was wrong. Undeterred, he put his grey matter to work again and decided to take another approach. He had also worked for many years with another organisation – the International Association of African American Music (IAAAM) – and he was sure he had enough influence to elicit a response. He contacted the woman who ran the organisation, Dyana Williams, and explained that Nina was due to perform in Philadelphia. Given her major contribution to both the civil rights movement and black music, he suggested it was time the IAAAM showed its appreciation. Dyana agreed, and although the Association had already finished producing the programme for the upcoming event, somehow it would make it work.

Several calls were made between the IAAAM and Nina's manager Clifton Henderson, and all was finally set up. Kenny Gamble, one of Philadelphia's top producers, would present her with the award. David recalled the event with much mirth. As he was due to attend the IAAAM event anyway, he had been trying to arrange to meet Nina beforehand. The only problem was that no one seemed to know where she was flying in from or where she was staying, which created a small drama on its own. Eventually she arrived at the venue, and David made his way to the green room in search of her and Clifton. Once inside he found the room packed, and was at an instant disadvantage as he had never met Clifton before. Finally, he announced he was David Nathan. Suddenly, from among this crowd of people came a familiar sound: '*David Nathan!*' He turned round to be confronted by Nina. She looked straight at him and said with a guffaw: 'Let me look at you! You're *faaat*, man!' Not exactly the comment he was looking for but he managed a fairly neat reply. 'Well, Nina, I haven't seen you for a while and I am getting older, you know.' She just roared with laughter and being her usual inquisitive self boomed, 'So, how old are you now?' This was a bit too personal for David's liking, and he was reluctant to let the entire room hear his reply, so getting as close to her ear as possible he whispered it: 'Well, I met you when I was 17.' Thinking that would do, he moved back, but then she announced to the whole room. 'Oh yes, that's right, we met when you were 17. And that's *35 years ago*, man!'

So the cat was out of the bag and the entire room now knew his age. It was all done with a huge amount of good humour and he knew she was just being her usual mischievous self. In fact, she then asked, 'How old do you think I am?' Having been around her for most of his life, he knew exactly what to say: 'Oh, Nina, you look like you're about 21.' Her response was immediate: 'See, David I taught you well.' Nina was on good form and the night had only just begun.

By this time most of the people in the room were looking at them. Suddenly her mood veered into a downward spiral. She looked at him with narrowing eyes and said, 'You know, you wrote something about me; you said I looked stoned!' She was indignant. Instantly David realised she was referring to the liner notes for *Baltimore* that he'd written many years previously. He had made a reference to the cover of the RCA album *It Is Finished*, specifically to a picture of her perched on some rocks staring straight ahead and looking slightly out of it. Apparently, attorney Stephen Ames Brown told the record company to delete the offensive reference, but he also told Nina that David had written it! Somehow, she had remembered this, and again turned to him: 'You wrote that I was stoned, man. I can't believe you wrote that, David, after all these years of knowing me. I don't want people to think I did drugs, you know. I don't, man.'

David was shocked – first, that she had remembered the incident at all and, second, that she had chosen now to scold him about it. He began trying to excuse what had happened but halfway through began laughing. He couldn't believe that he was standing there trying to justify himself after all this time. She knew he would never do anything to either discredit her or upset her intentionally, and he continued, 'Well, it was just a small phrase and they did take it out.' Suddenly, from out of nowhere, came the all too familiar sound, 'Ha! Game, set and match to Nina!' She had been playing with him and he had fallen for it. Again.

Nina had asked what was happening and David explained that she would be called and they would all go into the hall so that she could collect her award. 'Okay, man, that's okay.' Within minutes a man appeared and announced, 'We're ready for Dr Simone.' David smiled. Was anyone ever really ready for Dr Simone? Surrounded by an entourage that included Clifton, two burly bodyguards (one of whom was also a musician), her masseuse and several other people, she began walking towards the hall. David was striding along in typically British fashion when Nina suddenly shouted out, 'He's moving too fast! Doesn't he realise I'm older now?' With a humble apology, he slowed down and walked alongside her with a massive grin on his face.

Although David has never been one to blow his own trumpet, I knew that for him this was one of his proudest achievements. It was his determination that enabled this award ceremony to go ahead. Nina had given so much to him and knowing that he had provided the means for her to be recognised was special. A table had been reserved for Nina and her entourage, and she was thrilled to be sitting with Kenny Gamble, the poet Sonia Sanchez and several other dignitaries. Jill Scott, a new artist, performed a tribute to her, and during 'My Baby Just Cares', Nina began to smile. Following various tributes it was David's turn to take the stage. He recalled how they had known each other for more than a quarter of a century and, caught up in the moment, he retold the story of how Nina said he had to dance or have sex. Blushing crimson, he snapped back to reality and rushed off stage, not quite believing that he had shared such an intimate moment with the rest of the room.

Nina was helped on stage and beamed as Kenny Gamble handed her the award. The place went completely crazy, with yelling and screaming at a deafening pitch. Nina was still not lost for words. 'See, you love me, you *love me*! I'm just so glad to be here, man, so glad…'. The place erupted once more and, with a grin, she turned to the audience: 'Ha! You know why I've got them [looking at the bodyguards]? Because they're still after me. The Ku Klux Klan is still after me, you know. After all these years, I have to have the bodyguards with me.' People began cheering and she responded once again, 'It's not over, you know, it's still not over.' Standing there with a room full of people who had come to pay tribute to her work as a woman, an activist, a musical genius, and so much more, David was sure he saw the glimpse of a tear in her eyes – finally she had been paid some of her dues.

She was gently escorted off-stage and began walking (slowly) backstage. People were trying to shake her hands, to reach out to her and it began to get a little overwhelming. Still she found time to sit down with David for a moment. 'So, man, what are you doing now? We're going to eat and you must come with us.' He turned to her and began to laugh. When she had that look on her face and that tone in her voice, the request was more like an order, but one he was delighted to obey.

She left to change and returned looking resplendent. Summoning David to the waiting limo, they held hands as they sat in the back. Quietly he asked, 'So, Nina, how are you?' She replied softly, 'Oh, I'm good, man. You know I've got a South African boyfriend.' A gleam appeared in her eye. 'Yes, I can see you're glowing,' he told her, 'it really shows.' They were at peace with one another for the rest of the journey. The owner of the Japanese restaurant was a huge fan and had closed the place to the public, so she could eat and relax in private. The manager invited her to have some sake. 'Yes, get me some sake, I want some sake.' Clifton tried to intervene and suggested that it might not be such a good idea for her to drink, given she was taking medicine at the time. Nina was having none of it, and began pouring a generous quantity of the liquor into her glass.

During the evening she consumed a large amount of alcohol. The drink and her medication made her dangerously light-headed. David was sitting directly opposite her and said, 'So, Nina, you're in love?' She replied with a grin, 'Yes, yes... well I don't know, I don't think it's gonna last.' She then went into a graphic account of her boyfriend's private parts, which left almost the entire table in shocked silence. David, however, was not in the least bit shocked and knew she was just playing: 'Oh, Nina, you are naughty!' Out of the blue she turned to him and with a completely serious look asked, 'So, man, are you married?' To which he replied, 'Well, no.' She then responded with, 'So you have a girlfriend then?' Obviously, the copious amounts of sake were not helping matters and he told her firmly that they had already discussed this many years ago and that he didn't want to talk about his private life now. She was very respectful and didn't talk about it again.

Within minutes she had turned her attention to Clifton. He had now become the topic of conversation and she began to get a little too direct with her remarks. Obviously, Clifton knew she would occasionally overstep the mark, but he was unwilling to participate in this dissection of his sex life. Suddenly he rose from the table and announced, 'Look, Dr Simone, if you're going to continue talking about me like this in front of everybody, I'm leaving!' Nina didn't seem in the least bit worried by this and simply carried on talking. It was becoming pretty obvious that as the evening wore on she was getting more and more vocal. The comments had gone from personal remarks to her reminding everyone how she had been ripped off over the years. Having heard this many times before, David simply nodded and tried to steer the conversation round to more genteel topics. Sadly it didn't work. Nina began a tirade directed at another of her guests, Xavier, who worked with Clifton and was an up-and-coming photographer: 'You see him [pointing at Xavier], he just hangs around for the money, man. He's like all those white folk, he just wants the money, man. Of course, you want me to work, you want to make money off me.'

Things were beginning to turn somewhat ugly and the manager came over and announced that as it was now nearly 2am he was closing the restaurant. With a great sigh of relief everyone piled into the waiting limo and headed back to the hotel. David was staying a couple of doors down, and recalled how he was glad there was some space between him and the rest of the group. (It was an era marked by Nina's mental fragility. In 1995 she was given a suspended eight-month jail sentence after firing a scattergun towards noisy teenagers in a neighbouring pool. Her lawyer described her state of mind as 'fragile and depressed'. The court found she was 'incapable of evaluating the consequences of her act'.)

David called me the following day to 'relive' the previous night and how amazing it was to see Nina rewarded for her work. Obviously he relayed the rest of the tale in a bit more detail and we talked about the cause of these outbursts. My feeling was that as she had endured a strict upbringing and, being the daughter of a minister, she had probably not been able to express herself on sexual issues. Most teenagers tend to have a healthy interest in matters relating to sex, but it is likely that with Nina, being a child prodigy and spending most of her days sitting in front of a piano, such ordinary events just weren't part of her life. I felt that she had pushed her childhood away and as an adult finally felt it was time to 'play'. I reminded David that even now as an adult I made sure I had at least one childhood every few years, and would go off to Disneyland or buy stuffed toys, and so on, so that I always let the child in me play. Why should it be any different for Nina? He thought about this for a while and accepted that while I may not have all the answers, some of what I was saying made sense.

As for the remarks about race, again it was a part and parcel of Nina. Had I grown up in the Deep South and witnessed such overt racism I would be equally angry. Nina never disrespected me because I was white. We ended the call and David said he was looking forward to seeing her perform the following day. Having been involved in a serious accident a few years earlier, I was still unable to travel far, and once again had to live vicariously through David. I would, however, recover sufficiently to witness the Simone magic once more.

Clifton made arrangements for David to attend the show in Philadelphia and he arrived with a friend to a completely packed theatre. The audience was a mixture of both die-hard fans and a younger, hip audience. Interestingly enough, when she came on stage it was those in the younger age group that went completely wild. She had teamed up once again with two of her long-standing musicians, Paul Robinson and Al Schackman, and an African band. The place became totally still and as her hands brushed the keys the poetry of 'Black Is The Color Of My True Love's Hair' burst forth from her lips. Nina may have been older, but none of her sparkle had vanished.

Although she was now indeed more mature in years, Nina's movements seemed graceful and spirited. As she moved to the pulsing sound of 'Four Women', she mesmerised each and every person in the room. Being in Philadelphia she could not resist a verbal outburst and, grabbing the microphone, she glared out at the audience. 'Ha! I'm here in Philadelphia and as you know I was turned down by the Curtis Institute here. Well they regret it now! Look here I am all these years later, so Curtis Institute, let's forget about *you*!' The comments were followed by a tremendous laugh. Yes, she was right – look at what the Institute had turned its back on. But what it had rejected the world had embraced. (Strangely enough, the Institute would recognise its error in judgement and award Nina an honorary diploma shortly before her death.) Finally, the show came to an end, the audience was hoarse with screaming and, as she headed towards the wings, the sound of hundreds of voices could be heard 'We love you, Nina! *We love you!...*'

Backstage was a total zoo, but David managed to push his way into the room. (How many years had he been doing this now?) She was sitting engrossed in conversation with the poet Sonia Sanchez and, not wishing to interrupt them, he stood quietly to one side. It was still a wonderful thing to watch Nina holding court. She was nearly 70, yet she still had the ability to engage both young and old with her charm. As usual all memories of the 'night of the sake' had faded, and she was fondly teasing both Clifton and Xavier as if nothing had happened. Obviously, they too had learned that holding on to stuff around Nina was pointless. You either accepted her or used the door. Finally, David managed to grab a few minutes with her, and he began a major flattery assault.

She asked why I hadn't shown up, as she was sure I'd have wanted to see her get her 'dues' and he explained that, sadly, I was still unable to walk properly following my accident. 'Why didn't you tell me, man. Is she all right? What happened?' He explained in a bit more detail how I had had to endure two major back operations and had still not recovered but that I had been painting once again and had done a new portrait of her, which I hoped to present personally. This seemed to satisfy her curiosity and, once again, she made him promise to convey her love and best wishes, and to tell me to take good care of myself as she wanted to see me real soon. Her message sent my rather low spirits into a higher gear, and I determined that somehow I would get to see her when she next came to LA.

24 'Peace Of Mind'

Sadly, my recovery took a lot longer than anticipated, and I was beginning to wonder if I would ever get back to full health. David returned from Philadelphia and spent a day expanding on our previous conversations about Nina. I was determined to see her next performance, but the body doesn't always listen to the mind and mine was being stubborn. When David announced a week later that Nina was coming to LA within a few months, I set myself a goal to be there. I made great progress, but my doctors were still concerned that my sitting at a concert for nearly two hours would be too much for my back. I was banned from attending and despite this crushing disappointment I knew they were right. I would just have to content myself with David's colourful accounts once more.

Nina was performing at the Wiltern Theater on Wilshire Boulevard, and David, true to his word, recalled the entire event. She ran through a whole series of songs as if they were completely new, and improvised with such skill that even the standards sounded totally different. She was somehow able to give a totally new meaning to an 'old' song with just the slightest nuance. Of course, she treated everyone to her classics, and as she began 'See-Line Woman' the entire place became a seething mass of bodies moving as one. David got so caught up in the heat of the moment that he almost put his back out writhing to the beat! What he didn't know was that he was in fact going to witness a further treat. Towards the end of the show, Nina stood up and announced, 'I'd like you to meet my daughter, Lisa. You know, she's a singer too. She calls herself "Simone Superstar". That's *my* baby.' Smiling proudly she watched in silence as the lithe and beautiful figure of her daughter, Lisa Celeste, appeared.

David had seen Lisa perform quite a while ago at the House of Blues in LA, but she had certainly grown up since then. As she joined her mother, Nina began singing 'Compensation' from her album *Nina Simone And Piano!*, and they performed a duet. The audience nearly brought the house down (literally – it is, after all, an old building) and as they finished, Lisa stood centre stage and performed a song she had penned, with Nina accompanying her at the piano.

To see mother and daughter on stage was surreal, and Nina couldn't hide her admiration for her daughter. 'This is my baby, my baby Lisa. She's a superstar you know, don't forget, now: her name's *Simone* and she can sing!' As if the audience needed telling, Lisa had without doubt inherited her mother's talent and adapted it to create a style all her own. David went backstage and had a brief talk with both Nina and Lisa, and let Nina know that even though I had still not recovered sufficiently to be there in person, I was definitely there in spirit. That satisfied her and she told David that I had better hurry up and get better or else!

Due to unprecedented demand, Nina agreed to return to the Wiltern Theater in early 2001. At last I was able to sit down and walk without crying out in pain, and took my place in the theatre that day with great anticipation as her band assembled. The performance I witnessed was without doubt one of her finest. Added to this, from out of nowhere she began playing the opening bars to 'Pirate Jenny'. This was only the second time I'd heard her play my favourite song in almost 30 years. I was sure that David had been behind this magical moment, but he insisted he had nothing to do with it at all and that it must have been a coincidence.

I have no idea how long she performed for, or what other songs she sang, apart from 'Four Women'. I was totally lost in a world of my own. There were just the two of us: Nina and her magical voice, and me as her personal audience. It felt like everything around me had vanished except her. I even forgot for a while just how much pain I was in, but got a rather sharp reminder when I tried to get up from my seat. But, hell, it was worth every pang to witness such a sight and hear such heavenly sounds. Following what must have been her third encore, she disappeared from view. David and I were waiting backstage to meet her, and I began to get slightly irritable as my back was by now very painful. If it had been anyone else, I would have disappeared back to my sick bed.

Finally, her 'people' stopped rushing around and asked us to follow them. There, in front of me, was my friend and confidante of nearly 40 years, Dr Nina Simone, arms open wide and beckoning me closer. Her first words were delivered with a wicked grin: 'Sylvia, you know David's got fat!' Well, I almost collapsed with laughter. With that one small sentence she let me know that the years had done nothing to diminish her sense of humour. David was most indignant, mumbled something about having been on a diet, and opened his jacket to prove the point. We spoke for a few more minutes but I could tell she was tired and agreed to meet her the following afternoon to give her the painting

I had done. With a last hug and kiss, we left. I am sure that David wished secretly that it had been my mouth that was injured not my back, as I couldn't stop talking all the way home. I lost count of how many times I said, 'I can't believe how amazing she was.'

I woke early the following day and had just finished my morning coffee when the phone rang. It was Clifton and he sounded panicky. 'Sylvia, can you come over? Nina's upset and she wants to see you now. Something's happened and she won't listen to anyone, and I know she'll listen to you.' I told him that I'd be over as soon as I'd bathed and dressed. How was it possible that all these years later she was still involved in such drama? I wasn't too sure how I'd react, as during recent years I had begun a spiritual journey and, apart from becoming a doctor of metaphysics, had also become a minister. My life had undergone a transformation, and hearing Clifton was a reminder of some of the things I'd let go. I was feeling torn as I got in the taxi. I loved Nina, of that there was no doubt, but did I still want to be a party to her whims? I did a mini-meditation in the back of the taxi and prayed for extra guidance on the way.

I arrived at her hotel in the heart of one of LA's premier shopping areas, and quickly made my way to her suite. Clifton greeted me at the door and explained that while she had been performing the previous night, someone had broken into her suite and stolen her jewellery. She was understandably upset, and was threatening to cancel the remaining date in Chicago and fly home to France. He asked me to talk to her, although I explained that, under the circumstances, he might have to accept her wishes. I knew, too, that cancelling a show could create a major problem, not just with the promoters but also the expectant audience.

I went into her room, where she was being attended by her personal masseuse. For the first time, she looked old. I knew she was nearly 70, but had never really viewed her as an 'old' person. This day she looked her age and more. Having asked her assistant to leave, she began to shout, 'Goddam it, you know they stole my jewellery, man! I can't believe it. They even took my mother's ring. Can you believe that shit? I'm killing myself working and I get back to find I've been robbed. What kind of mess is that?' Sympathetically, I asked her a few questions about what had happened and whether the police had been informed. 'Ha! You know they ain't going to do a damn thing. This is still America and I'm still a black woman, so I don't expect them to help me, man. As usual, I'm on my own.'

It took a few minutes to calm her down and I also knew there was more going on here than the loss of her jewellery. She was angry, but it was more than that. Soon it was clear that, more than anything, she wanted to go home. 'I miss my dog – he's so cute you know – and I miss my home. I'm tired and I just want to go home, I've had enough. What should I do, Sylvia, tell me?' I sat for a moment and then calmly told her what I thought. 'Look, Nina, you'd be more than justified if you went home, and I can understand you're upset – you're entitled to be upset. But, the thing is, if you leave now with just one show left, it's as if you're leaving unfinished business. Also, think of all the people who have saved their money to buy tickets to see you – you know how disappointed they'll be. But you know what, at the end of the day, it's up to you.' She lay there quietly, and thought over what I had said. 'I know what you mean. You know I hate to let my fans down, but I'm tired, man, really tired.'

Finally I just said, 'Look, Nina, you know you always have some stuff to deal with in the States, not that that helps, but maybe if you finish this tour it will put an end to whatever karma you have here. I really don't know what else to say. It's up to you: if you really don't want to go to Chicago, then don't. It's your life and your choice. I can't tell you what to do, no more than anyone else. Just know that whatever you decide I'll always respect your choice.'

Rather than carry on discussing this issue, I decided to change the subject as whatever she chose would be up to her and was really not my business. I began telling her what had happened to me during our lost years, and that I was now a minister and a doctor of metaphysics. I gave her a copy of a small book I had self-published and, of course, the new painting. When she saw the painting her eyes lit up. I had painted her facing the Sphinx, surrounded by pyramids and the ocean. 'That's amazing, man. You have so many talents, I can't keep up with you. Thank you, it's beautiful. I'm going to hang it in my house in France. You know I've still got your pillows.'

I was a little taken aback by this torrent of praise and thanked her again for all the years of joy and love. I also confided that I had had my first ever drink around her, and lost my virginity to boot! Well, if I thought she was going to find that one amusing, boy was I wrong. She went completely mad. 'What do you mean you lost your virginity, man. How old were you? Who did it? You tell me, you hear!' Oh yes, I'd heard and was wondering what on earth had possessed me to be so open. I managed to garble something and she again roared, 'Did he know how old you were? Ha! If I'd have known, I'd have killed him. You were only a child.' Well, I wasn't exactly a child. I had been 17 at the time, and I'd had no idea my confession would cause such a strong reaction. I suddenly realised she felt responsible for me in some way and she believed

ROYAL FESTIVAL HALL
GENERAL MANAGER: JOHN DENISON, C.B.E.

CONCERT BY
NINA SIMONE
SATURDAY, 22 MARCH, 1969
8. p.m.
Management: Nems Enterprises Ltd.

STALLS
30/-

GANGWAY 3
ROW   SEAT
C   20

GREEN
SIDE
Please enter the
auditorium by
DOOR
3
LEVEL
3

R.F.H.
22
Mar., 1969
8. p.m.

STALLS
30/-
C 20

GUEST
GUEST

The High Priestess,
relaxing at London's
Mayfair Hotel in
1969

Following in her mother's footsteps:
Lisa takes her turn at the keyboard

Surrounded by fans on Human
Kindness Day, 11 May 1974.
Nina received an award for
her contribution to humanity

A proud mother and daughter
at the Human Kindness Day
ceremony

Chris White (bass), Al Schackman (musical director/guitar), Nina and Paul Robinson
(drums). Oviedo, 1989

Nina flanked by Odetta (left) and Miriam Makeba (right) on stage in 1990

Nina salutes her audience:
Olympia Theatre, Paris,
9 April 1990

Nina with members of the A-Team, Luxembourg, March 1990. L-r: Roger Nupie (carrying bag), Nina, Gerrit De Bruin (carrying flowers) and Raymond Gonzalez

Nina performs in Paris in April 1990, with a beaming Chris White looking on

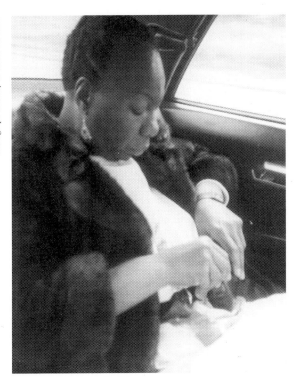

Nina keeping a close eye on
her money, London 1991

With long-time friend
Miriam Makeba, pictured at
Nina's housewarming party
in Amsterdam, June 1991

Nina with Gerrit De Bruin (standing) and guitarist Al Schackman, Amsterdam, 1992

The smiling doctor: A photograph
sent with a letter to Sylvia in 1992

Nina hides in furs from the
European cold in 1992

Original artwork from
The High Priestess Tour

that she should have protected me. I managed to convince her that it was my decision and it was fine. I had only told her to try to make her laugh. 'Ha! Well that wasn't funny, man. If I'd have known back then I would have let loose, you know.' Yes, I knew, and in a way I felt closer to her in that moment than at any time in the past. Here she was, an international star, and yet she was still a mother figure, and that part of her felt protective towards me.

Having regained my composure and changed the subject, we began talking about God. I explained how I was on a spiritual quest and she looked at me with wonder. 'So, you understand about God. You believe in God, don't you?' I said that I had always known deep down that God existed and it was only now I had recognised just how important having faith was. I had endured my own share of personal upheaval and had come to know on a personal level that God existed, not in some fantasy realm but within everything. I told her that a lot of what I had learned was in the little book I'd given her, and she picked it up and began reading. 'Yes, I can see that you know what I've been telling you. You understand and that's good, honey, that's real good.'

She had decided during the course of my visit that she would finish the tour, and recognising she was getting tired I stood up to leave. 'Nina, you know I love you. You are such a special person and I'm just glad I've been blessed to have had all these years with you. I know we've had our ups and downs, and been apart a lot, but no matter how much time passes and where you are, you're always in my thoughts.' She looked me straight in the eyes. 'That's so sweet of you, honey, but you must promise me that you'll come and see me at my home in France. You ask Clifton for the number and call me when you get back to England, and come and see me. You better promise me, man. I want to see you in France so don't forget, you hear?' With that, she gave me one of her smiles and I kissed her cheek and said goodbye. That was the last time I saw her alive. It was one of the few promises I broke, and one I regret more than anyone can ever know.

I could make a list of reasons and excuses for why I never made it to her home, but it would be redundant. The truth is, I returned to England, got caught up in life and, sadly, assumed she would always be around and that I would visit her soon. Soon never came, and before I knew it the chance to spend time with her was gone. David managed to see her again the following year, but my own journey with the incomparable Dr Nina Simone had ended, nearly 40 years after it began. She had seen me grow from a naive child of 12 to a woman of nearly 50, and yet it seemed as if it were a mere moment in time, not a lifetime.

David saw her a few months later. I had returned to England and he had received a call to say she was appearing once more in LA, this time at the Greek Theater, an open-air venue favoured by many a superstar. Sadly her health had deteriorated since her last visit and she was visibly failing, but had been determined to go on regardless. It was clear to David during the show that she was not at all well, and he was genuinely upset and concerned. Why on earth was she performing if she was feeling ill? Following this somewhat lacklustre performance, he went backstage for what was to be his last face-to-face meeting with her.

They talked for a moment and he was able once again to tell her how much he loved her and that she was an amazing person. Following her death he told me that in some way he was grateful to have had the chance to say these things to her. He did manage to catch her one last time, although he did not go backstage on that occasion. His last memory of Nina was of her walking slowly but regally towards her waiting car. He called me later that night and I told him how worried I was that she was still performing while she was ill. We talked for a while about just how much she had given over the years and how we both felt that, by now, she should be resting and enjoying her life, not travelling from one place to the next.

I did manage to get an answer to my question as to why she refused to stop performing. Although the people around her were pleading with her to stop and rest, she refused. After all the years spent touring she loved the energy she received from her audiences. In a way they made her feel alive, and the love they transmitted somehow closed the gap that not having a man in her life had created. She gave a final concert in France just prior to her death, and even though she could only manage to perform for 20 minutes, the audience showered her with overwhelming affection. Even at the end, she knew her life had been filled with an abundance of love, and she was happy to receive it. Perhaps performing fulfilled an ambition she had confided to the *New Musical Express* in April 1969: 'I am carving my own niche in this world of craziness. I am into my own thing, man, and when I die I want to leave some kind of mark that is my own.'

The Guardian newspaper featured an obituary to Nina on 22 April 2002 written by John Fordham. He wrote, 'In conversation she was brooding, restless, oscillating between dignified deflections of personal questions and arias of indignation about the prejudices, aesthetic deafness and philistinism of the music business. She was an act to be handled like hot coals or priceless china. To her audiences, particularly in the later years, she emitted an aura of fearful expectation that made one uncertain that, as part of the audience, one simply might not be good enough for her.'

His words summed up the persona but not the person. Nina once sang, 'I'm just a soul whose intentions are good.' Well, she got that right.

'It Is Finished': The Interviews

During the writing of this book, I have been fortunate to talk to some of the people who knew Nina at different stages of her life. Obviously I could not include every person she touched, so I have chosen those that I feel best reflect who she was.

INTERVIEW WITH LISA SIMONE KELLY

One of the most difficult interviews was with Nina's daughter, Lisa. She had just lost her mother and, knowing how hard that can be, I was at first reluctant to intrude upon private grief. Yet I discovered after Nina's death that Lisa and I had travelled along very similar paths in life. On a spiritual level we have bonded, and I feel that the link to Nina will continue through Lisa. I admire Lisa immensely for attempting to answer my questions, and am grateful for her replies.

Lisa is a successful and talented artist in her own right, having recently played the lead role in Elton John and Tim Rice's musical Aida *in New York. Her mother's apt description of her as 'Simone Superstar' was not just the belief of a mother but that of a world-renowned performer who knew talent when she saw it. Lisa is hoping to write her own account of her life as the daughter of Nina Simone, and I'm sure when she does it will deal with some unanswered questions and offer another perspective on Nina's life.*

What was your first memory of seeing your mother on stage, and did it just seem normal to you?

Truthfully, I don't remember exactly where it was, but I do know that I always loved seeing her on stage and having a good time. I do remember one time when they were recording a live album. Mommy was on stage and she was talking to the audience. All of a sudden you can hear me calling from the wings, 'Mommy, can I have a hot dog?' She simply looked over at me and began laughing as if it were the most natural thing in the world. I think they cut it out, but I'm not totally sure.

What would you say was the most fun you had together?
The happiest time I can honestly recall (and trust me there were a lot of them) was our time in Mount Vernon. Being at home was great. She was always very loving, but this time was definitely the most fun. I had a very happy childhood and we did a lot of regular family things. To me she was just Mommy, not Nina Simone the performer.

What's the best advice she gave you?
She gave me a lot of good advice. Her way of advising me was to ask negative questions. She never suggested things; she wouldn't say things like, 'Well, I suggest you do this or that', but she would give me advice on a whole lot of different things. When I was growing into womanhood, she talked to me about the changes my body would go through and what type of feminine products to use. You know, regular mother–daughter stuff. As a mother myself, I'm remembering a lot of things that I'm now fighting for, for my child, that my mother fought for for me. All you remember is your mother never let you get your hair straightened when everyone around you had it straight. I've had to deal with people trying to interfere in my life, and I'm having to scream at them to let it be, and I remember Mommy doing the same things with me. We had a good laugh about that, how things go full circle.

I know your mother wasn't exactly happy that you chose to go into the business and she felt very protective towards you. What was her best advice on this subject?
As I said, she gave me a lot of great advice. She would say things like, 'Well, you know, they're going to expect you to be like me. They're going to try and challenge you.' For everything she said I had a good answer, and she realised that the decisions I made to go into the industry were not superficial or spur of the moment, but I was serious. One of the things she did say when I said I wanted to learn to play the piano was quite funny. 'Why do you want to play the piano? You can sing, and that's all you need to do.' When we did play together I know she was proud and so was I. Even though she had worried about me to begin with, deep down she knew I had to follow my heart, just as she had.

Do you find people treat you differently being Nina's daughter?
Now that I'm a grown woman, yes. It wasn't always in my best interests being referred to as 'Nina Simone's daughter'. I was never uncomfortable, but it's

not something I went around doing, waving a flag saying, 'I'm Nina Simone's daughter.' In trying to promote a show or something, I might use it, or in trying to get certain doors open, but I had to be careful. I never knew if I was dealing with a promoter or somebody she had fought with in the past, or had tapped over the head with a champagne bottle ten years ago. But it always raised eyebrows and it did open some doors that might not have otherwise opened. She did have the respect of a whole lot of people and any mention of her name would provoke an 'Oh!' sort of reaction. Let's just say it didn't hurt, and sometimes it didn't make any difference at all. I feel that I'm a performer in my own right, and Mommy respected that.

Did she ever discuss the whole civil rights issue with you?
Yes, of course. It's subliminal. What affected her, affected me. It's like a domino effect. I wasn't aware of a lot of the things that were going on at the time. She made sure I had all the basics: a roof over my head, food on the table, love and stability. She tried to make sure I had a normal sort of childhood and she was exactly like any other parent, making sure I did my homework, etc. So we didn't exactly sit and talk about her beliefs. As much as possible she tried to make sure I was just a regular kid, and looking back on it, she did a really great job.

A recent documentary discussed her battles with a clinical condition. Were you aware of it?
For me, when my father was around she had a certain schedule, which kept things balanced. When they separated and I went to live with her, she was not the same person I remembered living in Mount Vernon. I remember thinking that she had turned into a monster. Mommy was selfish in a lot of ways and I often felt if she had taken two seconds to consider people around her, especially me, who depended on her 100 per cent, she would have made a different decision with her behaviour. It's a double-edged sword; you can point the finger and you can defend. Once I knew it was a medical condition she had that couldn't be transmitted, things started to make sense. I knew I wasn't crazy. Knowing it was medical helped me understand why she behaved the way she did sometimes and that helped.

How did the death of her own mother impact on her?
Funnily enough, it was me who told her. It affected her really badly. I remember I had called her and we had been chatting for about 15 minutes, just like I'd

called her to say 'Hi!' or something. I asked her if she was sitting down, and told her to sit down. Then I just told her flat out 'Grandma died last night.' She began to wail, literally just wail. I know it hurt her deeply, but we never really spoke about it in depth… I could feel her pain and I now know how she felt. It's a pain that is almost indescribable.

Given that she's left the world a legacy with her music, what else should people remember about her?

Well, of course, there's her work with the civil rights movement. But her perfection as a pianist is something she will always be remembered for. I recall watching her as a little girl and I would watch sheer perfection. In all the years I watched her, she never missed a note, she played every one. It was so special to see.

Actually, I can understand that. I remember watching her and thinking it was as if God was moving her hands. Does that make any sense?

Yes, that's it exactly. When you asked what would I most want people to remember I was pretty general, but if you knew who I was talking about you'd understand what I'm saying. There were just so many layers; she was right about so many things. Her delivery may get messed up a lot of times, but once you got a chance to decipher what she was doing it was like 'You know that she's right.' She was just so powerful. She was fearless and she had so much love to give, just so much love. Yet at the same time she was also afraid. She was hurt by so much; that's why she seemed to have a dual personality. Part of her was fearless, but the other part was afraid; I mean from the time she came into the world. She had so much insecurity around how she looked. She would traumatise me at times for having lighter skin, and I'd remind her that she had chosen my father, I didn't. That was her stuff, and she had so much stuff around rejection. The whole Curtis Institute thing, being from the wrong side of the tracks, all that stuff just branded itself into her. There were just so many demons and so much pain that she brought to the table before she even became a star, or a wife or mother. Everything else that happened afterwards was only added on top of that. So much so that you didn't know how to get to the core or how to peel away the layers. She was like an onion with layers, but she was never fully ready to peel them away. I can imagine trying to clear away the layers would have been a very scary journey and who knows if she could have found her way back from it if she'd tried.

What are your own personal goals?
That's easy, I'm going to be a superstar! I started my quest about 15 years ago, and my friends in the military would literally laugh at me, but I'd say, 'When I'm rich and famous you won't laugh then.' If people asked I'd keep it all very general, but I've learnt from that. Sometimes you need to be more specific and I've had to learn that over time. That's why at times my career has veered off in so many directions, such as stage, musicals, etc. Now I'm much more focused and I know what I want. I want to do movies, to sing and also to go out and lecture to help others. The time is definitely coming and I'm ready. I'm working with my mother's foundation, the Nina Simone Foundation. It deals with many issues, including child abuse, cancer research and bringing music back into schools. It's important for me to carry on her work as well as carve out my own career. Yes, I've grown a lot and learnt a lot, and I'm ready for superstardom. I know that people may regard this as a flippant or egotistical remark, but it's not. It's just my destiny, and deep down I know it and am happy to take it on and embrace life.

I have to say how grateful I am that, given how difficult this must have been, you've given me just a small insight into how you felt about your mother. Thank you for sharing this with me and the people who will read it.
That's okay, Sylvia. Mommy often talked about you and David, and how she loved you guys. I hope that it lets people get a small idea of who Mommy was.

With that, we ended the interview. I wish Lisa love and peace now and always. I have no doubt that her future will be a golden one, and whatever avenues she pursues will see her succeed. I like to believe that things do come full circle and that the lifelong friendship I was blessed to share with her mother will continue with her.

INTERVIEW WITH MICHAEL ALAGO
During the course of her life Nina would, of course, be associated with a number of record companies. One of her final albums, A Single Woman, was recorded on Elektra, and I was pleased to be able to speak with Michael Alago, the executive responsible for signing Nina to the label.

When did you first meet Nina?
In 1969 at a nightclub in New York city called Irving Plaza. I was an A&R

man at Elektra Records at the time and wanted to sign her to the label. Her brother Sam had arranged for me to meet her that day during the soundcheck. She saw me standing in the shadows at the back of the room and called out to me. She wanted to know what I was doing, and reminded me that this was not a freak show and I was not going to watch her do her soundcheck for free. Nervously, I introduced myself (actually I was shit scared), and just shook her hand and said, 'Hello.' I told her I wanted to sign her to Elektra. With that, she stopped me and declared, 'Where's the money, man?' I explained to her that I was not toting around any cash and that it had not been finalised with the company yet. She was not amused. She asked how old I was; I told her 22, and she just began to laugh. Out of nervousness I began to laugh with her and went on to tell her how much I loved her music. I think she realised I was genuine and asked if I wanted some of her tea. I guess you could say that was the beginning of a friendship that lasted until her death.

How did you find working with her?
Working with Nina was a blast. She was my idol and, yes, there were difficult moments – the album we were recording, *A Single Woman*, involved doing some extra takes and having to comp vocals, which she didn't like too much – but almost every song turned into a vocal stunner. I hired André Fischer to produce it and he was brilliant. Nina and I fashioned the album so that it was like a homage to the Frank Sinatra album *A Man Alone*. Nina loved that album and we both adored Rod McKuen. It turned out to be a beautiful recording of love, loneliness and loss, as a homage to both Frank and her late father.

No doubt you have a funny story or two. Any that spring to mind?
Oh, this one is a hoot. I think it was July 2000 in London. I spoke to Nina from the States and let her know I was coming over for the show and she insisted I stay with her at her hotel. Even though it was nearly seven years since the release of the album, we stayed in close contact if not seeing each other, by mail and a lot of transatlantic phone calls. The shows were part of a series called *The Meltdown* produced by the musician Nick Cave, and she was performing at one of the evening shows. During the day of the show, she had gone to get her hair done in the morning and I had sat with her drinking her famous concoction of tea with honey and cayenne pepper (that drink was delicious and strong!). Afterwards we ordered some sushi and, having finished it, sat and relaxed. Finally she decided to get ready and I helped her run a hot

bubble bath. She had asked me to help scrub her back, and as I was doing it I was getting absolutely soaked. She began laughing and said, 'Michael just get in the tub with me.' So I stripped off to my boxer shorts and got in. We both had a fun time, laughing and joking and, of course, drinking champagne, and all the while the bubbles were flying all over the place! That was one memory I shall always treasure.

What would you most want people to know about Nina?
The laughter, yes, definitely the laughter. After the scene in the bathroom she had given a concert and we met up backstage. There was a knock at the dressing room door and in walk Nick Cave and Elvis Costello. Nina had no idea who Elvis Costello was and there was no time to explain. Suddenly he reached out and kissed her hand, and with an ever-so-sly look on her face, she turned to me and asked, 'Who is the white boy kissing my hand?' Well, we both just burst out laughing, and she looked at her hand and said, '*Daaarling*, just give me some more champagne.' This was typical of our nights together; there was always something to laugh about. I felt so privileged to know her for the last 13 years of her life. Our relationship went far beyond that of record executive and artist. We really loved each other as dear friends, and had just so many laughs during our long-distance phone calls. She was a wonderful woman with fire galore, and a one-of-a-kind artist. As a performer and interpreter of songs, each song – whether it was Dylan, Irving Berlin or George Harrison – she made them all her own. She was without doubt the most gifted and wonderful performer there ever was. She also had the most beautiful and wicked smile in the whole wide world...

INTERVIEW WITH GERRIT DE BRUIN

My next interview was with Gerrit De Bruin, a long-standing and dear friend of Nina's, and someone who had the opportunity to spend lots of time with her over the years.

When did you first meet Nina?
I met Nina in either 1966 or 1967. I can't be quite sure of the exact date. I was in Amsterdam and had gone to a see her perform at a concert in the Amsterdam Concertgebouw. I had known her music since 1962. This was her first big concert in Holland, although she had done a small TV special in the Mickey Theatre just outside Amsterdam in December 1965. Sadly, I found out later,

in 1989, that the TV archives had lost the film, so I never got to see that TV show. I had tried to buy a ticket for the 1967 concert but it was sold out. The concert started at just past midnight and I had decided to go along anyway. I was waiting outside the building near the stage entrance when, about 11pm, a limousine pulled up and Nina and Andy went inside. A while later a large minibus arrived carrying her musicians. As they got out I followed them, acting as if I was, in fact, a valet from the concert hall, grabbed a few of their instruments and headed inside. The guard at the door must have believed I was with them and didn't try to stop me. Once I got inside I decided no one was going to get me out again! I heard the sound of piano playing coming from the hall and walked in. Nina was sitting by herself at the piano rehearsing, so I walked up to her and introduced myself, and told her I was one of her most dedicated fans. She was very nice and asked me if I wanted to sit down next to her and watch what she was doing. She called for an extra stool for me, and for about 20 minutes I was able to see her play and ask her all sorts of questions. It was a really great experience. She seemed to like me, and when it was time to leave the stage she introduced me to her husband Andy and he invited me to see them after the show. That was to be the beginning of a deep friendship that lasted until the very end.

Given her fiery temper, is there any story that you feel highlights this?
There are a lot of bad things said about Nina and she had a lot of enemies. Nina was sometimes difficult, aggressive and downright impossible, and often her behaviour was shameful, but I knew this was not Nina. It was just the chemical imbalance in her brain that caused this behaviour; therefore I never felt this was directed at me personally. I did feel a lot of pity for her and would say to myself, 'Oh, another attack. I will try my best to help her.' I knew she was deeply ashamed following these outbursts, when she was back to normal. Can you imagine how hard a life it must have been trying to deal with a disease that left you feeling such remorse? It was hard, and there were times she almost drowned with shame. Nobody understood that. I remember one time in particular. We were in the central hall of the Grand Hotel in Paris. Nina was nervous and suddenly she got into an argument with this complete stranger. She got so mad she literally went to hit him, and I grabbed her with both arms and tried to stop her hitting this poor man. I dragged her outside into the street and managed to push her into a taxi, which was not easy. I told the taxi driver to just drive, and he asked, 'Where to?' I told him just go to the Eiffel Tower.

So we drove through Paris until Nina had calmed down. We finally drove back to the Grand Hotel, but as I knew Nina was by now upset at what she had done, we slipped in through a side door. She never said a word. About three months later, when we were back home in Nijmegen, she turned to me and said, 'Gerrit, thank you for getting me out of that situation in the Grand Hotel in Paris.' Beneath all the bullshit caused by her disease there was a very intelligent and, above all, honest and warm person, who always showed her deep friendship for me. Personally there has always been the question that Nina was a genius, but would she have been a genius without her disease? I don't know, but I'm sure her music would have been less intense.

No doubt you have many stories to tell, but what would you say showed her sense of humour?
We once went out to eat at this Japanese restaurant in Nijmegen. Nina decided that the second course was taking too long and began to shout. This went on for some time and the owner came over to Nina and me, and asked us to leave. He didn't ask for money for the bill. He just wanted us to go. Nina got really angry and said, 'You don't like me because I'm black.' The man smiled and replied, 'No, madam, I don't like you because I'm yellow.' Well, there was nothing Nina could say to that, and so we left the restaurant and never went back. Nina told me later it was a shame because she liked the food there, but couldn't really go there again. All the while she was saying this she was laughing. She had a great sense of humour.

What would you say best shows Nina's intense passion?
In the 1960s Nina did sometimes let herself go emotionally during her concerts. I mean, she would get caught up in the emotion of her music. It activated her feelings, and while playing or singing she would be telling a story that was so intense she would make herself cry, or laugh, depending on the song. That went so deep sometimes that not only would Nina cry but the audience would get caught up in it and cry with her. The audience was very lucky to be there at just the right concert, and at these shows she was a real genius. Miles Davis told me that Nina Simone is the greatest interpreter of sadness and feelings of our times, and he was right. Personally I've seen well over 500 Nina Simone concerts, being on the road with her, and during most of them she would ask me to stay at least three metres behind her in the wings. She often came off stage for a few minutes to smoke a cigarette, and when she felt it was a good

concert she would ask me, 'Gerrit, did I make you cry?' and when I said yes she would kiss me and whisper things like, 'I know, I felt like crying too. I'd better go back now, Al [Schackman] has almost finished his solo.' These times she let me know just how emotional she felt, and I felt the same way.

What would you say is your personal favourite Nina song?
She was about to appear at the Royal Albert Hall in December 1968 (I'm sure you were there), and she was resting before going on. I was reading a paper and she turned to me, 'Gerrit, what do you think are the most important songs I sing?' I told her there were a lot, but for me 'Dambala' (from her RCA album *It Is Finished*) still cuts my heart in two when I hear it. She thanked me and carried on resting. That night she performed 'Dambala' for the first time in 25 years of performing, and it was just her way of saying how much she appreciated our friendship. I also have a couple of tapes of concerts she did while in Paris at the Palais de Glace. She had started playing 'My Father' on the piano and began singing 'Ne Me Quitte Pas' over it, it was amazing to hear and see. Later she switched it around and played 'Ne Me Quitte Pas' while singing 'My Father'. I let Miles Davis listen to that recording and he summed it ups, with tears in his eyes he said, 'Nina you make me break my own heart.'

Nina is your daughter's godmother. How did that come about?
The relationship with my ex-wife Juliska started while we were listening to Nina's music. When Nina came to Holland we used to see a lot of each other. She would come over with her husband Andy and we'd have fun. Nina would play the piano and we'd dance to her boogie-woogie tunes. She was just like one of us. So when our daughter was born we named her our 'little' Nina. We asked Nina if she would be her godmother. She was happy and said, 'Yes, of course.'

What do you believe was the one thing she most wanted in her life, and do you think she found it?
Nina wanted to find love, protection and a home where her brain would not attack her. Of course, that was impossible, being the Nina she was. That led her to search for substitutes and be hurt by deception a lot of the time. She once told me that she lived in the South of France all alone, and she should not have left Amsterdam but that because she was Nina Simone she could not admit that she had done wrong in going there. That was Nina, she hated to

let people see her vulnerability in any way, even though those closest saw it anyway. Another thing about Nina was that she really wanted her parents to be proud of her, especially her mother. She had an early publicity photograph sent to her parents that she had signed 'Eunice'. Years later when she became a doctor of music and doctor of humanities, she began signing her name Dr Nina Simone. This meant a lot to her and she had the inscription on the photo she had given her parents changed to Dr Nina Simone. It was rather strange, but in a way it was [because of] her desire to make them proud of her achievements. Being known as Dr Nina Simone was important to her as it was a symbol of recognition that she richly deserved.

As to her life, finally, she understood and accepted she would have to live alone, helped just by her employees. In 1989 we had a discussion about life and death and she told me that she would die when she was 70. I said that when 70 approached she would postpone her death another ten years, but she said, 'No, no, I will die when I am 70. I don't want to live any longer, it's just more pain. Sadly, towards the end, the people that loved her the most were unable to get near her. Many times I would call to be told she was asleep or was out. One time I went to her house and called her on my mobile while standing at the gates. I could see her sitting by the pool and yet I was told she was not at home. I got very angry at this and began to shout her name and so she heard me and welcomed me in. She was so happy to see me and I realised that she was also lonely. Sometimes she came to visit, but most times she waited for you to go to her, and I don't know if she knew I had called many times without speaking to her and that makes me sad.

Nina died when she was 70, at Easter. This was a sad end to a somewhat tragic life. It broke my heart, but I have done what I could to make her life as good as I could for her. I always felt her gratitude and a very deep friendship. Thank you, Nina! You have given me a lot; I hope I gave you all I could have.

As our interview ended I said to Gerrit that Nina had told several people she would die at 70, and, like him, most did not believe it. Sadly, she was right.

INTERVIEW WITH ROGER NUPIE

My final interview was with Roger Nupie, a life-long friend and president of the International Dr Nina Simone Fan Club. Roger took over what David and I had begun, and is dedicated to continuing to let the world know who Nina Simone was.

When did you first meet Nina?

I spoke to her a few times after concerts, but, in fact, I was first introduced to her in the late '80s by her dear friend in Holland, Gerrit De Bruin. Gerrit was taking care of her while she was living in Nijmegen. He wanted to know who this guy was who was always there with flowers waiting for her after her concerts. He called me one day and I told him I was a fan from the moment I was 14 years old, and that since then I had kept an archive on her. When he said they were trying to sort out the copyrights of her songs, I said I was quite sure I had all the information they needed. So he invited me to come and see her in the apartment in Nijmegen. I was dead nervous, but all of a sudden Nina came out of the bedroom dressed in a white nightgown. She smiled and said in her famous deep voice, 'Hello, *daaarling*.' The intention was that Gerrit would come and get me that evening and I should stay with him, and possibly he would bring me back for a second visit the next day. But when he came back Nina said, 'Oh no, you're not going to steal him away from me.' So I stayed with her for the weekend. We got along quite well from the very beginning, and it was an experience similar to when her music came into my life. I felt like I had already heard it, as if I recognised and knew it in some way or another. When we began talking first about music, then about life, love and everyday things, it was as if I'd known her all my life. I was in love with the 'star' Nina Simone for many years, but this was the start of a friendship with the woman behind Nina Simone.

Given all the many stories, which would you say are the ones that best describe Nina's humour, passion and laughter?

It is funny that you should put these three together, Sylvia. Humour, passion and laughter were often all combined. There are just so many incredible anecdotes, but I will keep to three of them.

The first was the very first time I was on tour with her. It happened in Montreux. She had locked herself in the bathroom, and when I arrived ready to go out to eat and help her dress before the show, she said she did not want to do the concert. I tried to convince her in every way possible, but she said I was just like all the rest, 'only interested in seeing me perform'. I gave up the discussion and pretended I was packing my suitcase. After some time had passed she asked me what I was doing. I told her I was packing my suitcase; since she was not performing I'd just go back home. After a few minutes she came out. She looked angry and somewhat astonished when she saw I was pretending to pack *her* suitcase, as mine was in my own room. I told her I had to do it this way, by pretending. She smiled and started to laugh, 'That's very clever of you, *daaarling*!' I ordered some food and asked her which of her African dresses she would like to wear and, of course, she agreed to do the concert.

The second story began when we were getting ready to leave the hotel. The press was waiting for her in the lobby, as she was doing a television show that was hot news. Just then the heel of one of her gold high-heeled shoes broke. She continued answering questions as if nothing was happening, and asked me to find the glue she had in her handbag. I repaired the heel on the spot and she turned to me and said, 'When you have fixed it, I have to stand on it for a minute, and then we can go. If you can't fix it, I'll go back to my room.' The reporters could see what was happening, but no one dared to laugh or even say anything about it. She stood up and began looking at her watch. After a minute she checked the shoe and said, 'You did it very well, *daaarling*.' With that, she walked gracefully to her limousine, leaving the press standing there looking astonished! After the concert we had dinner with the staff from the Montreux Festival and she retold the story of the shoe and the glue. Some of the people dared to giggle in a slightly nervous way, but she began to smile and laugh her devilish laugh at the thought of what had happened. You could say that was one case of not walking on pins and needles, but glue on the shoe!

The third story has to do with her down-to-earth attitude towards men, love and sex. Once when she was staying with me in Antwerp, we went out to an African discotheque, where many wealthy Africans went. We met this ambassador and his son, and they offered us both champagne and Baileys, and a whole lot more, to drink. He was very entertaining and charming, as was his son. But after a while Nina started to get bored; she wanted some real action, if you know what I mean. Next thing I know, she got up and said, 'Come on, Roger, you take the son and I'll take the father. Can we go now?' The ambassador was not quite sure he'd heard right, and asked madam if she could repeat what she'd said. Nina repeated what she had said, shouting at the top of her voice. Both men looked puzzled, and the next thing they decided was they suddenly had to leave. I thought Nina might be sad, as she seemed to be really interested in the ambassador, but she was fine. She looked at me for a moment and then started to laugh. 'Well, sugar, if we can't find a lover tonight, we may as well dance,' and that's what we did. After that we went to one of her favourite Chinese restaurants. It was a cheap and slightly dirty place, but they served huge portions and that's what she liked. She also liked the owner. The first time we went there she asked him if we could eat for free, as she was Nina Simone. The owner said quite indifferently, 'Oh, no, because when I go to one of your concerts, I have to pay.' His answer, and the fact he was not scared by her (as many people were when they first met her) impressed her. She once told me, 'Too bad he's married. I'd love to run a Chinese restaurant with him and curse people out.'

There were many funny incidents along the way and some were just casual things she'd say that made you laugh. One time we were driving to a housewarming for Gerrit, and Nigel Bartlett had come over from London with his son. They went to pick us up at the airport in Dusseldorf in Germany. On the ride back Nina asked his son what he wanted to be when he grew up and he said he wanted to be a singer. Nina told him that was a very bad idea and asked if he had another. He replied that his other 'wish' was to be a gangster. Nina's reply was brilliant. She said, 'That's a very good idea, you sweet thing. You're a very clever boy. I wish I'd been a gangster instead of a singer.' So, you see, Nina's sense of humour was like a lot of people's its just that most of the time people misunderstood her or got things wrong. If this story had been reported in the press no doubt it would have been very sensational and not at all like the actual event, and that's why she was often very guarded.

With her lifetime of work on behalf of the civil rights movement, did she ever talk about this with you?
Not really all that much. She was surprised that me being a white boy from a small village in Belgium I was so well informed about the civil rights movement (CRM). It certainly pleased her that people from other parts of the world were concerned with this problem, and were grateful for the message she spread with her music. As with many other things, she had a love/hate relationship with the whole period of her life she devoted to the CRM. Her reactions on this subject were often contradictory, but to me this was proof that she was still concerned, maybe even more than she would care to admit. On the other hand, I think it would be a mistake to pigeonhole her as a 'civil-rights-movement singer', as much as it is a mistake to pigeonhole her as a 'jazz singer' or a 'soul singer'. She combined the political songs with all other kinds of music from the early beginning to the very end. One thing that does stand out regarding this part of Nina was connected to an incident at a memorial for Dr Martin Luther King. She was given two beautiful jogging suits with the words 'Keeping the dream alive' embroidered on them. She said during the ceremony that she

was going to keep one and give the other to a 'boy in Belgium'. The interviewer was puzzled and said they didn't know there were any black people in Belgium. Nina's reply was that of course there were but she was giving it to a white guy, which puzzled them even more. I was the 'white' guy and was totally thrilled when she gave me the outfit. She kept the red one and I have the 'black one', which I still treasure to this day. This whole incident summed up Nina's attitude.

What would you most want people to know about Nina as a person and artist?
As an artist there was only one Nina Simone, and there will never be anyone like her, that's for sure. Not only because she had such a broad repertoire. She had this remarkable combination of vocal and musical ability. The impact she had on people's lives emotionally was remarkable. So many people have tried to analyse and describe her, but this was only a part of the story of Nina. The Nina Simone experience was more of a religious one. It is close to real black magic, maybe even voodoo in a sense. I remember one time when Nina had been with staying with me in Antwerp and her friend Miriam Makeba called and asked if she would sing on her new record. Nina agreed and a week later Nina, Gerrit and I drove to Brussels through a really bad snowstorm. The record was the Bob Dylan song 'I Shall Be Released' and it was being done in African and English. Nina asked me to write down the words and she just glanced at it once and that was it. The producer told her where to come in as it had been pre-recorded. Nina sang and it was clear that as she began there was definitely a magic in the air. Later when I listened to the result it was so moving, but that was Nina.

People should also know that behind the 'diva' Nina Simone, the one described as moody or difficult, was a single woman who was trying very hard to find love. There was just so much love hidden inside of her, that when it did come out there was such tenderness and warmth it was almost overwhelming. When she did the session with Miriam Makeba it was so wonderful to see the two friends together and it really showed how warm and loving she was. To those who knew the real Nina this was who she was – a very loving and kind woman, not the angry, bitter woman many described her as. She was sometimes both, but beneath it all she really was beautiful.

What will you most miss about her?
Her smile. Her wicked, devilish laugh. The way she would call you *daaarling*. But most of all, the moments when the love came out. It was not easy for her

to find peace in her life, but when it happened you felt you were at one with her. That was a wonderful feeling. That was true love.

Finally, as the president of the International Dr Nina Simone Fan Club, can you tell me a bit about how it came into being?
I had discussed the idea briefly with Gerrit De Bruin. Following a series of five concerts in Paris at the famous Olympia Theatre, Nina was holding a press conference (organised by agent Raymond Gonzalez) in her suite at Le Grand Hotel, when she suddenly introduced me as the president of her international fan club. Afterwards we celebrated by going out and dancing to her favourite African music. During the many years of running the fan club, we worked on many projects, including the documentary film *The Legend* with Gerrit and Stephen Cleary, the co-writer of her autobiography. In 2000 Clifton Henderson, her manager, made the international fan club a part of the official Nina Simone website. I am still running the fan club and, following her death, Aaron Heidemann invited members to go online to his brand new website, www.high-priestess.com, and read newsletters and exclusives available only to members. Together our aim is to keep the memory of Dr Nina Simone and her music alive for all time...

Epilogue: 'Consummation'

And now it is done – my soul has been released

When I made the decision to write this book it was my way of honouring the woman I had known for almost 40 years. What it became is not just a tribute to an outstanding woman, but a look at a life that could inspire, anger and create a reaction on many levels. Personally, it has been so much harder than I could ever have imagined. My emotions have run the gamut: I've cried endless tears for my friend who is no longer with me; I've laughed at the memory of the countless stories; but most of all, I'm grateful. Yes, I'm grateful that almost 40 years ago my brother David introduced me to Nina's music, and then went one step further and let me meet and know the woman herself.

Along the way I made a discovery, one that altered my life. Not only was Nina a friend, but there is no doubt we were connected on a much deeper, soul, level. Having spent many years on a spiritual quest, I have come to understand that we are all connected on some level. However, there are a few with whom the connection goes beyond mere knowing – it is as if we are one. I recognised that with Nina, and one of the reasons I am still unable to come to terms with her death is that my soul feels as if part of it is missing. I am a great believer in reincarnation, and have also learnt that death is not an end, merely a transition. Nina has left the world a legacy, a wealth of music that will never die and that will keep her memory alive for generations to come. But even though I accept all of this, on a purely human level I miss her deeply.

Yes, we had our ups and downs – like any friendship it went through several incarnations – but it survived them all. During the course of writing this I've sat with Nina singing in the background, and I've remembered it all: the concerts where I stood in shock and awe at what she was able to accomplish musically. I can see her hands as they caress the keys of her piano. I can hear her as she pleads for us to be more compassionate and to stop the hatred and bigotry. I smile as I listen to her tempt us with her sexuality, and dare us to love her. Even now as I sit with my memories, I am still unable to play 'See-Line Woman' without my body responding to the rhythm. Yes, all these years after my 'rehearsals' in Nina's presence, as soon as I hear the drums heralding the opening lines, my body automatically begins to move and I am transported back in time. I have such an abundance of memories and am blessed to have them, but I would trade them all for one more glimpse of the woman I knew and loved.

To the world, Nina was described as a 'diva', 'difficult', 'moody', 'angry' and a whole lot more besides. Without doubt she was no angel, but she was one hell of a woman. Regardless of the cost, she decided long ago that the plight of her brothers and sisters the world over was far more important than daily trivialities. For her it began back in the Deep South; a child prodigy, but none the less aware of the injustice racism and hatred engendered. She took those beliefs and made them her personal crusade, never willing to sell out, never willing to compromise, always staying true to her belief that despite the colour of a person's skin we are all just human beings. She taught me well, inspired me to look long and hard at life and to use all the wisdom she gave me. I know there were times that I let her down, but she accepted my weaknesses and encouraged me to keep on trying. I learnt much at the Simone School of Life and regret none of it, not a single moment.

The woman I knew had an abundance of love to offer and despite her own challenges, and her difficulties in finding true love, she never quit. Through the tough times, she continued to grin and bear her woes and, if sometimes the mask slipped and her own vulnerability was on show, there was a prevailing sense of pride. To describe Nina Simone is like trying to describe the wind – it's almost impossible. There were so many facets to her life, as a mother, activist, wife, musical genius and life-long humanitarian. She was all of these and yet so much more.

Oh yes, and the laughter – that was a whole other ball game! To be in her presence when her grin appeared and that husky laugh rushed forth from her lips was indeed a sight to behold.

Not only did Nina battle a system that was filled with injustice, she battled her own personal demons. Fighting her inner torment was never easy, adhering to a regime of drugs to help her deal with a clinical imbalance was equally challenging. The media often portrayed her as 'crazy', having no understanding of what she was dealing with, and yet she refused to be a victim then, and I would not have her be one now. Nina was never a victim. She fought battles with life – some she won and some she lost, but she never gave up.

Her quest for love was another area that would see her continue to believe that one day her prince would come. He may well have done so more than once in her life, but she either let him go or lost him along the way. Was she bitter? No. She had a God-given talent, a beautiful daughter, many loving relationships with friends and family and, above it all, she had faith.

Nina's faith was one part of her that was unshakeable. Even when it seemed that she had hit the ground, she would simply turn to God and rise again. Her music is filled with songs that praise God, that encourage others to seek God and to know God. Regardless of religious beliefs, Nina saw God as universal, neither one faith nor another, but proof of a love everlasting. Yes, she believed in God, and regardless of what opinions people formed about her, her faith remained at the core of her being. To me, Nina was a remarkable woman, a spirit of great compassion and humanity and, yes, as with all human beings, slightly flawed.

Her suggestion that I was an old soul and that we had met in a previous life, may have fazed me initially, but as the years went by it was something I would come both to accept and acknowledge. Strangely enough, her insistence that she was a reincarnation of the great Egyptian Queen Nefertiti may have seemed ludicrous, but who knows? What I do know is that literally within months of Nina's death, a British archaeologist uncovered what is believed to be the missing tomb of Nefertiti, so who can truly say who Nina was? It could be nothing more than sheer coincidence, but then again...

There are so many songs that could be used to describe Nina, and yet for me there is one that stands out above all the rest. 'Don't Let Me Be Misunderstood' *is* Nina. The words fit like a glove, and so to end my personal tribute to my friend, I ask you to read the following lyrics and decide for yourself. Who else could they have been written for? Nina may have been misunderstood by the world at large, but for me she was quite simply someone who hated conformity with as much passion as she loved music. Being a true rebel is just one of the ties that bound us in friendship, and for that I'm for ever grateful.

'Don't Let Me Be Misunderstood'
(Bennie Benjamin, Gloria Caldwell, Sol Marcus)

Baby, you understand me now, if sometimes you see that I'm mad.
Don't you know no one alive can always feel injured, when everything goes
wrong, you see some bad.
But I'm just a soul whose intentions are good – Oh, Lord, please don't let me
be misunderstood.
You know sometimes, baby, I'm so carefree, with a joy that's hard to hide,
And then sometimes again it seems that all I have is worry and then you're
bound to see my other side.
But I'm just a soul whose intentions are good – Oh, Lord, please don't let me
be misunderstood.
If I seem edgy I want you to know, I never mean to take it out on you.
But life has problems and I get more than my share, but that's one thing I
never mean to do 'cos I love you.
Oh baby, I'm just human, don't you know I have faults like anyone?
Sometimes I find myself alone regretting some little foolish thing, some simple
thing that I've done.
But I'm just a soul whose intentions are good – Oh, Lord, please don't let me
be misunderstood.
Don't let me be misunderstood. I try so hard so please don't let me be
misunderstood. I don't want to be misunderstood.

Having written what is my final chapter on a life lived to the full, I now turn
to David, to try to put into words his thoughts and feelings.

'Some days, it's just hard for me to listen to Nina. That voice, sometimes
dark and brooding, sometimes clear as a bell. On the days that I can, I
often go back to the very beginning of my musical relationship with a
woman who had such a major impact on my own development as a human
being. I listen to songs from the *At Town Hall* album, like "Black Is The
Color Of My True Love's Hair" or "The Other Woman", and I'm
transported back to my parents' bedroom in the flat we occupied above a
fish and chip shop in Kilburn where my father worked. That's where my

first record player was located and, after school, I would seek refuge from the turmoil of the household in Nina's music.

'There was something in that voice, a pain and a world-weariness that forged the connection. More than anything, I wanted to belong and every word of that song, "Don't Let Me Be Misunderstood", rang true. For those – like Nina and me – who believe in reincarnation, the 1965 coming together of a skinny, bespectacled, spotty-faced little kid from working-class London, and the black and sometimes haughtily regal then-darling of American supper clubs and concert halls makes complete sense. The innate sense of "knowing" each other was there from the very start and the karmic inevitability of us being in each other's lives for 38 years was unquestionable.

'If Nina taught me anything, it was that in the matter of creative expression, integrity and taking a stand we must never give into the dictates and whims of others. Of course, I learned so much more besides. I discovered that music could not be contained or constricted, that being true to one's self was the ultimate pathway. Nina was a complex individual but not unlike so many of us in that respect. Beyond any lofty conversations about music – which were relatively few and far between considering the original nature of our relationship as fan-club founder and diva of the first order – it was the hilarious chats about love and sex that I remember with the most fondness. In one of the many liner notes I've written for reissues of Nina's music, I wrote, "She smiled...and an angel flew around heaven." And when I say that – to quote Nina in "Mississippi Goddam" – I mean every word of it. Beyond the tough manner and sombre expression that she sometimes wore to protect herself from the madness of the world (much like "Peaches" in her classic "Four Women"), Nina was a vibrant, funny, earthy woman with a smile that could light up a room.

'I cried when Nina passed away, for I felt a member of my family had slipped away to the other side. While death is a part of life, it still hurt to know I would never again see that sly grin or hear that unique voice on the other end of my phone or on a stage somewhere.

'Of course, I know that any time I want to summon her up, I can. I can close my eyes, put on "Don't Smoke In Bed", "Love Me Or Leave Me", "Since I Fell For You" or "Feeling Good" and Nina is right there, listening with me. As I worked on the last section of this book, which focuses on Nina's music, I had the chance to revisit all of her recorded work, save for those plentiful bootlegs and unauthorised recordings that seemed to be a part of the Simone legacy: the bone-chilling bite of her version of "I Put A Spell On You" (next to "Don't Let Me Be Misunderstood", my favourite Nina recording), the world-weariness of "Ain't No Use" and the rage and fury of "Backlash Blues" or the live recording of the songs on *'Nuff Said!*, recorded days after the assassination of Dr Martin Luther King Jr. There's darkness in "Blue Prelude", lightness in "July Tree", humour in "Forbidden Fruit" and sadness in "Middle Of The Night", pathos in "Images" and passion in "Sinnerman", laughter in "Go Limp" and tears in "Just Say I Love Him", the stark honesty of "Strange Fruit", the lusty joy of "Gimme Some", the hope in "Tomorrow Is My Turn" and the despair in "Ne Me Quitte Pas". Yes, there is every kind of emotion, for Nina Simone could conjure up almost any aspect of the human experience through that sometimes magnificently strange voice and that unforgettable keyboard artistry.

'There was no one like Nina. Putting aside for a moment the wealth of amazing experiences I had with her over the years, there remains the music, always breathtakingly brilliant. No other artist has ever been able to run the musical gamut quite like Nina Simone: from the rhythmic chant of "Zungo" to the slow grind of "In The Dark". The world will never again see anyone of her kind. Referencing one of her last '60s recordings for Philips, she was indeed the "keeper of the flame" for so many of us.'

Nina Simone: A Musical Odyssey
By David Nathan

1. BEYOND JAZZ

Nina Simone's 'official' recording career began in late 1957, with what turned into a marathon 14-hour session in New York that would have a lasting impact on her life. 'Official' only because, as was the case throughout her career, Nina Simone's music was bootlegged before she ever signed a contract. An authorised live taping of a performance, likely cut at the Atlantic City venue where she first morphed from Eunice Waymon into Nina Simone, was released by Premier Records in the wake of her 1959 success 'I Loves You, Porgy'.

That LP – which has resurfaced from time to time throughout the years – was the subject of a lawsuit Nina initiated and won in 1965. *Starring Nina Simone* contained four songs: 'Black Is The Color Of My True Love's Hair' (originally a Norwegian folk song), 'Baubles, Bangles And Beads' (from the musical *Kismet*), 'Lovin' Woman' and 'Since My Love Has Gone', a song co-written by New Orleans star Aaron Neville. Some versions of the album (which featured completely separate recordings by Vince Guaraldi or, in some incarnations, George Wallington) also included 'I Loves You, Porgy' (from Gershwin's *Porgy And Bess*). According to Mauro Boscarol's excellent website (www.boscarol.com), all five songs were also part of an even earlier bootleg live session in Philadelphia that included 'Blue Prelude', 'Near To You', 'Remind Me', 'The Thrill Is Gone' and 'You Don't Know What Love Is'. Of note, versions of all but 'Lovin' Woman', 'You Don't Know What Love Is' and 'Baubles, Bangles And Beads' are available on the Tomato 1994 two-CD collection which does not offer any recording data, leaving speculation as to whether tracks on this compilation are actually from the original Philadelphia or Atlantic City bootleg live recordings.

Nina's work with Bethlehem Records, a subsidiary of King Records, came after label owner Sid Nathan heard a demo of songs she had made during a performance at a venue in New Hope, Pennsylvania. According to Nina's autobiography, Nathan originally wanted her to record songs of his choosing, but when she refused he relented and Nina chose material, much of which she had been performing at nightclubs up and down the US eastern seaboard.

In all, 14 songs were recorded in the session at an unknown studio in Manhattan, with Nina on piano accompanied by Albert 'Tootie' Heath (brother of saxophonist Jimmy and bassist Percy) on drums and Jimmy Bond on bass. Eleven tracks were used for the 1958 LP release *Little Girl Blue*, also released at various times under the titles *Jazz As Played In An Exclusive Side Street Club* and *The Original Nina Simone*. The repertoire – as would always be the case with every subsequent Simone recording – would be drawn from a wide array of musical sources: two songs, 'He Needs Me' and 'Don't Smoke In Bed' (recorded with just piano accompaniment) had been popularised by Peggy Lee; 'Plain Gold Ring', was a song previously sung by Kitty White, who had begun recording a year or two earlier. The LP also included Duke Ellington's 'Mood Indigo'; the popular jazz and pop standard 'Love Me Or Leave Me'; and 'I Loves You, Porgy', from the 1935 Gershwin opera *Porgy And Bess*, a song Nina first heard recorded by one of her own favourite vocalists, Billie Holiday, which would provide Nina with her first hit in the summer of 1959, after airplay first in Philadelphia and then in New York literally forced Bethlehem to release it as a single.

The album's original title track, 'Little Girl Blue' was from the songbook of writers Richard Rodgers and Lorenz Hart: in Nina's hands in took on a new meaning, using an inventive interpolation from the Christmas carol 'Good King Wenceslas'. Three of four instrumentals – focusing on Nina's brilliant classically trained piano style – were also a part of that first Bethlehem album: Rodgers and Hammerstein's 'You'll Never Walk Alone' (from the musical *Carousel*); 'Good Bait', co-written by band leader Count Basie; and 'Central Park Blues', a Simone original, so-named she referenced in her autobiography, because she had just finished a photo session in the New York park.

Rounding out the LP was 'My Baby Just Cares For Me', done by Nina with a loping ska-like beat which made it an instant favourite among Jamaican listeners who first heard in the early '60s. The song was originally written for a musical film, *Whoopee!*, and while it was supposedly part of Frank Sinatra's repertoire, he actually didn't record it until after Nina had done in 1957. Other versions that pre-date the definitive Simone recording include those by Nat King Cole (1943), singer Lorez Alexandria (1957), Woody Herman and Count Basie. The tune was not a regular part of Nina's repertoire until after the Chanel perfume company decided to use it for a highly successful UK ad campaign in

1985; thereafter, it became a fixture in live performances and, ironically – since it had originally been recorded at the very end of the sole Bethlehem session when an upbeat song was needed – one of Nina's most important and globally popular recordings.

In the wake of Nina's success with 'I Loves You, Porgy', Bethlehem took the three tracks remaining from that first 1957 session, threw in her 1959 hit and added tracks recorded by Chris Connor and Carmen McRae for the label to form *Nina Simone And Her Friends*, released in 1960. The three songs were the traditional spiritual 'He's Got The Whole World In His Hands'; the standard 'For All We Know', a song Nina often used as her final number in live shows in the '50s; and a Simone instrumental original, 'African Mailman'.

While Bethlehem chose to categorise Nina as a jazz performer, the repertoire on her one session for the company clearly took her beyond such categorisation. Her natural instinct for choosing songs that worked for her, and the stand she took on artistic integrity – expressed at the very start of what would be a prolific recording career – would become the hallmark of all her future work.

2. NO LIMITS

Nina was signed to Bethlehem Records for just one album, which in retrospect proved to be fortuitous. At the start of 1959, after she had moved to New York from Philadelphia, Nina pacted with Colpix Records, then a division of Columbia Pictures. In fact, it was a movie connection that led to the deal: Joyce Selznick, cousin of the famed Hollywood director/producer David O Selznick had brought her to the attention of Paul Wexler at Colpix, and by the spring Nina was ensconced in the studio to begin recording the first of what would be nine complete albums and some seven single sides that were never issued on LPs.

For her Colpix debut, *The Amazing Nina Simone*, the label assigned arranger Bob Mersey (who would go on to work with Andy Williams, Barbra Streisand, Julie Andrews, Johnny Mathis and a young Aretha Franklin at Columbia Records), and producer Hecky Krasnow (possibly a relative of industry executive Bob Krasnow).

The resultant sessions produced some tunes that featured big-band arrangements (on Benny Goodman's 'Stompin' At The Savoy') juxtaposed with gospel workouts (via the spiritual 'Children Go Where I Send You', an obvious throwback to Nina's church upbringing in North Carolina). The mix of tunes was dazzling, from the poignant theme from *Middle Of The Night*, a 1959

Columbia Pictures' movie based on a Paddy Chayefsky play starring Kim Novak), to the old English folk tune 'Tomorrow (We Will Meet Once More)'. Other highlights included the Marilyn Bergman co-penned torch song 'That's Him Over There' and Nina's reading of classics like 'Solitaire' and 'Blue Prelude'. The album was a veritable tour de force for an artist at the very start of her recording career.

While her first LP was well received, Colpix executives knew that the energy and spontaneity that occurred during Nina's live performances really captured the essence of her artistry. Thus, five of her albums for the label were recorded at clubs (such as New York's Village Gate) or prestigious venues such as Carnegie Hall and the famed Newport Jazz Festival. The first of such outings found Nina at Town Hall, a midtown Manhattan theatre perfectly suited to her, accompanied by Al Heath and Jimmy Bond, the latter the same musician who had worked with her on her Bethlehem debut.

Recorded on 12 September 1959, *Nina Simone At Town Hall* is universally considered one of Nina's best recordings and certainly one of the highlights of her Colpix years. Produced by Bob Blake and Jack Gold and arranged by Nina herself (as were all her Colpix albums), the focus was again on torch songs like 'The Other Woman' (previously recorded by Sarah Vaughan), 'You Can Have Him (I Don't Want Him)', an Irving Berlin composition found on albums by Peggy Lee and Ella Fitzgerald, and 'Exactly Like You', a very popular tune of the '40s recorded by a variety of artists from Carmen McRae to Louis Armstrong. Nina put her own stamp on Billie Holiday's 'Fine And Mellow' and turned in stellar performances on 'Summertime' (from *Porgy And Bess*) and 'Wild Is The Wind', the theme song from the 1957 film of the same name. But it was her beautiful arrangement of 'Black Is The Color Of My True Love's Hair' which, as the opening track for the album, set the mood for an amazing show, which also featured two Simone-penned instrumentals, 'Under The Lowest' and 'Return Home'.

A month later – possibly because the quality of live recordings in 1959 was not as advanced as it would become – Nina and her musicians were in a New York studio recording new versions of 'Exactly Like You', 'The Other Woman', 'Wild Is The Wind' and the folk song 'Cotton-Eyed Joe', which were then used for the final *Town Hall* album. At the same session, Nina also cut 'Since My Love Has Gone' and the Bessie Smith blues classic 'Nobody Wants You When You're Down And Out', which became Nina's first of just two charted singles during her Colpix years.

Clearly, the label knew that Nina's music didn't fit neatly onto the airwaves at the start of the '60s, but, nonetheless, Colpix made a couple of attempts by having Nina record singles such as 'If Only For Tonight' (coupled with 'What's Wrong With You And Me') and later, in 1961, 'Come On Back, Jack', an 'answer' song to Ray Charles's massive hit 'Hit The Road, Jack'. Nina had been assigned Stu Phillips, a new employee at Colpix, as her producer and Phillips – who would have one of the label's biggest hits with The Marcels' 'Blue Moon', as well as working with such varied artists as The Ronettes, The Monkees and The Chad Mitchell Trio – recalled making those early singles. 'I was a novice as a producer,' remembered Phillips, the author of *Stu Who?* (published by Cisum Press) in a January 2004 interview. 'I was aware of Nina from her success with "I Loves You, Porgy" and the guys at Colpix told me my job was to try and make money with her. We tried a couple of things – an aria with English lyrics ["If Only For Tonight"] – and then the answer song to the Ray Charles hit...'

Unfortunately, neither produced any significant sales activity, so sticking with a formula that worked, the label recorded Nina's auspicious debut at the Newport Jazz Festival on 30 June 1960, released as the album, *Nina At Newport*. While Phillips' name was listed as producer, he says that his role in the album was 'sequencing and mixing it'.

With guitarist Al Schackman, who had originally started working with Nina before her first Bethelehem album, Bobby Hamilton on drums and Chris White on bass, the seven-song set captured Nina in fine form on a selection of music that ranged from Cole Porter's 'You'd Be So Nice To Come Home To' (given a nearly six-minute workout that once again showcased Nina's incredible dexterity as a classically trained keyboardist), to the old blues tune 'Trouble In Mind' (issued by Colpix as a single in early 1961 and became a Top 10 R&B hit). Unlike on *At Town Hall*, music buyers were treated to Nina's ad libs (like her hilarious request for a tambourine at the start of 'Little Liza Jane') and introductions to certain songs like the poignant 'Porgy', a song about the same character in *Porgy And Bess* but not taken from the musical itself; and 'Flo Me La', an African-styled loping rhythmic piece credited as a Simone composition. A rousing version of 'In The Evening By The Moonlight' demonstrates that Nina was having a good time at the show, and we can assume the audience was having just as much fun! *Nina At Newport* is a brilliant showcase for her singular talent as a unique singer, whose ability in accompanying herself at the piano is almost unparalleled, and became her first and only Colpix album to make the US best-selling charts (in the spring of 1961).

Bassist White, who had joined the Simone band just months earlier, recalled in a January 2004 interview, 'Newport was a very important date and we came on just after this amazing performance by Duke Ellington. We were watching Duke and his band from backstage and they were incredible. Then, here comes Nina... and she had only had that one hit ["I Loves You, Porgy"].'

White says the songs chosen for the Newport show were 'mostly songs we were already doing in performances at clubs. I do remember that Nina was starting to do English folk tunes and "Little Liza Jane" was one of them. It was interesting because there was a little more interaction between Nina and the musicians vocally on that tune.'

Generally speaking, White – who quips that Nina 'gave me my pass out of the ghetto!' when he joined her band – says that the musicians would rehearse material for shows 'without charts. When Nina would do new material, we would learn it but we might never actually perform it. We had about thirty or forty songs to draw from and on any given night, you never knew what the set would be. We usually had half an hour of bonding with Nina before a performance and we'd get related so you would get a feeling for where the set might go, but it was an intuitive thing. And once you learned the songs, she might change the key on you! She would give you one note on the piano and you had to get the key for the song from that – and if you didn't hear that note...'

While it does not seem to have been recorded in front of a live audience, Nina's next album was 1961's *Forbidden Fruit* and utilised what became the trio of musicians at her Newport show and on subsequent performances until 1963. Produced by Cal Lampley, who had worked with such notables as Miles Davis, Dave Brubeck and Art Blakey, the ten-song set is considered by many to be Nina's finest studio work for Colpix. There is a cohesiveness and, for the most part, a consistency to the choice of material, with such mellow selections as 'I'll Look Around' and 'No Good Man' (both originally done by Billie Holiday), 'I Love To Love' and 'Where Can I Go Without You' (both previously cut by Peggy Lee), 'Just Say I Love Him' (with an appropriate gender change, recorded by singers Vic Damone and Eddie Fisher) and 'Memphis In June' from the Hoagy Carmichael songbook. No doubt, the plethora of love songs may have reflected events in Nina's own life, for it was in 1961 that she met and married Andy Stroud. With love on her mind, Nina was at her tender best, and the treatment she gave to those six songs is beautiful.

Rounding out *Forbidden Fruit* was 'Gin House Blues' and three songs from the pen of Oscar Brown Jr, a brilliant black poet, playwright and social commentator who began his own recording career in 1960. Two songs from *Sin And Soul*, Brown's debut for Columbia Records, 'Work Song' (written with Nat Adderley) and the haunting 'Rags And Old Iron' were chosen by Nina for her Colpix album. The title track – which gave Nina a chance to express the wry and often sassy humour which would become so much a part of her onstage persona in years to come – was also written and recorded by Brown for his first LP, but was issued later. Says Chris White, 'I don't actually remember ever going into the studio with Nina so I think "Forbidden Fruit" may have been done in front of a live audience and the applause taken out – but I can't be sure. I do remember that we were running a lot with Oscar Brown Jr in those days and he provided a wellspring for new material for Nina…'

Nina's popularity at different clubs throughout the US seemed to grow with each new album release, and one such venue had become her 'home' in New York City. Located at 160 Bleecker Street, in the heart of Greenwich Village, and owned by Art D'Lugoff, the Village Gate was a performance haven for the then up-and-coming Bob Dylan, the likes of John Coltrane, and comedians Woody Allen, Dick Gregory (who was also on Nina's first UK tour) and Richard Pryor (who opened for Nina on the night in April 1961 when she recorded an album at the club). The Village Gate was frequented by notable members of the black cultural revolution such as Langston Hughes and James Baldwin, who both become close associates and friends of Nina's.

Produced by Cal Lampley, *Nina Simone At The Village Gate* featured the now-familiar mix of diverse music that audiences had come to expect from Nina. A melancholy reading of 'House Of The Rising Sun' (a traditional song popularised by folk singer Josh White) fits right between the Rodgers and Hart lament 'He Was Too Good To Me' and a powerful interpretation of the standard 'Bye Bye, Blackbird', which gave Nina another opportunity to showcase her artistry at the keyboards. Her plaintive reading of Oscar Brown Jr's 'Brown Baby' (first recorded by Mahalia Jackson) is actually her first 'civil rights'-related recording, and, clearly, 'Zungo' (written by famed Nigerian percussionist Olatunji reflected Nina's growing bond with her own roots as an American of African descent. Two spirituals – a nearly eight-minute version of 'Children Go Where I Send You' (first cut on her Colpix debut) and the sombre 'If He Changed My Name' (recorded by Roberta Flack on her first Atlantic album) – and 'Just In Time' (from the 1957 Broadway musical *The Bells Are Ringing*) complete a highly satisfying album.

Worth noting is that the UK company Westside Records re-issued *Nina Simone At The Village Gate* as part of a two-CD set (along with *At Newport*) in 1998, and included seven previously unreleased tracks which supposedly belonged to Nina's *Village Gate* taping. However, the presence of percussionist Montego Joe on at least four of the songs suggests that all seven were likely to have been taped during Nina's 1963 performance at Carnegie Hall.

In 1962, Nina entered the studio to cut at least one entire album; while no specific session data is available, we can surmise that the release of the single 'I Want A Little Sugar In My Bowl' that same year means she recorded more than once in '62. What we do know is that Stu Phillips returned once again as Nina's producer for the 11-track project, a tribute to the musical genius Duke Ellington. The album *Nina Simone Sings Ellington* featured some Ellington classics such as 'Satin Doll', 'Solitude', 'I Got It Bad And That Ain't Good', 'It Don't Mean A Thing', 'Do Nothin' Till You Hear From Me' and 'Something To Live For' alongside some lesser-known compositions such as 'Merry Mending' and the quirky 'Hey, Buddy Bolden', an Ellington-penned nod to a New Orleans musician credited by some as the 'father of jazz', which Nina chose to sing at a rare Hollywood Bowl appearance in tribute to Ellington in the '90s. Some other favourites, such as the perky 'The Gal From Joe's' (recorded by Ellington himself as well as Charlie Barnet and Johnny Hodges), 'I Like The Sunrise' (also to be found on albums by Frank Sinatra, Mel Tormé and Al Hibbler) and 'You Better Know It' (cut by Claude Bolling and Lena Horne prior to Nina's recording) completed the session for *Sings Ellington*. Recalled producer Phillips in 2004, 'It was Nina's idea to do the Ellington album. It was a nice album, one that I'm very proud of. She and I worked well together and she was open to suggestions. She reminded me of a mild-mannered Barbra Streisand in her approach to working in the studio: Nina was not a time-waster because she knew the longer you spent the studio, the less money you'd make as an artist!'

Returning to the tried-and-tested formula of recording Nina in front of a devoted and enthusiastic live audience, the last 'official' Colpix recording was cut on 12 May, 1963 at New York's Carnegie Hall on 57th Street in midtown Manhattan. For sure, Nina performed two shows that night, since a total of 15 songs were issued via two albums, 1963's *At Carnegie Hall* (featuring seven songs) and 1964's *Folksy Nina* (with nine songs). Add in the seven songs left in a New York studio and rediscovered for UK Westside's 1998 re-issue, and it seems that Nina worked hard that May night, performing some 22 numbers.

At Carnegie Hall includes no less than three cinematically inspired pieces: 'Black Swan' from the musical opera and film *The Medium*; the Saint-Saëns' theme from the 1949 Cecil B De Mille's epic *Samson And Delilah*, which finds Nina accompanying herself at the piano on this beautiful piece – a reminder that many a classical musician had sat in the same spot at Carnegie Hall before her; and the Irving Berlin-penned theme from *Sayonara*, a 1957 movie starring Marlon Brando, in which Nina faithfully recreates the Japanese flavour of the film's setting. We can deduce from such choices that Nina loved to go the movies; after all her stage name was in part derived from her admiration for the work of French actress Simone Signoret!

A lovely Simone original, 'If You Knew' (featuring members of the Malcolm Dodd ensemble), is one of the album's highlights, along with 'The Twelfth Of Never' and 'Will I Find My Love Today' (both recorded and popularised by singer Johnny Mathis), while a medley of 'The Other Woman' and 'Cotton-Eyed Joe', tunes originally cut on Nina's *Town Hall* album, rounds out the LP. Since Nina had left Colpix in late 1963, the label wanted to make use of material left from the momentous shows at Carnegie Hall, thus 1964's *Folksy Nina*. The reprise of 'Twelfth Of Never' confirms that Nina did more than one performance at Carnegie Hall in May '63, as do a couple of versions of the spirited Israeli tune 'Erets Zavat Chalav'; one included on the original album and two found in the vaults and used on the 1998 Westside re-issue. For those who may be curious: the translation of the song from Hebrew into English reads 'The land flowing with milk, milk and honey.'

Folksy Nina was aptly named, for it featured bluesman Leadbelly's 'Silver City Bound'; two old English odes, the saucy 'The Young Knight' and the sorrowful 'Lass Of The Low Country'; and the traditional 'Hush Little Baby', combined in an interesting Simone-derived medley with 'You Can Sing A Rainbow' (previously recorded by The Four Freshmen) and 'Mighty Lak A Rose' (also cut by Paul Robeson and Frank Sinatra). A standout was the folk tune 'When I Was A Young Girl' (also recorded by Odetta), with Nina's keyboard mastery evident on the instrumental 'Vanetihu'.

The remaining songs from the *Carnegie Hall* sessions issued on Westside's *At Newport, At The Village Gate – And Elsewhere* are another version of 'Little Liza Jane'; an over-ten minute workout on 'Work Song' (previously recorded on the *Forbidden Fruit* album), which also features an interpolation of 'Good Bait' from her very first Bethlehem LP; a slow and ponderous piano-only version of 'You'll Never Walk Alone' (from *Carousel*); a torrid 'Sinnerman', a forerunner to the version Nina would do during her years with Philips Records, after she left Colpix; and the old spiritual 'Will I Find My Resting Place?', which finds Nina inviting her avid audience to clap along. She was accompanied at the New York venue by Al Schackman and Phil Orlando, both on guitar, Lisle Atkinson on bass (who replaced Chris White, who was responsible for introducing Atkinson to her and who would become a fixture in the Simone band until 1966) and as previously noted, renowned percussionist Montego Joe.

While the original recording dates are unknown, at least 11 more songs were recorded during Nina's Colpix years; what we do know is that the label took ten songs that had been 'in the can', added strings to some of them and released the set as *Nina Simone With Strings* in 1964, after she had signed with Philips. The resulting LP is a very strange mix of songs, ranging from what sounds like live recordings of 'I Loves You, Porgy' and 'Porgy, I Is Your Woman' from *Porgy And Bess*, the latter with strings added, and later without, to a rhythmic 'Blackbird' (not The Beatles' song but a Simone original) which actually does *not* feature strings at all! In fact, not a single violin can be heard on the old blues 'Gimme A Pigfoot (And A Bottle Of Beer)', which also has the feel of a live recording, or on an incorrectly named 'Chain Gang', which is not the Sam Cooke song but, in fact, Oscar Brown Jr's 'Work Song!'

Other tracks on the peculiarly sequenced LP: 'Falling In Love Again' (a song always associated with Marlene Dietrich), 'Baubles, Bangles And Beads' (from *Kismet*), the standards 'That's All', 'Spring Is Here' and 'The Man With A Horn', a song Nina would later record at RCA Records. Nina's reading of the Cole Porter standard 'Every Time We Say Goodbye' was issued for the first time on a 1992 Blue Note release, along with 'Baubles, Bangles And Beads'(without strings) and an alternate version of 'Gimme A Pigfoot' (with strings). At least six more songs, 'My Ship', 'Od Yesh Mama', 'Lonesome Valley', 'Golden Earrings', 'Ain't Nobody's Business' and 'Try A Little Tenderness' remain in EMI's vaults, where all the original Colpix masters are now stored.

That last selection of such varied songs perfectly sums up Nina's 70-odd recordings for Colpix: an impressive and ambitious pot-pourri of music that stretched the bounds of categorisation, incorporating African chants, Israeli folk songs, jazz standards, old English odes, movie themes, Ellington classics and old blues. It was just a taster of what was to come as Nina made the all-important move to an international label.

3. WEAVING SPELLS AND MAKING MAGIC

Nina's signing with Philips Records in late 1963 heralded a new and important period in her career. While Colpix offered her a consistent opportunity to record on a regular basis, the label's international reach was very limited: in the UK, for instance, Colpix's licensee was Pye Records and almost none of Nina's albums had been issued in Britain. As Nina herself recalled in her 1991 autobiography, Philips' label Wilhelm Langenberg flew from Holland to New York to sign her to the label, showing up in her dressing room at the Village Gate and unwilling to leave the city until Nina had put her signature to a recording contract with the company.

The Dutch-owned company was an established entity in Europe and had purchased Mercury Records in 1960, so the label also had a strong distribution system in the US. It was Philips's ability to market and promote Nina's music on a global basis that would alter her career definitively. Once signed, Philips decided to use the Colpix approach for Nina's first recording for the label, capturing her in concert at New York's Carnegie Hall on 21 March 1964. With the trio of Bobby Hamilton (drums), Lisle Atkinson (bass) and Rudy Stevenson (guitar) – which would become her consistent touring unit throughout her three years with Philips – Nina was in fine form that night, turning in a brilliant performance that included material that would become indelibly associated with her.

In a 2004 interview, bassist Atkinson noted, 'Nina basically came in prepared with the material and we would learn it at the rehearsals. I remember "Pirate Jenny"in particular because I played piano on the song. I was a bassist who played a little piano so I really had to get my chops up for that one!'

While she was clearly becoming more and more involved with the civil rights activities of the late '50s and early '60s, Nina's music had not necessarily reflected the stance she had taken as a pioneer for freedom and justice. Once she began recording for Philips, that changed dramatically: *In Concert*, her first release from the label, contained four of seven songs that were musical statements articulating her views. The highlight was unquestionably her own 'Mississippi Goddam', a riveting diatribe against the South, inspired by the killing of four young girls in a church bombing in Birmingham, Alabama, in September 1963: Nina had performed the song at the Village Gate to standing ovations, a scene that was repeated wherever she went. Once committed to wax, it became her first real anthem, banned in parts of the South and marking her as an artist unafraid of controversy.

On the same album was 'Go Limp', a tune she co-penned, which was a humorous take on the marches and demonstrations that were bringing people of all races together in the name of equality throughout the US at this critical juncture in the nation's history. 'Old Jim Crow' was another stark and clear indication of Nina's feelings on the struggle African-Americans faced in their daily lives, while a biting, bone-chilling, dramatic reading of 'Pirate Jenny' (written by Kurt Weill and Bertolt Brecht) from *The Threepenny Opera* continues to be one of Nina's most spectacular performances. She gave the song a whole new meaning in light of the civil rights struggle and left no one in any doubt that she meant business.

According to session information, the Carnegie Hall concert also included versions of 'I Loves You, Porgy', 'Plain Gold Ring' and 'Don't Smoke In Bed', all three songs from Nina's debut Bethlehem album. Other tunes ('Chilly Winds Don't Blow', 'Images', 'Wild Is The Wind', 'The Other Woman' and 'See-Line Woman') were recorded as part of the same concert but used on subsequent Philips albums without any indication that they were from a live performance.

Nina's first studio session for Philips took place from 16 April 1964, under the supervision of producer Hal Mooney, whose name would appear on many of the six albums the label would release between 1964 and 1967. Mooney's extensive credits included work with an illustrious list of artists that included Sarah Vaughan, Louis Armstrong, Dinah Washington, Dizzy Gillespie, Quincy Jones and Mel Tormé, so being in the studio with Nina was in keeping with the kind of performer he'd produced. More so than practically anyone else, however, Nina's penchant for being an artist without musical borders presented Mooney with a challenge, and while he masterminded the six songs cut in April '64 (including two, 'The Thrill Is Gone' – not the BB King tune but a '50s standard – and 'Near To You', which seems to be unreleased), Mooney was not the only arranger for Nina's first Philips studio album.

None of the songs Mooney recorded in April were used for *Broadway–Blues–Ballads* but ended up on subsequent albums; however, he did arrange five of the LP's 12 tracks. Horace Ott, a well-known and much-respected R&B arranger and conductor, worked on six songs and was also responsible for the more 'commercial' sides Nina recorded in '64 and '65. Key among the tracks was 'Don't Let Me Be Misunderstood', an original tune written for Nina by the team of Bennie Benjamin and Sol Marcus (with Gloria Caldwell), who penned half-a-dozen more songs for her during her Philips years. Of course, as pop music historians know, the British group The Animals (with Eric Burdon as lead singer) heard Nina's original almost as soon as it was released in the US and did their own version, making it a massive US and UK hit in early '65. Burdon is also quoted as saying that it was Nina's version of 'House Of The Rising Sun' (recorded on her *Village Gate* LP) that had inspired the group to do it themselves, giving them their first major hit single in '64.

Other Benjamin-Marcus tunes on *Broadway–Blues–Ballads* included the sassy 'Don't Take All Night', the plaintive 'I Am Blessed' and 'How Can I?', with Benjamin (not the renowned Motown drummer but a songwriter with many credits to his name) offering 'Our Love (Will See Us Through)' to the Ott-arranged session, which featured the New York backing vocal group heard on most R&B-related records, whose line-up included Dee Dee Warwick (sister of Dionne and future Mercury artist herself) and members of what would become The Sweet Inspirations. One Benjamin-Marcus song that did not make the LP, the strange 'A Monster' was used as the flipside of 'Don't Let Me Be Misunderstood'. Clearly, Philips and Nina's husband (and then manager) Andy Stroud, felt that the material she was cutting with Ott had a shot at being played on R&B radio of the day; while only one of the Philips tracks released as a single ever made the charts, the material was certainly up to par.

Mooney's work on *Broadway–Blues–Ballads* was marked by the kind of lush string and band arrangements clearly missing from Nina's Colpix recordings. Finally, Nina was being treated with the respect she deserved as an artist, and she rose to the occasion by selecting a stunning diversity of songs including an obscure Cole Porter tune, the sassy 'The Laziest Gal In Town'; Rodgers and Hammerstein's 'Something Wonderful' from *The King And I*; the old Scottish air 'The Last Rose Of Summer'; the Broadway show tune, 'Night Song' and; 'Nobody', a turn-of-the-century classic originated by Bert Williams, considered by *All Music Guide* as 'the recording industry's first important and enduring black artist'. An eclectic mix, indeed, rounded out with the hypnotic 'See-Line Woman', recorded at Carnegie Hall in March '64, a rhythmic tour de force that would remain in Nina's repertoire until her last few performances.

Bassist Atkinson played on the sessions Mooney arranged and conducted for *Broadway–Blues–Ballads* and recalls, 'We were working with ultra-learned musicians [in the orchestra]. The arrangements on songs like "Nobody" were beautiful and so well prepared. Nina was at the piano for most songs and we did the tunes mostly in one take.'

In January 1965 Nina was back in the studio for an album that would become her first international bestseller. The lead track and title cut was an unforgettable, intense, passion-filled rendition of Screamin' Jay Hawkins' 'I Put A Spell On You', considered by some (including this writer) as perhaps her finest-ever recording. The 12 tracks on the LP once again ran the musical gamut, but without any doubt the highlights included a haunting version of 'Ne Me Quitte Pas', a Jacques Brel composition that took on a life of its own in Nina's hands; 'Beautiful Land' and 'Feeling Good', two Anthony Newley–Leslie Bricusse tunes from *Roar Of The Greasepaint, Smell Of The Crowd*, the latter revived in a UK ad campaign and a club hit in 2002 because of its inclusion in the *Verve Unmixed* collection; two more French songs, 'Tomorrow Is My Turn' and 'You've Got To Learn', both originally recorded and co-written by Charles Aznavour; and 'Gimme Some' and 'Take Care Of Business', a pair of lyrical, risqué up-tempo tunes, credited to Nina's husband Andy and arranged by Horace Ott. Guitarist Rudy Stevenson contributed two songs, the tender 'One September Day' and a wonderful instrumental, 'Blues On Purpose'; and the entire *Spell* LP was completed with 'July Tree', with its childlike nursery-rhyme theme, a far cry from the stark soulfulness of the album's title track. Says bassist Atkinson, 'I only played on the Hal Mooney stuff and I do remember "I Put A Spell On You", but "Ne Me Quitte Pas" was truly a moving performance.'

By now enjoying her first taste of European success thanks to a 1965 visit to the UK and a subsequent appearance at the Antibes Jazz Festival, in France, Nina was hitting her stride as a recording artist when it was time to release another album. Tagged *Pastel Blues*, with a loose thematic concept, Nina's fourth LP forsook the big band and lush orchestral approach of her two previous Philips albums and focused instead on the stellar musicianship of her working trio (Stevenson, Atkinson and Hamilton), augmented by long-time associate Al Schackman on guitar. The nine tracks included a percussive, hypnotic, African-styled 'Be My Husband', credited to Andy Stroud; new recordings of 'Chilly Winds Don't Blow' and two blues songs, 'Trouble In Mind' and 'Nobody Knows You When You're Down And Out', all of which Nina had also recorded during her Colpix years; a wonderful contemporary blues tune, 'Ain't No Use' written by guitarist Stevenson; and the plaintive 'End Of The Line', a song previously done by singer Al Martino.

Unquestionably, the three standout pieces on *Pastel Blues* were a tension-building nearly 11-minute workout of the traditional 'Sinnerman', previously recorded live at Carnegie Hall by Colpix in 1963 but only released in 1998 on the UK Westside label; and Nina's treatment of two Billie Holiday songs: the smouldering 'Tell Me More And More And Then Some' and the classic 'Strange

Fruit', written for Holiday by Lewis Allan. The latter represented Nina's return to recording songs that reflected her feelings about the treatment of her fellow African-Americans, a stark and chilling recounting of the appalling lynchings that took place in the South way into the '50s. Nina's piano-and-vocal-only reading of the song is one of the most remarkable recordings she ever made and is undoubtedly the singular highlight on *Pastel Blues*. Atkinson says that several of the tunes on the album 'were songs from Nina's live repertoire that we recorded in the studio'.

Thanks to the kind of exposure and promotion Philips could offer, the LP became Nina's highest R&B-charting album in the US, reaching the Top 10 in late autumn 1965, and earning much acclaim among music buyers and critics in Europe who, by now, were increasingly aware of Nina's prodigious talent. Determined to keep the momentum going, she was back in the studio six months after completing work on *Pastel Blues* to cut tracks for what would be 'Let It All Out'. The album's title derived from a composition by well-known R&B songwriter and producer Van McCoy, written specifically for Nina: the brisk and bouncy 'Break Down And Let It All Out' was recorded on 1 October 1965, at the same time as another McCoy composition, the almost-classical 'For Myself', but for whatever reason was left off the final 'Let It All Out' set, and used on Nina's second 1966 release, 'Wild Is The Wind'.

Five tracks on the LP were recorded at the New York session that started on 30 September and ended on 1 October. Two of the tunes, 'Mood Indigo' and 'Love Me Or Leave Me', were also part of Nina's debut Bethlehem LP, the latter given a much more perky reading than in it original incarnation; another cut that Nina had done for that same album, 'Little Girl Blue', was left over from Nina's April '64 session and included on *Let It All Out*. The other tracks from '65 included a poignant reading of Billie Holiday's 'Don't Explain'; the explicitly raunchy blues 'Chauffeur', originally done by Memphis Minnie and credited to Andy Stroud; and Irving Berlin's enchanting 'This Year's Kisses'. The remainder of Nina's fifth Philips album consisted of two songs from a May 1965 session, Bob Dylan's 'Ballad Of Hollis Brown' and the traditional spiritual 'Nearer Blessed Lord'; a revisiting of 'The Other Woman' and Nina's own thought-provoking, 'Images', cut at her 1964 Carnegie Hall concert.

'Wild Is The Wind' was not a proper album in that – unlike earlier Philips' LPs (like *Broadway–Blues–Ballads* and *I Put A Spell On You*) – it was a conglomeration of tracks left from sessions done in 1964 and 1965. It could well have been that Nina was so busy touring both at home and abroad that there was little time to record. In fact, there was almost a year's gap between the October '65 session and Nina's final Philips recording date (August 1966). Surprisingly, even though the album, released in September 1966, was made up of 11 songs cut at different times, there was a consistency and flow to it, likely because many of the tracks were arranged by Horace Ott, whose penchant for cutting more R&B-flavoured material was evident in 'I Love Your Lovin' Ways' (left from the *I Put A Spell On You* sessions) and 'Why Keep On Breaking My Heart?', a pair of Benjamin–Marcus compositions. Ott, himself, contributed two songs: the hidden gem 'That's All I Ask' and 'What More Can I Say?'. On the same 1 October date when Nina cut *Break Down And Let It All Out*, she revived 'Either Way I Lose', another Van McCoy tune, originally recorded in 1964 by Gladys Knight And The Pips, giving it her very own special soulful flavour.

One of the perennial favourites from her live shows, 'Black Is The Colour Of My True Love's Hair', was left from the 1964 Carnegie Hall concert, while Nina's tour-de-force rendition of 'Wild Is The Wind' stemmed from her 6 April 1964 session and 'If I Should Lose You', a song also recorded by Dinah Washington (and one Nina would record almost 30 years later for her one-off Elektra album) was part of her May '65 recording date. However, the album's highpoint was the enduring classic 'Four Women', a one-of-a-kind Simone composition that was still one of the most requested songs in her repertoire until her last concerts in 2002. Recorded in September 1965 along with the ponderous 'Lilac Wine', the nearly five-minute razor sharp description of four different black women was simply outstanding, ending with all the intensity and passion for which Nina was known. No surprise that Nina could rarely do a show without including 'Four Women', guaranteed to bring the house down every time she performed it.

The High Priestess Of Soul (named no doubt in light of Aretha Franklin's crowning as 'The Queen Of Soul'), Nina Simone's final album for Philips, saw her working with Hal Mooney (credited as producer on all of her LPs for the company) as an arranger on 12 songs cut in a mammoth session on 26 August, 1966. Two tunes were new takes on Colpix cuts, Duke Ellington's 'The Gal From Joe's' and the Oscar Brown Jr–Nat Adderley composition, 'Work Song'; the rest of the album was Nina's usual heady mix of music from such different sources as Chuck Berry (via frisky 'Brown-Eyed Handsome Man') and her own guitarist Rudy Stevenson, represented with the brilliantly frantic 'I'm Gonna Leave You' and the gospel-flavoured, tambourine-waving 'I'm Going Back Home'. There was the traditional spiritual, 'Take Me To The Water', and the African-flavoured 'Come Ye', and two compositions penned by the team of Angelo Badalamenti and John Clifford: 'He Ain't Comin' Home No More' and 'I Hold No Grudge', a song delivered with an emotion-filled vocal from Nina that could have been interpreted as a statement on a personal relationship or a comment on racial injustice.

The mysterious 'Keeper Of The Flame' was one of the album's highlights, as was 'Don't You Pay Them No Mind', a song also recorded by Dee Dee Warwick during her stint with Mercury Records. A finger-snappin' 'I Love My Baby' completed Nina's seventh album for Philips, a song that was also part of a three-track session (along with 'Ding Song' and 'Sinnerman') apparently recorded during a live show at Washington DC's Cellar Door club in 1965, but never released. With Nina depicted more like an Egyptian queen than a high priestess on its outer sleeve, her swansong album for Philips may not have had the brilliance of *Pastel Blues*, the flow of *Wild Is The Wind*, the magic of *I Put A Spell On You* or the bite of *In Concert*, but it was a fitting end to a highly significant and important chapter in Nina's ascendancy as an artist continuing to develop an international profile, a profile that would reach new heights with her signing to RCA at the end of 1966.

4. THE SUN, THE MOON AND A STAR!

With the foundations that had been laid through her seven albums for Philips, Nina Simone was ready to move to the next level of global popularity, and signing with RCA Records would facilitate that. Her work with Philips had set her up for expanding her audiences, and while it took a few albums to get there, by 1968 she had reached a new plateau with audiences worldwide.

The emphasis at RCA was on finding material that would give her greater access and yet, ironically, two of the nine albums she cut for the label from 1966 to 1974 were more concept-driven: 1967's *Sings The Blues* and the 1969 classic *And Piano!* Nina began sessions for her debut set for RCA on 19 December, 1966 using the label's 'B' studio in Manhattan for a two-song session, working with some of New York's finest musicians: drummer Bernard Purdie, guitarist Eric Gale, bassist Bob Bushnell, Ernie Hayes on organ and Buddy Lucas on harmonica (featured heavily on the sessions) and tenor sax. As always, Nina accompanied herself at the piano and included touring guitarist Rudy Stevenson on the first RCA recording dates which continued on 22 December and then again on 1 and 5 January 1967.

Produced by Danny Davis (who had a background in country and jazz), the 11 songs that comprised *Nina Simone Sings The Blues* (released in the summer of '67) included two bona fide, highly suggestive, blues tunes, 'I Want A Little Sugar In My Bowl' and 'In The Dark' (a song associated with Lil Green). The '30s classic, 'Since I Fell For You' (written by Buddy Johnson and recorded by him and his sister Ella) was soulfully Simone-ised, while Nina's revival of 'The House Of The Rising Sun' was notably different from her previous take on the song, now transformed into a driving, upbeat ditty. Referencing the musical opera that had jumpstarted her own recording career, the emotion-filled 'My Man's Gone Now' is from *Porgy And Bess* and one of the outstanding performances on the album.

Biting and bristling with intensity, 'Backlash Blues' was co-written by Nina with famed black playwright Langston Hughes; it became a fixture in Nina's live '60s repertoire, a no-holds-barred statement on the pervasive racism that continued to impact on black men and women fighting for economic power and civil liberties in America at a time when the nation was deeply divided over the war in Vietnam. Nina worked with another popular black song stylist, Abbey Lincoln, in crafting the slow 'n' deep 'Blues For Mama', and, as had become customary on a number of her previous albums, she referenced her own upbringing, singing and playing in church, via an adaptation of the traditional spiritual 'Real, Real'.

Moving from the sacred to the secular, her own 'Do I Move You?' and 'Buck' (penned by Andy Stroud) were straight expressions of lust and desire. While critics tended to focus on her political statements, particularly through the '60s, Nina's humour and penchant for singing songs with unabashed sexual connotations (try 'Gimme Some', 'Chauffeur', 'Don't Take All Night' and 'Tell Me More And More And Then Some') didn't stop when she signed for RCA. Perhaps more than any other LP she cut for the label, *Sings The Blues* explored that side of Nina's personality. 'Day And Night', written by guitarist Stevenson, was an upbeat cut that fitted neatly into that category and was the first single released by RCA in the hope of gaining some R&B radio airplay in the US. Worth noting: there was a second, slightly faster and less raw version of 'Do I Move You?' cut on 5 January which was eventually released on the 1997 RCA CD re-issue, *Saga Of The Good Life And Hard Times*.

Producer Danny Davis recalled in a January 2004 interview his first meeting with Nina: 'She came into my office at RCA – which was not large – wearing a white turban and turned to me and said, "Do you know my music?" I replied,

"Yes, but not as well as you do, Nina." Then she asked, "Do you know my people?" and I answered again, "Yes, but not as well as you do!" She looked at me and said, "Well, I've heard some nice things about you but you're white." Then she smiled and said, "Maybe we'll be friends," and then walked out! That was our first meeting and the first album we did together went very smoothly. She liked the musicians I hired – like the guitarist Eric Gale – and we did two or three takes on most songs and that was it. Recording with Nina was a very enjoyable experience and she was easy to record: if I had a suggestion, she would listen...'

Nina's next trip into RCA's studio came in June 1967: once again working with producer Davis, the ten songs that formed *Silk & Soul* were derived from a variety of musical sources, with the aim to present Nina in a more sophisticated setting with a full complement of strings and brass players (Davis's forte). Contemporary tunes of the day – Burt Bacharach and Hal David's 'The Look Of Love' (from the James Bond movie, *Casino Royale*) and 'Cherish', an autumn 1966 hit for the pop group The Association – were given Nina's royal treatment. Producer Davis had spoken with songwriter Hal David, a good friend, about possible Bacharach–David songs he could do with Nina and David suggested 'The Look Of Love' which, Davis says, 'she knew and liked'.

The real gold on Nina's second RCA LP – less silk and more soul – lay in songs like 'Go To Hell', a somewhat restrained recording (given the lyrical content!), which came to life when Nina performed it in concert; jazzman Billy Taylor's 'I Wish I Knew How It Would Feel To Be Free', an anthem that Nina took on and made very much her own; and John D Loudermilk's suggestive 'Turn Me On' which producer Davis had suggested.

Martha Holmes's 'Turning Point' was a well-crafted song that illustrated the impact of racial prejudice, recounting the story of two little girls who become friends only to be separated by the ignorance and bias of one of their mothers. Producer Davis says the song was actually given to him by an air-hostess: 'I met her on a plane trip and she told me she wrote songs and sent me that one. I thought it was perfect for Nina because of its subtle message and I played it to her when we were preparing to do the second album and she agreed to do it immediately.' Standouts on *Silk & Soul* was Nina's own stately 'Consummation', in which she shared her personal belief in reincarnation (a theme explored again on her fourth RCA LP) and the possibility of the reuniting of soulmates. The album included two snappy upbeat tunes, 'Some Say' and 'It Be's That Way Sometime', which came from the pen of Nina's talented musician brother, Sam Waymon; and husband Andy contributed the bluesy 'Love O' Love' which sounded more like it belonged on Nina's first RCA LP.

Producer Davis says that a live album done during a rare Simone performance in Las Vegas was planned, but three days before the gig, Nina nixed the idea and she completed 1967 with a three-song session in New York on 20 December. Delving into the songbook of the brothers Gibb, known the world over as The Bee Gees, she chose two tunes: 'To Love Somebody' (which would become a Top 20 pop hit for her in February 1969) and 'I Can't See Nobody' (the flipside of the single); the third tune was the old standard 'The Glory Of Love' (revived by Otis Redding in 1967), which remained un-issued until it was used on a 2003 BMG two-CD anthology covering Nina's entire career, compiled by this writer.

Following the example set during her Colpix and Philips years, RCA decided next to record Nina live in concert at an early April 1968 show at Westbury Music Fair in upstate New York. This would become the album 'Nuff Said!. No one could have known that three days before, on 4 April, the world would be shaken by the assassination of the pre-eminent civil rights leader, Dr Martin Luther King. The impact on Nina – who knew Dr King personally – was deep and profound. With angry riots taking place all over the US in wake of his passing, Nina decided the best course of action was to move forward with the concert on 7 April, the day President Lyndon Johnson had declared a national day of mourning. In memory of Dr King, to whom Nina dedicated the whole concert, she recorded a song composed by bass player Gene Taylor. 'Why? (The King Of Love Is Dead)' is sung with the honest sense of loss that Nina clearly felt. The original emotionally charged dialogue that was part of Nina's live performance was edited, as was the song itself; in 1997, re-issue producer Paul Williams restored the original take as part of a three-song piece he named *Dr Martin Luther King, Jr Suite*.

Included in the suite were an extended version of 'Sunday In Savannah' and an understandably angry reprise of Nina's 'Mississippi Goddam' (in which at one point she substitutes 'Alabama' with 'Memphis', the city where King was killed). Both songs were filled with the kind of authenticity that audiences could always expect from her, and while it was not part of the suite that Williams created in 1997, Nina's live version of 'Backlash Blues' from the Westbury show was just as furiously real.

The original concert at Westbury featured a remarkable 17 songs: the *Saga Of Good Life* re-issue included one previously un-issued cut, and a revival of 'Come Ye' (previously recorded on her last Philips LP); other songs that remain in the can include a rare live version of 'Don't Let Me Be Misunderstood', 'Go To Hell' (from *Silk & Soul*), the spiritual 'Bless The Lord' and two unknown tunes, 'Cause I Know' and 'You've Got To Move'. What was released on *'Nuff Said!* was typical of a Simone performance, an imaginative mix of songs from Broadway to blues. Nina chose another pair of Bee Gees songs, 'In The Morning' and 'Please Read Me', added 'I Loves You, Porgy' (a seemingly mandatory item in her repertoire), offered the time-honoured hymn 'Take My Hand, Precious Lord' and went to town with a rousing 'Gin House Blues'.

'Peace Of Mind', a song also recorded by Nancy Wilson, was recorded at Westbury as was a medley of 'Ain't Got No – I Got Life', two songs from the Broadway musical *Hair*.

But as re-issue producer Williams discovered many years after the 1968 issue of the original LP, what was actually heard on the final album were re-recordings of the *Hair* songs and of the Bee Gees' 'In The Morning', all cut on 13 May. Additional studio recordings of 'Peace Of Mind' and 'Ain't Got No – I Got Life' were also done on 24 June, along with Nina's memorable cover of the Jim Webb song, 'Do What You Gotta Do', which became one of her three Top 50 US R&B hits for RCA. Somewhat unexpectedly, the *Hair* medley became a massive hit in the UK at the end of '68, giving Nina's European career a major boost. It virtually made her a household name in Britain and assured her of a loyal audience for the duration of her career.

According to the website of Simone expert, Mauro Boscarol, Nina did a studio session in Rome in June 1968; we can presume that this may have been Italian language versions of three songs, but the results of the recording date were never issued, and nor were the four tunes cut live during Nina's emotional appearance at the Montreux Jazz Festival on 16 June, which she comments on in her 1991 autobiography: 'As I walked out on stage the true weight of the last month's events hit me. I tried to gather myself – but it didn't work. I sat down at the keyboard and tears started rolling down my cheeks, one after another, unstoppable...' Nina was responding not just to the April assassination of Dr King but to the murder of Bobby Kennedy on 5 June, just two months later.

Constantly busy on the road, both at home and abroad, Nina finally returned to making a new record in September 1968. This time, it was about creating an album that was an expression of her artistry, with little regard for charts and sales. Ironically, of course, within months of recording the 14 songs for *Nina Simone And Piano!*, she found herself with a big UK pop hit. However, when she sat down at the keyboards to cut the LP, hit records were not on her mind! At the grand piano in RCA's Studio B on 16 September, Nina was in rare form, accompanying herself on a brilliant selection of ten songs (the number of tracks finally included on the album).

The first song on the session was the old spiritual 'Nobody's Fault But Mine' (also recorded by the late Otis Redding), which was given a wonderful workout. The five tunes that followed were perfect vehicles for Nina to stretch vocally: Randy Newman's 'I Think It's Going To Rain Today', which expressed the sense of outrage she felt at what seemed like the lack of caring she experienced in a culture increasingly emphasising materialism above human contact; British pop star and latter-day impresario Jonathan King's somewhat bizarre 'Everyone's Gone To The Moon', on which Nina's sense of drama and commitment to quirky self-expression is in full evidence; the stately 'Compensation' (marked on the original tape box as 'Compassion'), which finds Nina double-tracking her own voice with an overdubbed organ part, based on a poem by African-American 19th century writer Paul Lawrence Dunbar; Hoagy Carmichael's 'I Get Along Without You Very Well (Except Sometimes)', a bitter-sweet love song that had been recorded by a number of other artists including Frank Sinatra, Chet Baker, Billie Holiday and Peggy Lee, given a melancholy and poignant reading by Nina; and 'The Desperate Ones', co-written by one of Nina's favourite French artists, Jacques Brel, an eerie, marvellously mysterious tune that could be about the lonely, the unloved, perhaps addicts or everyday human beings dealing with a certain hopelessness about life. Nina's performance on the song is simply outstanding, unbridled, unrestrained, and completely free of any constraint.

Four other songs that Nina recorded that September day in '68 remained unreleased until BMG put out an expanded edition of the critically acclaimed album in 2001, an album Nina claimed (in a 1999 interview) as the one piece she would most want to be remembered for. Accompanying herself at the organ, Nina offered 'Music For Lovers', a song previously recorded by '50s vocal harmony group The Hi-Los, virtually transforming it into a hymn; she would re-record the tune for her famed *Baltimore* album in 1978; and 'In Love In Vain', a tune that Sarah Vaughan and Gloria Lynne among other song stylists had done before Nina tackled it: in her hands, it is a little dark and sombre.

Nina also decided to re-do Billie's Holiday's 'I'll Look Around' for the *Piano* session. A tune she had originally recorded for her Colpix album, *Forbidden Fruit*, it was notably different from the '61 version; this time more pensive. Nina had cut 'The Man With The Horn' for Colpix and it was issued on the

Strings album in 1966: this version is more expansive and, once again, an opportunity for Nina to sing without any restriction or restraint. To some ears, the vocal performance is a little 'off', but then Nina's modus operandi was always to go for emotion over technique!

On 1 October, Nina returned to RCA's studios to finish off the album with another four songs, three of which she had tried on 16 September; the final LP included the takes from that October date. Aretha Franklin's sister, Carolyn, had written the song 'Seems I'm Never Tired Lovin' You' and, in addition to Nina's warm reading of the ballad, the group The Swordsmen, a male duo originally signed to Ninandy Records (a label started by Nina's husband-manager Andy Stroud) who occasionally opened for Nina on US and UK shows, had released it as a single. Several tunes on *And Piano!* dealt with eternally heady questions such as the purpose of life, ageing, life after death and death itself: Leonard Bernstein's 'Who Am I?' leaves one in no doubt as to Nina's viewpoint on reincarnation! Delivered with intensity and passion, she asks if she may have lived as 'a rooster or a hen'.

'Another Spring', penned by Badale and Clifford, the same team who had written songs for Nina's *High Priestess Of Soul*, was a remarkable piece: an African-American woman reflecting on a full life, on what the future holds, and concluding with an expression of gratitude for seeing one more year. It is classic, pure Nina, as is 'The Human Touch', the final song cut for this unparalleled album. As she did with 'I Think It's Going To Rain Today' and 'Everyone's Gone To The Moon', she chose a song that asked whether the rush towards material gain was at the expense of a basic and essential tenet of life itself. Thirty-five years later, in an age of reality shows and on-line sex, the question seems even more valid.

As brilliant as *Nina Simone And Piano!* was, it was strictly for hardcore devotees. Fortunately, in hindsight it has achieved prominence and stature as one of Nina's most stunning works, but in February 1969, it didn't fit any radio formats and had very limited sales impact. While RCA had been happy to indulge Nina's desire to express her art, the company was aware that, finally, Nina was enjoying unbelievable mainstream success in the UK thanks to 'Ain't Got No – I Got Life' and 'To Love Somebody' (released at the suggestion of this book's authors). Anxious to cash in on such activity, Andy (by now acknowledged as producer on all of Nina's albums) set up another RCA session in January 1969, covering three dates and a total of seven songs, to become the album, *To Love Somebody*. While that may have been the idea, Ms Simone must have had some other ideas! Rather than finding a suitable follow-up to her British hits, Nina focused on material written by contemporary songwriters and artists of note, such as Bob Dylan, Leonard Cohen and Pete Seeger. There was an almost folksy approach to the selection of the songs, which in many ways continued Nina's tradition of finding tunes that expressed her feelings about the social conditions of the day. Dylan's 'I Shall Be Released' and the magnificent 'Times They Are A-Changing' (with a beautiful organ accompaniment) typified this, as did Seeger's classic 'Turn! Turn! Turn!', a 1965 chart-topper for The Byrds.

In keeping with the general drift of the material there was Nina's own 'Revolution'; far from folksy! A strange mix of funk, gospel and psychedelia, the song – written with new collaborator, keyboardist Weldon Irvine Jr – was not well received in Britain; it was maybe a little too 'out there' for UK music buyers, who liked their Simone a little tamer. US R&B radio played the song when it was issued as a single in April 1969, and it made the soul charts; one wonders in hindsight whether disc jockeys ever played Part 2 of the song, which ends with a touch of musical insanity, Nina thumping away at the piano in wild abandon, bringing the tune to an almost apocalyptic ending, as UK writer Mike Butler stated in liner notes for the 2002 re-issue of the LP.

Nina's melodically pleasing version of Leonard Cohen's 'Suzanne' may have served as the model for future readings of the poetic song by such artists as Roberta Flack and, many years later, Dianne Reeves; while scribe Butler describes Nina's cover of Bob Dylan's epic 'Just Like Tom Thumb's Blues' as 'more faithful to the subject matter than Dylan's original'.

The versions of both 'Suzanne' and 'Turn! Turn! Turn!' were redone respectively on 5 March and 22 April and used for the final LP, which also included the pair of Bee Gees songs (the title cut and 'I Can't See Nobody') from the December 1967 session; the original January take of 'Suzanne' surfaced for the first time in 1998 on the two-CD RCA set *The Very Best Of Nina Simone: Sugar In My Bowl*.

Since the *To Love Somebody* LP was originally designed to capitalise on Nina's European success, it made little initial impression in the US, even though 'Revolution' did make the R&B charts. Looking for a possible follow-up hit, Nina was back in the studio in August 1969 for a four-song session, accompanied by such stellar musicians as Richard Tee on organ, guitarist Eric Gale, bassist Jerry Jemmott and percussionist Montego Joe, among others. Weldon Irvine Jr was now an integral member of Nina's touring band, and arranged the session as well as co-writing one of the quartet of tunes recorded. The song was 'Young, Gifted And Black', and the title was inspired by Nina's friend, playwright, Lorraine Hansberry; it would become a real anthem for people of colour the world over, and in addition to giving Nina her last US–charted single (No. 8 R&B, No. 76 in the pop charts), the tune would also be recorded by Aretha Franklin as the title track for her 1972 gold album and by the late Donny Hathaway on his 1970 Atco debut.

Other songs from the same session were a funky remake of 'Save Me', a song co-written by Aretha, her sister Carolyn, and sax master King Curtis, featured on Franklin's historic Atlantic debut LP, *I Never Loved A Man (The Way I Love You)* and used as the flipside for 'Young, Gifted And Black'; and two tracks released as a single in 1970, a remake of 'Whatever I Am (You Made Me)', a Willie Dixon tune previously recorded by blues diva KoKo Taylor, and 'Why Must Your Love Well Be So Dry?'. Nina's performance on these latter two songs is less than inspired, considered by some her worst recording for RCA, and if the purpose was to create another 'hit' for her, it failed miserably.

Far more inspiring and satisfying was the work Nina did at Philarmonic Hall in New York City on 26 October 1969 preserved through the release of 'Black Gold', her sixth album for RCA. Nine songs were recorded that night with special guest musician Emile Latimer (known for his work as a percussionist with Ritchie Havens) sitting in with drummer Don Alias and percussionist Jumma Santos; Weldon Irvine Jr played organ, and on certain songs, the male duo The Swordsmen provided background vocals. Nina opened with the Simone staple 'Black Is The Color Of My True Love's Hair', segueing into another version of the song written and performed by Latimer: the contrast is interesting, with Latimer's mournful vocalising taking the song to a new place. A somewhat harried and hurried 'Ain't Got No – I Got Life' followed and, at the original show, Nina moved onto 'Suzanne', which is still unreleased. The Afro-Cuban rhythmically hypnotic 'Westwind' was an almost ten-minute-long epic Nina described as 'a prayer', noting that she was told to sing the song by long-time friend, South African singer Miriam Makeba. It is one of the album's centrepieces, featuring the masterful work of Alias and Santos.

A version of Richie Haven's 'No Opportunity Necessary' that followed was never issued; *Black Gold* continued with a ten-minute-plus rendition of 'Young, Gifted And Black', which received an appropriately enthusiastic response from the audience. Nina ends the concert with two interesting choices: 'Who Knows

Where The Time Goes', written by Sandy Denny of the British folk group Fairport Convention, beautifully executed and also recorded by Judy Collins; and 'The Assignment Sequence', a Jen Hendin composition which took on a personal meaning for Nina as she noted, 'The song is about the gap between lovers...especially married lovers!' In an earlier comment, before introducing 'Who Knows Where The Time Goes', Nina makes a clear reference to 'being tired', quoting actress Faye Dunaway's comment on her appearance in the popular movie of the day, *Bonnie And Clyde* and how important it is to 'give people want they want'.

Cryptically, Nina disagrees and notes, 'You use up everything you got trying to give people what they want. But I will learn my lesson soon,' she adds, 'and then you will buy more records and you won't see me!'

What the packed audience didn't know was that Nina's marriage to then-manager Andy Stroud was unravelling; she felt that there was too much pressure for her to continue working, and in the year that followed the spring release of *Black Gold*, her best-selling RCA LP, Nina and Andy split up. In the wake of what was a major change in her life, Nina's January 1971 return to the studio to record *Here Comes The Sun* found her in a different space musically. Working with renowned arranger and producer Harold Wheeler, and Nat Shapiro, a well-known author and writer, Nina took songs of hope and inspiration like George Harrison's 'Here Comes The Sun', 'O-o-h Child', a 1970 hit for R&B group The Five Stairsteps, Tin Pan Alley writers Cynthia Weil and Barry Mann's 'New World Coming', and even the Paul Anka-penned Frank Sinatra anthem, 'My Way' (with an outstanding arrangement by Wheeler), and made them very much her own, turning in stellar performances.

The personal ache she might have felt in the wake of the end of her marriage was evident in Nina's interpretation of Bob Dylan's 'Just Like A Woman', a song she continued to perform into the 21st century. Rounding out what is still considered by some as her best album for RCA were a heartfelt performance of 'Mr Bojangles', a Jerry Jeff Walker song popularised by Sammy Davis Jr; 'Angel Of The Morning', a UK hit for former Ikette PP Arnold, revived by Merilee Rush in 1968, given a completely different take by Nina, with a soulfully slow reading that emphasises the lyrical beauty of the song; and the gospel-like 'How Long Must I Wander', penned by Weldon Irvine Jr, tailor-made for Nina, a song that in retrospect had an air of fate about it, for – in the years that followed – she would indeed 'wander' the globe, living in Barbados, Liberia and Europe, a world-weary (and sometimes soul-weary) traveller in search of love and peace of mind. She invests the song with such honesty and passion that the listener is left in no doubt that it reflects her personal feelings.

Here Comes The Sun is a Simone masterpiece, with Wheeler providing perfectly suited, beautiful orchestral arrangements and just the right musical balance. With all the turmoil Nina experienced in the years that preceded its creation, the album is possibly Nina's most personal; the songs seemed to reflect what she was experiencing, from 'My Way', a statement of no regrets, to the bright and joyful 'O-o-h Child'. It is simply stunning, as were four songs ('My Father', 'Jelly Roll', 'Tell It Like It Is' and '22nd Century') recorded during those February sessions that were never logged and could have stayed lost for ever had it not been for the work of re-issue producer Paul Williams, who uncovered them in the vaults while doing research for the 1998 2-CD set *Sugar In My Bowl*.

Nina attempts Judy Collins's 'My Father', but after a verse or two stops, declaring she doesn't want to sing 'this song…it's not me. My father never promised we'd live in France…he promised we'd live in peace… Okay, we have to skip that one…' She would eventually tackle the song on her 1978 album, *Baltimore*. Skipping indeed, she moved to a wonderfully funky, jazz-flavoured eight-minute-plus workout on the song 'Jelly Roll', a brilliant showcase for her keyboard mastery that includes an interpolation of 'In The Evening When The Sun Goes Down'. Nina is having big fun with the musicians, as she shares her thoughts on contemporary black life, referencing everything from soul food to the music of the day, declaring 'Ain't that bad, ain't that black, ain't that fine!' It is one of Nina's finest recordings, a free-form liberating piece that shows the essence of her artistry.

Aaron Neville's 1966 classic, 'Tell It Like It Is', was given a bluesy reading by Nina, and with the accompaniment of a sympathetic rhythm section, she sings with verve, even though she does forget to change the song's gender early on, declaring she is 'not a little boy!' While this particular cut was good, it pales in comparison with the nearly nine-minute monumental opus '22nd Century', in which Nina considers the fate of humanity with 'ghosts and goblins walking this land', a world in which there would be 'no more babies born, there is no one and there is everyone'. It is sheer brilliance – Nina at her most expressive – backed by a Trinidadian steel drum, '1990', she says, 'was the year when the plague struck the earth', a chilling prediction that, in hindsight, could have referred to the AIDS epidemic. There is a 'liberation of women, liberation of men' and Nina declares the 22nd century will be a time when there will be 'a revolution of music', a time when 'man is woman, woman is man, even your brain is not your brain'. It is without parallel in her recorded legacy; Nina at her most creative, lyrically explosive, performed with the kind of zest and passion only she could bring. Big kudos to re-issue producer Williams, for allowing us to hear what is certainly a complete Simone gem.

In case anyone was in any doubt that with *Here Comes The Sun*, Nina had lost any of her political and social conscience, she was back with a vengeance with the 1972 release *Emergency Ward*. The album's cover art made it perfectly clear: Nina was addressing the bitter struggle over the unpopular war in Vietnam. Performing for a primarily black military audience at Fort Dix, she took George Harrison's 'My Sweet Lord' and backed by the Bethany Baptist Church junior choir, featuring brother Sam Waymon and daughter Lisa, turned it into an almost 20-minute opus segueing into 'Today Is A Killer', a tune based on a poem by David Nelson, predicting the 'reality of today, grinning its all-knowing fiendish grin...pressing its ugly face against mine...' The track ends with a fierce declaration: 'Today, who are you, Lord? You are a killer!'

While it appears to be a live album, the other three songs that comprise *Emergency Ward* came from recording sessions with accomplished producers Harold Wheeler and Nat Shapiro: 'Isn't It A Pity', another George Harrison tune, cut for the *Here Comes The Sun* sessions, which takes on a new dimension extended to an 11-minute piece with additional highly potent lyrics by Nina; and 'Poppies', recorded in February 1972, a four-minute song whose subject matter is stark and real, referencing the ravages of drug addiction.

Had *Emergency Ward* been her final RCA album, it would have been a somewhat curious end to an extremely important chapter in Nina's career. Instead, her eight-year stay with the label ended fittingly with *It Is Finished*, released in 1974, based for the most part on a live concert at New York's Philarmonic Hall. With long-time musical associate Al Schackman on guitar and Nadi Quamar on an exotic variety of African percussive instruments (including the guinee kuna, the Madagascar harp, the mama-likembi and the tal viha), Nina opened the show in fine form with the traditional spiritual 'Com' By H'Yere-Good Lord', moving into a couple of songs from her existing repertoire, 'I Want A Little Sugar In My Bowl' and 'Mr Bojangles'. The show's highpoint came with two tunes: the undulatingly evocative 'Dambala' and the menacing 'Obeah Woman' (in which Nina exhorts, 'To get to Satan, you gotta go through me!'), both with an Afro-Caribbean flavour. No surprise, given Nina had been spending more and more time in Barbados.

A couple of songs, a Simone original, 'A Charge To Keep I Have', the standard 'After You've Gone' and a version of Bert Williams' 'Nobody' (a song Nina recorded for the *Broadway–Blues–Ballads* album in 1964) appear to have been part of the original show, but have never been issued.

For whatever reason, RCA gave the impression that the entire *It Is Finished* album was recorded live: in reality, one of the songs, 'Let It Be Me', a warm and tender cover of a song popularised by the Everly Brothers and later Betty Everett and Jerry Butler, featuring Nina's brother Sam was from the 1971 *Here Comes The Sun* sessions; while a tantalising, heavily percussive reading of 'Funkier Than A Mosquito's Tweeter', a 1971 Ike and Tina Turner original, and a no-kidding, biting rendition of Hoyt Axton's 'The Pusher', were from a studio session Nina herself produced at RCA's Manhattan studio on 24 June 1971.

With a front cover depicting Nina looking somewhat stoic sitting among what appear to be shells and stones, *It Is Finished* (actually a quote from the New Testament) seems to be Nina Simone's declaration of the end of an era. Indeed it was: she would spend the years that followed living in different countries, occasionally recording and performing in Europe, returning to the US from time to time. She would virtually become the spell-weaving 'Obeah Woman' of whom she sang, a free spirit, a soulful adventurer, living her own truth...

5. END OF AN ERA

From 1974 until her passing in 2003, Nina Simone's output as a recording artist was minimal, consisting of some half a dozen 'official' releases, and countless albums that were unauthorised. Indeed, looking at any complete list of everything released during the nearly 30 years she was without a consistent recording contract, it is amazing that she may have been one of the most bootlegged artists in music history.

Sorting out which releases may have been sanctioned by Nina herself is nigh on impossible, so mention of any of the following albums does not imply they were bootlegs! We do know that some (52) master recordings were returned to Nina in 1995 in a judgment by a San Francisco court against San Juan Music, beginning at least to offer some redress for the dozens of LPs and CDs that bear her name and for which she, no doubt, received no compensation.

Starting in the early '70s, three LPs, *Sings Billie Holiday*, *The Gospel According To Nina Simone* and *Live At Berkeley* – were issued through ex-husband Andy's Stroud Productions. A 1974 live LP, *Portrait Of Nina*, consisting of ten songs, on the Trip label, made the R&B charts. In 1977 the same company issued the 12-song set *Live In Europe* (also released as *The Great Live Show In Europe*), apparently based on a 1968 performance at the Olympia Theatre in Paris, and possibly the same recording released as the *Suzanne* CD in 1990 by Moon Records. Orginally taped for an April 1968 German television show, an album entitled *A Very Rare Evening* was issued in 1979 and re-issued on a Japanese CD in 2003; it consisted of eight songs, including rare live versions of 'Save Me', 'I Think It's Going To Rain Today' and 'Revolution'.

Nina's first contract-related recording following her departure from RCA came in 1978, when she signed with jazz veteran Creed Taylor's CTI label. While Nina herself had reservations about the album after the fact (expressed candidly in her *Blues & Soul* interview with Sylvia [Hampton] in September of that year), the one-off album she recorded for the New York-based label remains one of her best recordings. With beautiful string arrangements by conductor David Matthews (whose credits included work with Bonnie Raitt, Grover Washington Jr, George Benson, James Brown and Earl Klugh, as well as a slew of albums as a saxophonist in his own right), some masterful playing by such New York session stalwarts as bass players Will Lee and Gary King, guitarists Eric Gale and Jerry Friedman, drummers Jim Madison and Andy Newmark and percussionist Nicky Marrero, aided and abetted by the cream of Manhattan background vocalists, *Baltimore* is superbly produced. Nina's long-time musical associate, Al Schackman, was on hand (playing piano on the title cut and tambourine on 'If You Pray Right') and Nina herself arranged four of the ten tracks on the album, accompanying herself at the piano. As producer Taylor noted at the time of the session, 'When Nina walks into the studio, she radiates the most magnificent intensity of any artist I have ever seen...'

The choice of songs for *Baltimore* was brilliant, ranging from the Randy Newman-penned title track with its loping reggae-like beat, to Nina's poignant reading of 'My Father', the Judy Collins' tune she had briefly attempted at a 1971 RCA recording session. Another revisit from her RCA days was 'Music For Lovers', and just as she had for the *Nina Simone And Piano!* session, she accompanied herself at the piano, supported this time by a sympathetic string arrangement from Matthews. 'Everything Must Change', the Bernard Ighner classic made famous by Quincy Jones in 1974, has an understated pathos, Nina emoting as only she knew how. Two 'up' tracks, 'The Family' (previously recorded by pop/country star Billy Joe Royal) and soul/pop duo Hall and Oates' 'Rich Girl', have a decidedly funky flavour, the latter imbued with a hint of reggae also to be found in the nifty David Matthews' original, 'Forget'. 'That's All I Want From You', a hidden gem from Aretha Franklin's 1970 LP, 'Spirit In The Dark', is given a more ponderous, reflective reading by Nina.

The album ends on a triumphant note for Nina, with a pair of traditional spirituals, 'Balm In Gilead' and the righteously rousing 'If You Pray Right', two songs she herself had clearly chosen for the album (in spite of her protestations to Sylvia in '78 that she has 'no say whatsoever in the selection of songs'. After the album's release, to strong critical acclaim, Nina even complained that the cover art was not to her liking: in fact, the LP depicted her smiling, clapping her hands with joy, a far cry from the mournful look that had adorned her final RCA album, *It Is Finished*. It's hard to discern why Nina disliked *Baltimore* so much because, almost 25 years after its release, it sounds better than ever: the sound clean and clear, the songs a perfect match, the string and background vocal arrangements completely supportive, and Nina in great vocal form.

There was no second CTI album, doubtless because Nina was not pleased with the outcome of her first experience with Taylor. Now living in France, fresh from experiences in Barbados, Liberia and Switzerland, Nina ventured back into Studio Davout in Paris in January 1982 to record 13 songs for what would be her sole release for the independent Carrère label, the LP *Fodder On My Wings*. Accompanied by three musicians – Sydney Thiam on congas, bells and woodblock, Paco Sery on percussion and timpani and Sylvain Marc on bass – Nina cut a highly personal record, writing 12 songs (including two remakes of songs from the CTI album, a French language version of 'Balm In Gilead' and 'If You Pray Right' retitled 'Heaven Belongs To You', with lyrics in both English and French), and adapting Gilbert O'Sullivan's classic 'Alone Again Naturally', which Roger Nupie, long-time president of Nina's International fan club, describes as 'a milestone in the Simone repertoire, bitter-sweet reminiscence of her father's death'.

Roger notes that the hard-to-find CD re-issue of the album features three songs not included on the original LP version, based on her self-imposed exile from the US. More than ever determined to make her own music, Nina wrote, adapted and arranged the songs, played piano and harpsichord and sang in English and French. 'I Sing Just To Know That I'm Alive' is inspired by carnival in Trinidad; 'Liberian Calypso' revives the time she spent in Liberia, and 'Le Peuple En Suisse' (combined with Weill-Brecht's 'There Is No Returning') is about Switzerland. The song 'Fodder In Her Wings' is about reincarnation.' Roger says that if Carrère had released 'Vous Êtes Seuls, Mais Je Désire Être

Avec Vous' ('You Are Alone But I Long To Be With You') as a single, 'it could have been a huge hit in discothèques', adding that the track 'Stop' is 'based on her dislike of the song "Send In The Clowns", and "You took My Teeth" is a short ode to Bob Marley'. The song 'Thandewye' is actually a new version of 'A Charge To Keep I Have', a tune Nina recorded during her live show at Philarmonic Hall in 1973 during her RCA years, that remains un-issued. 'Color Is A Beautiful Thing' was also cut during live performances as 'The Ding Song' and issued on the 1974 *Portrait Of Nina* album.

While it may be among her most obscure recordings, *Fodder On My Wings* is an album that Nupie says 'is among her most important'. Certainly, it captures Nina expressing whatever experiences she was having at the time, making it a precious musical commentary of the life she was living in Europe in the early '80s, seldom returning to the US except for occasional concerts.

That changed in 1985 when Nina decided to spend an extended time in California, living in Hollywood in the condo she had purchased. During a two-year period, she would make a total of three albums: *Nina's Back* and *Live & Kickin'* for the independent VPI label and *Let It Be Me*, a live recording done at the now-defunct Vine Street Bar & Grill and released by Verve in 1987. Cut at an LA studio, Rock Steady, *Nina's Back* (re-issued on CD under countless other names since 1985) was an interesting musical departure for Nina: the album finds her in a contemporary '80s setting, backed by four-man brass section, veteran guitarist Arthur Adams, percussionist Luke Metoyer, arranger and keyboardist Hence Powell and the famed Waters family on background vocals. There are some uncharacteristically upbeat tunes like Adams' 'You Must Have Another Lover' and two songs from former Motown executive, producer Eddie Singleton's 'Touching And Caring' and 'It's Cold Out Here', which, one can speculate, might have achieved a greater response had they been released on a major label.

Nina rewrites history with opening dialogue for a remake of her very first hit, 'I Loves You, Porgy', claiming that, 'It was back in the early '60s when I first travelled north to Philadelphia when a friend of mine told me about an engagement in Atlantic City, New Jersey' – referring to when she got her start in show business! In fact, such events took place in the early '50s but, Nina's 'convenient' memory lapse is forgiven, since her recording of the song includes a rare and very touching spoken interlude that, in light of her passing, is more precious than ever.

The other cuts on *Nina's Back* were 'For A While', brother Sam Waymon's 'Saratoga' and a new version of 'Fodder In Her Wings' which features a fine guitar solo from Arthur Adams. As an entire piece of work, the album had some uneven qualities but, 15 years after it was recorded, it sounds better now than it did when first released, with Nina sounding upbeat and confident, a quality also present on *Live & Kickin'*, which according to the CD notes was cut 'in Europe and the Caribbean'. With selections from virtually every era of her recording career – starting with 1959's 'I Loves You, Porgy' and ending with 1982's 'I Sing Just To Know I'm Alive' – the album works really well: highlights include chestnuts like 'The Other Woman', an intense 'Pirate Jenny', a joyous 'Sugar In My Bowl', a no-holds-barred 'Backlash Blues', a rare live reading of 'Do What You Gotta Do', the perennial 'See-Line Woman' and the inevitable encore 'My Baby Just Cares For Me', at the time revived thanks to the success of a Chanel perfume ad and a massive pop hit in the UK. In true Simone style, Nina commands the audience, 'This is Saturday night – get loose!' as she insists on audience participation.

In retrospect, *Live & Kickin'* (which features Al Schackman on guitar, Cornell McFadden on drums and Leopoldo Fleming on percussion) is an excellent representation of the kind of performance that made Nina so popular amongst audiences on both sides of the Atlantic. In a different mood and mode, a show at London's famed Ronnie Scott's in November 1984, months before she returned to the US, was also captured on tape. With British drummer Paul Robinson as her sole accompanist, the results of Nina's performance surfaced in a 1987 album, *Live At Ronnie Scott's*, a 13-track set that reprises a number of well-known Simone staples (such as 'Mississippi Goddam', the 1963 original 'If You Knew' and the 1965 recording 'Be My Husband') along with some new material, notably the Weill-Brecht composition, 'Moon Over Alabama', and uncredited songs 'Mr Smith' and 'God, God, God'. A DVD of the performance (complete with a backstage interview at the club) was re-issued by the UK company Quantum Leap in 2003.

Not quite as exciting but still a good example of Nina's compelling work as a live performer, 'Let It Be Me' was a ten-track album that became a 12-track CD with the addition of two songs ('Mississippi Goddam' and 'Four Women'). The set featured Nina with Arthur Adams on guitar and bass, and Cornell McFadden on drums, and while many of the songs were once again familiar items in Nina's repertoire (such as 'Four Women' and Bob Dylan's 'Just Like A Woman'), there are some notable additions, like an ominous reading of 'Baltimore' and a reflective, almost painfully honest cover of Janis Ian's 'Stars'. The latter song was also part of a seven-song set recorded in July 1980 and released on CD as *The Rising Sun Collection* in 1994.

While one album, *Madame Nina Simone*, derived from a 1990 live performance at Montreux, Nina actually stayed away from the recording studios until 1993. After then-Elektra Records executive Michael Alago saw her in concert in New York in 1992, he relentlessly pursued her. Finally, in January of '93, Nina began working with Andre Fischer, former drummer with Rufus, who had made his mark as the Grammy-winning producer of his then-wife Natalie Cole, on what would be Nina's last studio album, *A Single Woman*. The musical match was really strong: her voice deeper than it had ever been and sometimes a little more world-weary than usual, Nina turned in amazing performances of hand-picked tunes such as a trio of tunes penned by '60s poet and singer Rod McKuen – the poignant title track, the perky 'Lonesome Cities' and the majestic 'Love's Been Good To Me'. Nina revisits 'If I Should Lose You' from her Philips years, this time giving it a more melancholy flavour, supported by the stellar musicianship of pianist Michael Melvoin, bassist John Clayton, guitarist John Chiondini, drummer Jeffrey Hamilton and special guest Gerald Albright on sax, with a sympathetic orchestral arrangement by veteran Richard Evans.

The Hammerstein-Kern standard 'The Folks Who Live On The Hill' (dedicated to the memory of Earl Barrow, the prime minister of Barbados, who Nina reveals in her 1991 autobiography was one of the true loves of her life) benefits from a fine arrangement by Britain's Jeremy Lubbock. 'Papa, Can You Hear Me?' from *Yentl* opens with a few bars from 'Swing Low Sweet Chariot' before Nina turns in what is the emotional highpoint of the album. After reading her comments on the passing of her father, there is no doubt that the song has deep personal meaning for her.

The remaining songs that ended up on the original version of *A Single Woman* include the French tune 'Il N'Y A Pas D'Amour Heureux' ('There Is No Happy Love'); a standout version of 'Just Say I Love Him' (which Nina originally cut for her 1961 *Forbidden Fruit* album) featuring Al Schackman on guitar; a foot-tapping jazzy version of 'The More I See You' (a 1945 hit for Dick Haymes from the Betty Grable movie *Billy Rose's Diamond Horseshoe*, revived by Chris Montez in 1966); and Nina's own witty 'Marry Me', sung with the kind of spark that was often her trademark.

There were several more songs cut at the sessions for *A Single Woman* including versions of Nina's own 1967 tune 'Do I Move You?', a lushly-orchestrated cover of The Beatles' 'Long And Winding Road', Nina's take on Bob Marley's 'No Woman No Cry', the perky ditty 'Baseball Boogie', the old standard 'I'm Gonna

Sit Right Down And Write Myself A Letter' (done much in the style of 'My Baby Just Cares For Me') and, arguably the pièce de resistance, a funky, let-it-all-loose reading of Prince's 'Sign O' The Times', which found Nina at her most expressive. At the time of writing, Rhino Records plans the 2004 re-issue of an expanded edition of *A Single Woman* with all previously unreleased tracks.

As a final studio recording, *A Single Woman* was a major achievement. Challenged by the beginning of health conditions that would affect her for the decade that followed, Nina still turned in the kind of performance long-time fans expected. By 1993, there was also a whole new body of fans, thanks to the inclusion of Nina's music on the soundtrack for *Point Of No Return*, a popular movie starring Bridget Fonda, whose character is inspired by Nina's albums. While *A Single Woman* didn't necessarily achieve the sales levels Elektra had hoped it might, Nina's popularity among music buyers had reached a new plateau, thanks to the re-issue of virtually all her work for Bethlehem, Colpix, Philips and RCA. Total global sales for her CDs were said to top one million units worldwide, and that figure is probably now considerably greater because the plethora of unauthorised recordings and the subsequent repacking of Nina's work since her passing in April 2003.

6. COMPILATIONS

It's virtually impossible to name Nina Simone's best recordings, for the choices are simply too vast. In conclusion, we simply recommend the following compilations as prime examples of the magnificent legacy of one of the greatest musical artists to have touched our lives.

Jazz As Played In An Exclusive Side Club (UK Charly)
Anthology: The Colpix Years 2-CD set (US Rhino)*
Sings The Standards (UK EMI)
Four Women 4-CD box set of all Philips recordings (US Verve)
The Very Best Of Nina Simone: Sugar In My Bowl 2-CD set (US RCA)*
Anthology 2-CD set (covers track from all labels) (US BMG)*
* Includes liner notes by David Nathan

A discography, including special guest appearances and other recorded performances, can be found at:
http://www.boscarol.com/nina
We also recommend referencing the official discography at:
http://www.ninasimone.com/discography.html

Acknowledgements

Sylvia Hampton

First and foremost I would like to give thanks to God for the creative energy, inspiration, love and strength I have received in my life. I am truly blessed and writing this book has afforded me the opportunity to share a small part of my blessings.

To my parents: Although no longer here, on some level I know they are aware of this project and were a part of the story. Thank you both for giving me life and love. To my brother David: Without his exquisite taste in music this book would not exist. Thank you from my heart for the countless years of love and support. We have had our battles, but through it all one thing remains: a deep respect and love that will never diminish. You're simply the best!

Thanks to all my family: Each of you has enriched my life and your support is gratefully received.

To Cherri Classe: Always ready to give me a shoulder to lean on and support me in my many endeavours – a big hug and many blessings. Marilyn Kasserer, Glen, Georgina and Tim Phillips, Linda McAfee, Michael Critchley and Romey: Thanks for the years of friendship. The LA Gang – Jan Lipsky, Forrest Wilson, Michael Shelebian, Faith Cole, Rebecca Sherrick, Leon Cohen, Toia Hicks, OT Hernandez: Thank you for your support and love.

A very special thanks to Lisa Simone Kelly: Thank you, Lisa, for trusting me with this project and enabling me to honour your mother. I look forward to our continued friendship and know that on a soul level we share so much. May the love you give to life sustain you in all you do, and as you attain your goals know that I am supporting you 100 per cent.

Archbishop Carl Bean: Thank you for setting me on a new path and encouraging me to reach for the stars. You are a blessing and an inspiration to so many and I am forever grateful for your wisdom.

Dr Mable John: Your charitable works, and care for those in need is a true blessing. Thank you for allowing me to be a small part of it. From your music to your ministry, you are one of life's angels.

Roger Nupie: *Daaarling*, Nina may have left us, but she created a bond between us for which I am eternally grateful. Thank you for allowing me to dig into your personal archive and share 'our' Nina with the World.

Gerrit De Bruin: I am forever grateful that you were willing to share Nina with me. As one of her true friends, I know you miss her but I also know on some level she's still watching over us. Thank you for your generosity.

Paul Robinson: Thanks for helping me to know the depth of feeling Nina's music created, and for your contribution to this book and, of course, the world of music!

Ray McCammond (Virgin Atlantic Airways): Thank you for helping me to travel in comfort and style.

Patsy Phillips: I'd never have got through it without you – thank you for your love and support.

Blues & Soul magazine: A Special thanks to Bob Kilbourn for your contribution and the years of dedication to black music.

Sanctuary Publishing – Michael Wilson, Iain MacGregor, Chris Harvey and Laura Brudenell: Thank you for trusting me with this project, and for all the support and enthusiasm you have brought to it's creation.

Last, but definitely not least, Dr Nina Simone: a friend, mentor, inspiration and one of life's true musical magicians. My life has been so much richer for knowing you. I miss you more than mere words can convey. Even though I can hear the unique sound of your voice whenever I choose, I miss that mischevious grin, the roar of your laughter and, yes, even the veritable temper tantrums. There will never be another to fill that void – you gave me so much. I just hope that this book conveys just a part of who you were. Nina, I have loved you since childhood and will do so forever more. Thank you from my heart.

David Nathan

Firstly, to my sister, Sylvia, whose idea it was to do this book. I am so proud of what you did, expressing your talents and skills as a writer and so faithfully portraying Nina as so human, yet such an amazing spirit. Thank you for your love, support, encouragement and enthusiasm. I am honoured to have been a part of this book and thrilled that we got to work together this way. I love you.

To Lisa Simone Kelly: Thank you for giving us your words of wisdom and your blessing to move forward with this love-filled testament to your mother. You are beautiful, soulful and strong.

Thank you, Archbishop Carl Bean for being such a friend. You know how important Nina was to me and your words of wisdom made all the difference.

'Mama' Doris Troy, one of a kind, a friend always. Thank you for your love.

Stephanie Jourdan, for guidance, insight and counsel: you keep me on track and in tune. Much love!

Much appreciation to the soulful divas, Dionne, Chaka, Bonnie and Alicia, for adding your kind words; and thanks to Stu Phillips, Danny Davis, Chris White and Lisle Atkinson for your insight into working with Nina. Thanks to Ashley Kahn for the hook ups.

The guys and gals in my Team Management and Leadership Program, Jen Herda, my coaches, course leaders and friends at Landmark Education in Los Angeles for empowering me and training me as 'Captain Adventure'! You rock!

Nestor Figueroa: You started this mess but I love you for it and always will!

Byron Motley, for hanging tough with Ms Simone back in the day and keeping her always present in my life through the laughter and the smiles.

Vivek Mathur and Teo Martinez, for sharing your love of Nina with me and reminding me why she has been such an important force in my life; and Louis Washington for the opportunity of sharing about her on MLK Day this year – a reminder of the pioneering role Nina played in the civil rights movement.

Giovanna Imbesi for musical support and giving me the opportunity to express my love for Nina through music.

To the Spirit That Lives Within: Thank you for the many gifts.

To Sandara, Pythagoras, Akhenaten, Billie Holiday, Esther Phillips, Big Maybelle, Phyllis Hyman, Judy Clay, Lorraine Ellison, Hayden Sealy, Eric Brogdon, Gary Walcott, John Simmons – smiling down on me, always.

Mother Frances and Father Mark: I know I was two hours and fifteen minutes late getting here, but thanks for giving me life and the opportunity to learn so many wonderful lessons. I love you.

And, finally, to Nina, who will always be with me. I may never know how providence brought us together – me a skinny teenager from London and you a musical high priestess from North Carolina. All I know is that you helped me understand the importance of taking a stand, of being myself fully and completely, of artistic integrity and unbridled passion. My life would not have been the same without you, your music, your magic or that unforgettable smile. Ne Me Quitte Pas.

The Nina Simone Foundation

The Nina Simone Foundation (NSF) was established in May 2003 by Nina Simone's daughter, Lisa. The Nina Simone Foundation is a non-profit organisation, established for the preservation and celebration of the music, socio-political contributions and overall legacy of the late Dr Nina Simone. NSF is also a philanthropic initiative established to raise money in support of the three, most personal and life-long pursuits of Dr Nina Simone, which are: Cancer research and awareness in underserved communities, music education restoration in the public schools and child abuse prevention.

For further information contact:

The Nina Simone Foundation
156 W 56th Street
New York
NY 10019
USA

Other organisations that were close to Nina's heart and that the reader may wish to contact are:

Minority AIDS Project
5149 W Jefferson Blvd
Los Angeles
CA 90016

www.map-usa.org

NAACP (National Association for the Advancement of Colored People)
4805 Mt Hope Drive
Baltimore
Maryland 21215

ww.naacp.org

ANSA (Artists For A New South Africa)
PO Box 1616
Los Angeles
CA 90034

www.ansafrica.org

Index

ERYKAH
BADU

THE FIRST LADY OF NEO-SOUL

Joel McIver

ERYKAH BADU: THE FIRST LADY OF NEO-SOUL
Joel McIver

Erykah Badu stands at the forefront of a whole new genre of music. Before Macy Gray, Alicia Keys and Angie Stone, Erykah was bringing the unique sounds of neo-soul - the classic vibes of Motown and Stax smoothed by jazz and toughened by hip-hop - to the people. Quite simply, there is no other artist like her.

- Grammy award-winner for Best Female R&B Vocal Performance and Best R&B Album
- Producer of two platinum-selling albums that have won her worldwide accolades, on a par with Lauryn Hill and Macy Gray
- *Baduizm*, her 1997 debut album, entered the US album charts at the highest ever position for a female solo artist.

1-86074-385-4 | £12.99/$18.95

YOUNG GIFTED AND

THE STORY OF TROJAN RECORDS

BLACK

Michael de Koningh & Laurence Cane-Honeysett

Free 12-track CD of rare grooves

YOUNG, GIFTED & BLACK: THE STORY OF TROJAN RECORDS

Michael de Koningh & Laurence Cane-Honeysett

Recently resurrected and now enjoying chart success in the 21st century, when it was formed Trojan Reocrds epitomised the punk DIY ethic over a decade before 1976. With a blizzard of individual labels and a marketing strategy that involved selling product out of the backs of vans, the company spearheaded the injection of reggae and ska into the vein of British youth consciousness.

Complete with first-hand interviews, a comprehensive discography and an exclusive 12-trackCD, *Young, Gifted & Black* is the official story of Trojan Records, lifting the lid on the scheming, backbiting and sheer seat-of-the-pants inspiration that made the label such a powerful force for black UK music.

1-86074-464-8 | £12.99/$17.95

www.ninasimone.com